Imagining Teachers

Imagining Teachers

Rethinking Gender Dynamics in Teacher Education

Gustavo E. Fischman

ROWMAN & LITTLEFIELD PUBLISHERS, INC.
Lanham • Boulder • New York • Oxford

ROWMAN & LITTLEFIELD PUBLISHERS, INC.

Published in the United States of America
by Rowman & Littlefield Publishers, Inc.
4720 Boston Way, Lanham, Maryland 20706
http://www.rowmanlittlefield.com

12 Hid's Copse Road, Cumnor Hill, Oxford OX2 9JJ, England

Copyright © 2000 by Rowman & Littlefield Publishers, Inc.

British Library Cataloguing in Publication Information Available

Library of Congress Cataloging-in-Publication Data

Fischman, Gustavo.
　Imagining teachers : rethinking gender dynamics in teacher education / Gustavo E.
Fischman.
　　p. cm. — (Critical perspectives series)
　Includes bibliographical references and index
　ISBN 0-8476-9181-0 (alk. paper) — ISBN 0-8476-9182-9 (pbk. : alk. paper)
　　1. Women teachers—Training of—Argentina—Case studies. 2. Women teachers—
Argentina—Social conditions—Case studies. 3. Student teachers—Argentina—Case
studies. 4. Feminism and education—Argentina—Case studies. I. Title. II. Series.

LB1719.A7 F58 2000
371.1'2—dc21
　　　　　　　　　　　　　　　　　　　　　　　　　　　　　　00-031105
Printed in the United States of America

⊖™ The paper used in this publication meets the minimum requirements of American
National Standard for Information Sciences—Permanence of Paper for Printed Library
Materials, ANSI/NISO Z39.48–1992.

To my parents, Jacobo and Livia,
To my loved Marcella,
To the living memory of the disappeared

CONTENTS

ACKNOWLEDGMENTS

As with all books this one owes a fair share to many people who have offered their time, enormous intellectual resources, and love and patience with me. Some of them are my friends and colleagues: Mauricio Andion, Karen Anijar, Ayelen Atias, Christopher Boyd, Pablo Cafiero, Silvia Calcagno, Marcelo Caruso, Alberto Cevese, Valeria Cohen, Daniela Comaleras, Gabriela Diker, Esteban Dicovskyi, Silvana Franzetti, Rosa Garza, Pablo Gentili, Zelda Grunner, Isabel Hernandez, Alberto Iardelewsky, Carina Kaplan, Veronica Kaufmann, Jorge Katz, Alejandro Lucangioli, Nancy Mateos, Jenny McLaren, Amaya Montes, Maria Ines Monzani, Graciela Morgade, Prosper Ngodonoo, Sandra Nicastro, Pilar O'Cadiz, Victoria Orze, Pablo Pineau, Javier Serrano, Jon Snyder, Daniel Suarez, and Lynn Winters.

There are also many teachers, researchers, and administrators who during my fieldwork were always ready to talk and share their knowledge: Andrea Alliaud, Alejandra Birgin, Cecilia Braslavsky, Maria Cristina Davini, Ovide Menin, Mariano Narodowsky, Adriana Puiggros. Many more remain anonymous as promised. However, Marta M., Marta C., Lucía and Adriana, I owe you forever.

I want to especially acknowledge Liora Bressler, Kris Gutierrez, Ana Inés Heras, Ann Lippincot, Vijitha Mahadevan Eyango, Douglas Hollan, Peter

McLaren, Diana Rhoten, Val Rust, Daniel Schugurensky, and Nelly Stromquist. They have been very insightful readers and generous scholars. Without their comments and critique this book would not have been as exciting to write as it was.

A very special thanks to Donaldo Macedo for trusting in me; to both Dean Birkenkamp, my thorough editor and Renee Jardine, in editorial production at Rowman & Littlefield for the often tedious and persistent job of transforming the book into a "publishable" form; and to my talented friend Roisan Rubio who used his skills towards the same goal.

My friends and gifted colleagues Inés Dussel, Lisa Laumann, Marc Pruyn, and Julie Thompson have always been there for me. Their attention, ideas, resources, and criticisms have made this work a better one. They are among the most talented colleagues I know, and their friendship is a source of joy and hope.

Thanks to my father, Jacobo; my mother, Livia; my brothers, Daniel and Guillermo; my sisters-in-law, Mónica and Ana; my aunt Mabel; my cousins, Enrique and Darío; and my nephews, Leandro, Andrés, Nicolás, Emiliano, and Ignacio. Thanks also to my new family, Ana, Mónica, Juan José, Patricia, María José, Jano, Sofía y Agustina. I want to acknowledge the contribution of my relatives to this project, not only for their love and constant support but also for their wise and thoughtful "why" questions with which on many occasions they challenged my ideas.

When I arrived in Los Angeles in May 1992, I was excited and terrified. I came here thinking about getting a Ph.D. and learning about theories and practices, books, and authors, but I did not know that I was going to find Marcella Harvey, my partner, teacher, lover, editor, and best example of love for life. Without Marcella, I am sure I would not have been able to arrive at this point. She knows that this book is ours. She knows that I love her. Now you know this, too.

Last but not least, I want to acknowledge that the original research project for this book was possible thanks to the institutional support of Fundación Antorchas (Argentina) and the UCLA Graduate School of Education. I also want to recognize the support of the College of Education at Arizona State University.

As with any book, all its shortcomings and problems are the author's responsibility.

FOREWORD

The feminization or, conversely, the masculinization of certain occupations provides important venues for the inculcation and regeneration of broad and widespread social representations of the kinds of competencies appropriate for women and for men, and the kinds of roles they should be allowed to play. Teaching, especially at the primary education level, is one such venue—all the more crucial given the nearly universal exposure to school environments at impressionable periods in our lives.

Gustavo Fischman's *Imagining Teachers* is a most welcome addition to our understanding of teachers' beliefs about their profession and practice. By focusing on student teachers, rather than teachers, Fischman catches them at a very revealing moment of their antecedent socialization.

As in most Latin American countries, in Argentina women represent an overwhelming majority of primary school teachers—about 90 percent. They are also very young: 90 percent are under thirty and half under twenty. What can be said about this overwhelmingly feminine profession? Using qualitative methods and, therefore, focusing on a small number of subjects, Fischman composes a complex picture with multiple voices, dimensions, and perspectives.

In this multiform set of perceptions and interpretations and variegated narrative, the reader learns—and will remember—a great amount.

Building upon the well-known notion that women teachers in Latin America are expected to show an inner calling to serve children, this book takes the reader into much less understood angles on teachers' aspirations, definitions, and construction of the real and the ideal students, classrooms, and teachers themselves.

It is in the uncovering and analysis of these subjectivities that Fischman's study makes its most important contribution. While employing several methodologies, ranging from a questionnaire to focus interviews, the use of subjects' drawings and their interpretation provides an uncommon contribution and positive challenge to conventional social science research. Images constitute a new terrain in the social sciences and certainly one that expands our sense of "evidence." They add nicely to our incipient, but growing use of the visual—now represented mostly by efforts at social cartography and the creation of conceptual maps to identify the location, connection, and distance among ideas, authors, or institutions. (In the field of comparative education the work by Rolland Paulston is a step in this direction.) By asking the student teachers in his study to draw pictures (in whatever form they could, from stick figures to quite descriptive representations) about the real and the ideal, and by asking them to express their interpretations through a group discussion, Fischman carefully weaves the conscious with the subconscious and the private with the social of the participants. Their subjectivities come to the fore as the representations are explained by the participants who created these drawings. Equally intriguing is the second layer of interpretation—sometimes coinciding with those of the participants, sometimes not—provided by Fischman himself.

It may be no coincidence that Fischman produces an inquiry method that resembles psychoanalytical techniques. In most of Latin America, Argentina has a strong reputation for the reliance of its people on psychoanalysis. Postmodernity has rescued the value of subjectivity, so researchers are becoming friendlier to the use of interpretive techniques and narratives that deconstruct both official discourse and our own everyday discourse. Fischman's study shows how these techniques can illuminate our understanding by highlighting the cumulative impact of "their stories, realities, languages, bodies, drawings, sounds, joys, pain, economy, poverty, laughter, madness, actions, backgrounds, dreams, resistances, and many more things." The book works subtly through many areas of ambiguity and shows successfully new and alternative ways of looking at our social practices and imaginary. Beginning with the title, we ask ourselves, is the book about teachers who imagine or about how we imagine teachers? And, if the former, it is more how teachers-to-be rather than actual teachers imagine teachers and teaching.

The role of gender, specifically being a woman or being a man, is found to permeate the discourse of these teachers-to-be. Imbued with received interpretations of "man" as conveyor of strength and order, future teachers readily associate leadership in schools with men. Simultaneously, notions of "woman" as soft, caring, and committed lead them to see women educators as mostly teachers, not administrators and much less policy makers. While these perceptions still dominate, their world is being inhabited also by an increasing number of young men moving into primary school teaching. As Fischman observes, this trend receives a guarded response, accompanied as it is by the fear of deviant heterosexuality (or "hidden homosexuality") reaching the schools. And the new phenomenon reveals a subtle conflation of gender and class, for men seeking to become primary school teachers tend to be from lower social classes.

Multiple inconsistencies in the lives of future teachers are detected. The reader should welcome them because all too often our research training calls for order and coherence, which we do produce, but often at the cost of bringing our data into shape with our initial intentions. Scratching the surface of the future teachers' perceptions, we see the vague contours of areas of acceptance of received knowledge coexisting with domains in which opposing and even conflictual beliefs and feelings operate. The use of visual sources greatly enabled Fischman to seek meaning and obtain from the future teachers their accounts of key elements in the educational system. It is indeed interesting to realize that, while the discourse of "commitment" and "vocation" (in the sense of innate calling) prevails, many study participants settled for teaching programs after having unsuccessfully sought admission to other university departments. It is also intriguing how wide the gap in their views of the ideal and the real can be, yet at the same time, how aspects of the ideal can overlap the real or are at least aspects under the student teachers' control. For instance, in describing students, the teachers-to-be characterize "real" students as "obedient and poor" (as 69 percent indicate), but all depict as "ideal" those students who are "receptive to teacher's instruction." Do the teachers-to-be see obedience and receptiveness as very different? When describing the "real" classroom, they portray student desks organized in rows facing the teacher; when depicting the "ideal" classroom, they place the desks in a circle, facing the teacher. Changing the layout of classrooms is certainly more possible than endowing the classrooms with technological equipment or having fewer students per class.

What are these future teachers revealing here? Is it their intention to introduce new concepts and small reforms when they become regular teachers, or merely a sign of their cognizance of alternative realities that they are not willing to introduce in practice? When describing teachers, substantial differences emerge between the emotional features of "real" teachers (frowning, stern, unable to control students) and "ideal" teachers (smiling and willing to play); yet, they are alike on a core dimension: "knowledgeable about content." Only 15 percent of the participants consider this a feature of "real" teachers and 20 percent consider it a feature of "ideal" teachers. The question we can raise is why does knowledge per se not receive major recognition? Is it perhaps because it is taken for granted or because knowledge matters much less than caring and order?

Tango in Argentina is a ubiquitous cultural expression. Some may not dance it but its lyrics have indelibly shaped Argentinean minds. Building upon the hegemonic form of masculinity represented in the tango (it is the man who uncontestably and forcefully leads the dance and it is often a man who sings the story), Fischman presents the tango as an ambiguous terrain in which men exude the external dominance and yet the stories reveal that it is a woman who had done something tragic and unforgettable to these men—abandoned them, left them for another, made them suffer for no reason, etc. Expanding the notion of the tango to an examination of the teaching profession, Fischman contends, and shows persuasively, that significant contradictions underlie the apparent homogeneity of understandings and norms. Here, Fischman invites us to exploit the contradictions and tensions (between freedom and authority, tradition and innovation, knowledge and affection, sexuality and motherhood), but warns us about "falling into ambivalent or naive explanations." His Freirean advice is to be "simple without being simplistic." A challenge, indeed, for all of us.

One of the key points in the book is that all too often we maintain a binary position toward teachers, tending to see them as either those who duly reproduce the status quo or those who act as change agents. Fischman proposes a modest but no less challenging position, to see teachers as persons "in the process of finding meaning." Such being the case, it is up to us to engage in constructive and clarifying dialogue with them, especially when they are still student teachers. In the end, Fischman produces not unequivocal findings but rather a kaleidoscope of perceptions, insights, and possible interpretations. This probing challenges many of our firm and unchallenged beliefs and understandings. The salience of subjectivity in the book, both on the part of the participants and the researcher, nags us again and again. While highlighting the expected and the unexpected to reveal the beliefs and preferences of future teachers, Fischman simultaneously probes our own norms of what teachers should be.

Multiple questions will haunt us after reading this book, and many interpretations will come to mind. Two questions that were important for me upon reading this study were: What are the possible positive and negative implications of a teacher force that continues to be composed mostly of women, but also of women who are poor and poorly educated? What spaces for transformative education are there when future teachers see themselves as transmitters of morality yet they are not overly concerned with appropriate teaching methods or the transmission of knowledge? This book provokes many ideas. I am sure that you, the reader, will also come up with challenging reflections.

Nelly P. Stromquist
Rossier School of Education
University of Southern California

INTRODUCTION

Imagination *n*. imagining, the ability to imagine creatively or to use this ability in a practical way (as in dealing with difficulties). **Imagine** *v*. (imagined, imagining) 1. To form a mental image of, to picture in one's mind. 2. To think or believe, to suppose. 3. To guess. (*Oxford American Dictionary*, 1980)

This book is about imagining elementary education teachers—their stories, realities, languages, bodies, drawings, sounds, joys, pain, economy, poverty, laughter, names, actions, backgrounds, dreams, resistance, and many other things. But more than anything, it is a book about the active processes involved in the political and pedagogical acts of educating teachers. And in doing so, imagining them.

In that regard, perhaps the first question we need to explore is: How do we think about teacher education programs? Following Raymond Williams's strategy in his *Keywords* (1976), I suggest that a good way of understanding the intricacies and complexities of teacher education programs, that is, their structural conditions, language, cultural patterns, and dissonance, is to take a common concept or figure employed by these organizations and investigate its changing meanings in the present.

1

Take the word "teacher" for instance. What comes to mind, a female or a male? Based on the examples provided by popular media (especially movies and sitcoms) the answer should be "male."[1] However, based on personal experiences most people would answer "female." In fact, since the twentieth century, in many countries around the world, elementary public education has relied on women to occupy the majority of teaching positions.

What does the image below represent for you? A mother and her child? A teacher and her student? Perhaps both? Indeed, these immediate connections exist in our imagination for as long as elementary public schooling has become extended to most children.

"Republican Schoolteacher." [1793]. Engraving. Bibliothèque Nationale, Cabinet des Estampes (cat. no. 149).

The examples of the word "teacher" and the image of an eighteenth-century teacher also help to explain why not only scholars but many people would agree that "teaching has become a feminine profession."[2] However, to define the advantages and privileges for women within such a feminine context requires a second look. In the United States more than 80 percent of the elementary school teachers are women, while only 10.6 percent of the superintendents and 43.1 percent of principals in elementary schools are female (Acker, 1996). Similarly, in the city of Buenos Aires, Argentina, men constitute 10.8 percent of all teachers in primary schools, but they are 31.6 percent of all the principals and 57.2 percent of the district supervisors (Morgade, 1997). The disproportionate presence of males in the higher echelons of school administrations reflects, in part, the traditional assumption that men are better suited to occupy those administrative and authoritative positions (Leonard, 1998). This inequality is also due to the preferential treatment granted to males by long-held educational norms and practices.[3] In many Latin American countries the situation is even worse, yet it does not seem to be a rallying point in the current educational struggles (Fischman, 1998).

These percentages give some indication about starkly different patterns of promotion, concepts of career, professionalization, masculinity and femininity. And yet, in order to clearly understand the complex dynamics of the genderized territory of today's schools, we need to move beyond statistics of distribution, representation, and promotion.

Teachers, Who Cares?

One of the latest and most quoted outlines for teacher education reform in the United States, *What Matters Most: Teaching for America's Future*, states, "By the year 2006, America will provide every student with what should be his or her educational birthright: access to competent, caring and qualified teaching" (NCTAF, 1996: 5). Although this sounds like a desirable goal, there is an important need for revising the educational and everyday understanding of what constitutes the *caring professional*, particularly because, as Sandra Acker has pointed out:

> It would not be necessary to belabor the obvious, were it not for the pervasive conceptions of teaching as "a sacred calling" and of teachers as individuals who "care deeply about children." The association of these images with women is important in shaping the occupational culture of teachers and the approaches of scholars who study teacher education. (1996: 102)

At the same time, when concepts of *caring* and *authority* are not redefined and critically analyzed they become part of complex mechanisms supporting structures of career discrimination, thus contributing to the impoverishment of the professional situation of the teaching workforce as a whole. Moreover, uncritical acceptance—or its counterpart, uncritical dismissing—of caring and authority, especially as they relate to teacher education, represent an important and urgent challenge to our imagination not only as educators, but also as citizens.

Caring, professionalism, and authority are among the most important concerns of policymakers, teacher educators, and the public in general. They also seem to be of great concern to most aspiring teachers. In fact, most student teachers report that they start their studies full of enthusiasm, moral purpose, love, passion, and a sense of hope. More often than not, they also have genuine goals related to social change and justice. "Scratch a good teacher and you'll find a moral purpose," says Michael Fullan. "Many, many teachers enter the profession because they want to make a contribution—they want to make a difference!" (Fullan, 1993: 10).[4]

Their passion and enthusiasm are often countered by a sense of skepticism or discouraging remarks on the part of friends and family.

> So, you want to be a teacher?
> Yes.
> Why? Don't you know that teaching is for losers, sissies, and geeks?
> I don't think so.
> Hmm?
> I love kids!
> So?
> I had such a bad experience at school, I really want to make a difference.
> Sorry, but I don't buy it!
> Think about the future. Teaching is crucial!
> Yeah, and is that why teachers earn so little, work so much, are laughed at and harshly criticized in every movie, TV show, and newspaper around the world?
> But I always wanted to be a teacher. . . .[5]

Despite this stubborn, perhaps even naive, sense of hope, by the end of their preservice training, many students will have replaced their hopes with fear, their desire for social change with dread, and their enthusiasm with a sense of apathy about their future profession. What happens with students in teacher education programs that is so powerful to transform hope and a sense of vocation into despair? Are their original dreams an expression of a romantic vision of teaching? Are they developing some sort of false consciousness influenced by the media or extraordinary high expectations? Or is the sense of burnout a direct result of stressful working conditions and disagreement with their salaries? Perhaps, but there is more to it than that.[6] A guiding hypothesis for this book is that gender dynamics are very important and often overlooked when the educational community seeks to provide answers to these questions.

In the context of teacher education, this book argues that gender appears to have special importance in organizing differences and related systems of classification, such as class and ethnicity (Melhuus and Stølen, 1996). The main focus here is to examine the realities of teacher education, using historical, political-economic perspectives that problematize and bring to the fore gender as a medium for the articulation, reinforcement, and resignification of systems of classification.

Understanding gender within a political economy perspective is an attempt to consistently locate gender processes in space and time. It is also an attempt to see the constant interplay between experiences and meanings of masculinities and femininities and the multilayered contexts in which both experiences and meanings are patterned by inequality, discrimination, and oppression. And it is an attempt to understand the emergence of particular expressions of masculinities and femininities and their connections with global histories, in order to place those local expressions in the larger currents of world history.

Using Images in Educational Research

In his wonderful book, *Blindness*, Jose Saramago tells the story of a city in which its people are suffering from a rare and sudden form of blindness. One of the characters in the novel, bitterly wonders at one point why they did become blind. What makes this question so bitter is its answer: "I don't think we did go blind, I think we are blind. Blind but seeing. Blind people who can see, but do not see" (Saramago, 1998: 326).

For some, the idea that we could become blind people who can see may seem, perhaps, utter nonsense. For me, the blindness in Saramago's novel is a suitable allegory that describes why during some periods societies seem to be blind to racism, economic exploitation, domestic violence, sexual abuse, oppression and discrimination. At another, and perhaps less dramatic but nonetheless surprising level, Saramago's allegory could be applied to educational research. This field seems populated by professionals who at best neglect the world of images and at worst, refuse to even consider that images and visual phenomena could be conveyers of relevant information.

What seems surprising is that majority of educational researchers, as many other social scientists, have relied on a scientific paradigm that claimed emotionally neutral and objective observation was the privileged method for conducting inquiries and arriving at the "true nature" of the phenomenon under study. This eye-dominated paradigm applied equally to quantitative and qualitative traditions. In both research traditions, what was observable by the researcher's eye (quantifiable for the first or naturalistically describable for the latter) warranted access to the true nature of the observed phenomena. And yet despite this seemingly unchallenged domination of the visual, infrequently we encounter educational studies in which images are critically used, or even presented as data and not simply "complementary" illustrations. As Thomas Popkewitz persuasively argues we need to:

> Understand that the eye does not merely see, but is socially disciplined in the ordering, dividing, and "making" of the possibilities of the world and the *self*. By asking how the *eye* sees, it is possible to ask about how the systems of ideas "make" possible what is seen, thought about, felt, and acted on. Such questions about reason itself—that is, the social construction of (and power relations embedded in) reason——are the principles by which the agent "sees" and acts to effect change. (1999: 22)

I, for one, following Popkewitz's reflections, want to critically incorporate the notion that we need to inquire and reflect on what we see, and how those images are constructed and reconstructed by the participants of the research project.

But I also want to acknowledge the existence of limitations to this attempt, specially if it is understood as the simple extension of the old saying "A picture is worth a thousand words." Granted, this saying may not be out-of-date as an explanation for a very immediate experience for most people around the world. Nevertheless, what should be noted is that if a picture is worth a thousand words it is also the case that in order to understand it, reflect about it or explain it, we may need to use a thousand and one words. And even then, there is nothing transparent or inherently truthful in the world of images.

This book analyzes gender and identity dynamics in elementary teacher education using historical and political-economic perspectives, qualitative interpretive methodologies, and a novel approach that borrows from image-based research techniques (Prosser, 1998). In today's world the increasingly more sophisticated use of images and newer forms of representation has been conceptualized at best as the "visual turn" and at worst as "the dictatorship of the images."[7] This is not the place to thoroughly evaluate the multiple perspectives developed around the impact and significance of these changes; nevertheless, I would like to refer to two connected problems.[8] First, most educational researchers are neglecting and thus underutilizing forms of visual information. Jay Ruby develops a clear argument about the need to increase the use of tools of visual anthropology that is equally important for education.

> Anthropology (*read education*) is a word-driven discipline. It has tended to ignore the visual-pictorial world perhaps because of distrust of the ability of images to convey abstract ideas. When engaged in ethnography the researcher must convert the complex experience of fieldwork to words in a notebook and then transform those words into

other words shifted through analytic methods and theories. This logocentric approach to understanding denies much of the multisensory experience of trying to know another culture. The promise of visual anthropology is that it might provide an alternative way of perceiving culture-perception constructed through the lens. (1996: 1351)

Second, in order to take advantage of images and the promise expressed in Ruby's words, we would need to abandon relatively simplistic understandings of the "visual" and "representation." Commenting on the difficult task of accessing the "truth" in any representation, Edward Said states that the "real issue is whether indeed there can be a true representation of anything, or whether any and all representations, because they are representations are embedded first in the language and then in the culture, institutions, and political ambience of the representor" (1978: 272–73).

When thinking about the representational value of images or, more specifically, their value as data in educational research, Said's contention is important because it directs our attention to the complex task ahead. The processes people tend to use in their understanding of the representational value of an image involve implicit operations of simplification that undermine the ambiguities and multiple meanings of any given image. In other words, in order to access (and this access is always fragile) to the representational value of something (a poem, portrait, film, and so on) we cannot ignore the cultural, social, and economical conditions surrounding the producers and users of the representation.

The twentieth century has been prolific in the production of art and images that do not seem to be located in any particular space or time—a bottle of Coke, the U.S. flag, the lightbulb, all of them seem to evoke meanings that appear to be without histories, location, bodies, or owners, and nevertheless, these are powerful images. These dislocated, disembodied, and thus reified images, are powerful in part due to their intrinsic aesthetic qualities, but also because their meanings are taken-for-granted.

There are, however, countless examples, which challenge the assumption of the transparency of images. Perhaps one of the best known examples is the "betrayal of images" by René Magritte. In this famous painting, Magritte told us in writing that his painting of a pipe, was in fact, not a pipe. By doing so, he explicitly questioned the often taken-for-granted effect of visualization as having unequivocal meaning, not grounded in historical and geographical locations.[9] Indeed, as Joan Copjec has argued:

There is and can be no brute vision, no vision totally devoid of sense. Painting, drawing, all forms of picture making, then, are fundamentally graphic arts. And because signifiers are material, that is because they are opaque rather than translucent, because they refer to other signifiers rather than directly to a signified, the field of vision is neither clear nor easily traversable. It is ambiguous and treacherous, full of traps. (1989: 68)

In a similar tone, considering the power of images Melhuus and Stølen (1996) have discussed, "[t]he force of images, then, can be understood only once the glue that makes them stick dissolves" (28). This research, with its combined use of images and words, attempts to dissolve the sticky glue that fixes and stereotypes figures and metaphors about teachers and gender. To do so it has developed a method of inquiry that takes advantage of "nonlinear" or "interpretive activities" (Ayers, 1989; Bolin and Falk, 1987).

These interpretive activities delve into areas that are often resistant to oral or written discourses, such as feelings and ideas about sexuality. In addition, they have two interconnected goals: The first is to facilitate the expression of certain topics without threatening or censoring the participants. The second is to allow the participants to actively reflect and (re)present important experiences, expectations, desires, and even fears. As William Ayers expresses, "Interpretive activities disengage people from conscious thought and can provide fresh insight and significant discoveries" (1989: 7). In this research, interpretive activities are tools that were devised with the goal of allowing the expression of perceptions about the body, experiences and emotions about how students in teacher education programs see others (such as teachers, students, parents) and how they project images of themselves and their future work.

Emotions and beliefs are not easily incorporated in educational research, not only because people tend to mask the expression of feelings, but also because emotion and expressions of desire resist the (very often) reductionist preconceived frameworks of researchers. Moreover, in order to imagine a different educational future, researchers need to incorporate the multifaceted dimensions of emotions, bodies, and feelings because ignoring them is impossible when dealing with the real problems of schooling. Furthermore, isolating feelings from thinking and understanding will not be of much help in imagining how to transform the inequalities occurring at schools and in society.

This research deliberately seeks to obtain multiform discourses (emotional, rational, spoken, written, pictorial, and the like) about gender dynamics in teacher education. These discourses, which this research has elicited and analyzed, indicate the subject's understanding of the reality of teacher education and provide clues that go beyond the subject's current understanding, not only in its connections with the past, but also into imagining alternative future scenarios.

Imagining these scenarios was in part elicited by the production and analysis of images, Therefore, I would like to stress that the drawings and other images used in this book should not be conceived as trendy accessories to the text, nor are they included here to occupy a passive space. These visual artifacts are not simple *illustrations* or light afterthoughts fortuitously distributed in the text to ease and please the reader. The shapes and contours of these images, forms and backgrounds, simplicity or entanglement, are demonstrations to their centrality and active presence in the organization of this project. These are ceaselessly puzzling images (at least for me, and hopefully for the reader), and yet they are premeditated. The premeditation of these images consists in the fact that they were created under calculated conditions, with very specific purposes and privileging a photograph-like format. A photograph-like format seeks to elicit images that represent what the author sees as the most pressing issues in her or his imagination about a given topic (in this case teacher education).

At this point, I would like to invite the reader to look again at the book cover, and reflect on the value and importance of intentions in the creation of images.

"Planting Semillas" by Marcella Harvey © 2000.
(Reproduction of painting used as cover of this book.)

The cover of this book was the result of a very engaging discussion with the artist, Marcella Harvey, about some of the issues tackled in this project. She rendered this image after reading the first draft of the book, translating her impressions and understanding of this research including the images produced by the students. In this case, Ms. Harvey's image was the only one influenced by results of this research, as opposed to being one of the images influencing the researcher interpretation of the phenomenon under study. Notwithstanding, the different contexts of production, I do consider the painting of the cover as being part of the research process, and contributing to the "content" of the book.

Considering the cover part of the "content" of this book could be seen as a paradoxical position, yet it is also justified because the production of drawings used in this project was modeled after Dick Hebdige's (1988) thought-provoking reflections about the world of images and reproductions. Hebdige points out that photographs and visual reproductions in general are paradoxical objects, because they have the haunting qualities of being at "once signs and objects, documents of actual events, images of absent things, and real things in themselves" (1988: 12). Thus, according to Hebdige's argument it is possible to consider that the images in this book, are embodying the paradox of being "on the one hand, quotations from an irrecoverable text (the world of yesterday, of the hour before last, of the second before this one) and on the other, they are ghostly emanations from the real" (1988: 12).

In this sense, the photograph-like images used in this project do not intend to have a monopoly on any "true" representation or an embedded transparency that prevents producers, researchers, or readers from having optical or textual distortions. On the contrary, in this project the effort to provide an environment conducive to the production of photograph-like drawings and their analysis in combination with other discursive formats, contends that they are well-suited to convey, suggest, indicate, describe, and imagine the "realities" and "idealities" of teacher education, not in an idealistic vacuum but always participating in discourses of power.

In short, with the critical incorporation of images in this project, I am committed to finding a new angle to look at education through a different lens without discarding the tools and methodologies of other more established approaches. The use of nonconventional methodologies—and their theoretical nuances—constitutes a challenge to the more traditional ways of seeing, and not seeing, the presumably well-known topics of teacher education and gender. The fact that in most of educational research there is an almost complete absence of the visual is not totally surprising. Educational research (as most of the social sciences) has relied on written and spoken words, and sources of information that are more or less easily quantifiable, or that at least provide the illusion of some sort of neutral process of description and classification. Images, drawings, and pictures are always in need of interpretation, always having a surplus of information that seems resistant to simple operations of data reduction and analysis.

Mine is a personal challenge, not a deliberate attempt to reinvent educational research nor a wise way to proclaim, as in the old Spanish saying that I am a one-eyed king in the land of the blind. My motivation is to investigate ideas and tools in order to overcome some limitations of current educational research, a search for developing new questions and suggesting possible answers to our problems. This challenge I face has many colors, figures, voices, and modalities, which nevertheless may provide useful tools, ideas, and resources for researchers and teacher educators alike.

The Local, the Global, and the Problems

> For better of for worse, we have entered the global age and we entered it together. . . . Our social conditions may appear to be altogether different, but as we push below the surface of our everyday lives, we find that the questions we are asking ourselves require the same type of considerations. (Carnoy, 1997: 8)

Although this book analyzes data collected in teacher education programs in Argentina, thus dealing with particularities and local stories, it also shares common problems and challenges with teacher education programs in other contexts. Indeed, the literature on teacher education reflects the emergence of trends, and similarities between the strategies implemented (or resisted) throughout the world (Zeichner, 1999).[10] One of the most common trends involves proposals for changing teacher training and accreditation systems and catapulting them to the fore of the new blueprint for many countries' educational futures (Tatto, 1999). These proposals are made not only by think tanks, the media, and government officials, but also by international financial organizations and different sectors of civil society. Undoubtedly, these proposals are happening in contexts in which "neoliberal" policies and the continuous attack and dismantling of the structures of the welfare state operate at the level of the reconfiguration of governing practices (Popkewitz, 2000a; b). These changes in governing practices are having direct effects not only on the working conditions, symbolic roles in society, and professional status of present and future teachers, but also on the future of public education as a whole.

Teacher education reform proposals combine various discussions that reflect forces and struggles in related economic, demographic, cultural, and political arenas. Issues ranging from the role of the state, prejudice and multiculturalism, gender roles, regional autonomy, and national identity are always present and provide strong arguments for the development of the ideological and pedagogical frameworks of diverse models of teacher training (Fischman and McLaren, 2000).

Without doubt, agendas for teacher education reform are not isolated experiments (Steiner-Khamsi, 1999). They are important components in larger and far-reaching programs of educational reform. Worldwide, most of these reforms are centered on "restructuring" educational systems, with the dual goals of producing financial savings as well as the thorough transformation of objectives, epistemological bases, methods, and procedures of schooling (Brunner and Puryear, 1995; Darling-Hammond, 1993, 1997).

These reform agendas are being carried out during times of serious financial austerity for public education and amidst extremely severe criticisms about the quality and performance of public schools and of the teaching workforce in particular (Berliner and Biddle, 1995; Dussel, Tiramonti, and Birgin, 2000; Whitty, 1997). Some of the efforts in reforming teacher education have involved the application of tighter systems of accountability in the context of the de-skilling, standardization, and changing rationales of the teaching profession (Popkewitz, 1996 and 1998b). Pressure to do more work in the same amount of time, to do more work for less money, or to increase the number of students per classroom are clear manifestations of what has been termed the "intensification of teaching" (Apple, 1996).

Both de-skilling and intensification are phenomena well known to teachers around the world (Guinsburg and Lindsay, 1995). Because much of the "schools-are-failing" literature blames teachers for the so-called current decline in student achievement, the relationships between teachers and parents and teachers with administrators and educational authorities are under increased pressure (Berliner and Biddle, 1995). As Alan Jones (1998) has noted, teacher education programs have been under severe scrutiny from the media, legislatures, at "blue chip" governors' conferences, and in federal reform initiatives (Darling-Hammond 1997).

Not surprisingly, in some regions of the United States and Argentina, teacher education programs are increasingly having difficulties recruiting students, and well-known educational researchers like Frank Smith refer to teachers as endangered species:

> Teachers are in danger of becoming an endangered species. They are criticized, disparaged, accused of dereliction of duty, and blamed for declining standards. At the same time, their resources are reduced and they are frequently told exactly what, when, and how they should teach. They are trapped between inflated expectations and diminished autonomy. (1995: 65)

Even in those contexts where there is less focus on blaming teachers, attention is directed toward issues involving more control and accountability, as in the case of teacher competency testing, certification, and national exams (Goodlad, Soder, and Sirotnik, 1997). In short, diverse attempts are being made to improve aspects of teachers' activities judged as central to the quality and excellence of instruction. However, in this context, excellence becomes tantamount to attempts at reducing the expenditures of financially overburdened school districts and at making them more cost-effective. This process usually involves layoffs and the substitution of fully trained, more expensive teachers for lower paid teaching personnel (Carnoy and de Moura Castro, 1996; Whitty, 1997).

In this scenario, some people see teacher education programs as condemned to be reduced to a subsector of the economy, perhaps, waiting to be rescued of its critical conditions by tougher standards, more accountability and much more technology. In reviewing North American and South American newspapers and popular magazines published in the period 1999–2000, it is easy to find that the new hopes for reforming education rest in the apparition of technological heroes, specially in teacher-proof, internet delivered and assessed materials.

The rationale for this romantic idealization of the development of technologically-prodigious, teacher-proof materials is also guided by financial goals. The dream of replacing teachers by some magical combination of internet-based education and expert manufactured materials is oriented primarily by cost-benefit analyses in which the maximization of profits has emerged as the driving force for achieving educational "excellence." Currently, achieving educational excellence equals doing well in standardized tests, which will in turn improve the human capital of a country, and alas, such a society will be ready to accommodate and succeed in this triumphant global society.

Processes of globalization (in economic, financial, social or cultural terms), have been framed as the manifestation of the changes initiated in a dramatic yet unstoppable new era (Rhoten, 1999). The relevance of understanding this framing of global-local processes for educators cannot be understated. When the discourses about globalization, restructuring, and market liberalization are presented on public arenas as autonomous entities, these discourses acquire quasi-divine characteristics. Globalization is now heralded as an autonomous and miraculous process of salvation through which the world's destiny will be realized, as it happens in so many adventure movies. The reference to the movies is not accidental, because in most discourses about globalization it appears that almost the entire population of the world has the role of being part of the audience. We the audience, only need to sit in the back rows waiting for the miraculous power of global technocapitalism to defy misery, racism, sexism, violence, and even improve the shattering systems of public education on behalf of a patiently observant humanity.

However, can we afford to sit back and watch peacefully, waiting for the magic to happen?

What Is in This Book

This book does not pretend to determine a set of well-defined predictions for the future of teacher education. Rather, it attempts to rethink these institutions as they relate to gender and processes of professional identity formation, searching for partial answers with the spirit of a detective.

The detective model I have in mind is not the classical intellectual—clean and always successful, like Sherlock Holmes—but rather the detective of the noir genre. Slavoj Zizek (1991) points out that the main difference between the classical versus the noir detective is not based on the dichotomy intellectual versus physical activity, but on the level of personal engagement between the detective and the mystery.[11] As a former school teacher, popular educator, and university professor in Argentina and in the United States, I am concerned and committed to be engaged with the struggles for social justice and radical democratic change in public schools, in working with public school teachers and students. Thus the lack of involvement that classical researchers/detectives, those whom Mr. Holmes exemplary personifies in the detectivesque genre and many intellectual researchers exhibit in the field of education, is not a viable option for me.

This personal involvement is also based on the theoretical assumption that one of the conditions for conducting better educational research is that investigators should abandon totalizing schemes that pretend to predict the whole complex that concerns teaching by largely ignoring the diversity of the teaching workforce (Kanpol and McLaren, 1995). Rather, I want to suggest a more humble, yet perhaps more productive approach. Educational researchers, I want to suggest, should approach the data collected in the field as indications not only of economical and ideological confrontations, political struggles, but also bodily manifestations and discursive practices that are not predestined to reproduce the scripts that larger structures of authority and privilege seem to dictate for the individuals (Rust, 1991). That is one of the never-ending challenges of conducting research in education: the arduous task of positioning and assuming ourselves as political and ethical subjects who respect our own heterogeneity and the multiplicity of the Other in order to learn and transform our realities (McLaren, 1993; 1995).

This book is organized in five chapters. Chapter 1, addresses four thematic areas: identities and gender, schools as gendered spaces, the concepts of caring and dialogue, and context and power.

Chapter 2 presents the methodological considerations that have guided this research and a series of methods developed during the fieldwork, particularly the use of pictorial productions by students as a valid method of educational research.

Chapter 3 is devoted to the sociohistorical reconstruction of the ideological system that has portrayed teaching as a natural extension of motherhood. It examines teacher education from a double perspective: (1) the historical development of teacher training institutions, and (2) the social representations of teaching advanced by the institutions of teacher training in Argentina.

Chapter 4 is based on the theoretical premise that in educational research it is essential to comprehend and scrutinize how past trends are manifested in the present, locating breaks and permanencies, ruptures and stable traditions in the institutional life of the institutions of teacher education. The initial section of this chapter chronicles the changes in teacher education enrollment and how they are perceived by teacher educators and researchers. The discussion of those trends intertwined with other sources of data (interviews, institutional observations, analysis of the news) will contribute to a reconstruction of the general profile of how current teacher education program (TEP) students are perceived. The second section discusses teacher education students as a social group, and their perceptions about teachers and teaching. The third and last section of this chapter presents the information obtained through a collection of drawings, other interpretive methodologies produced by the students, and the results of several group discussions that followed the creation of the drawings.

Chapter 5 concludes the book by revisiting the main theoretical premises and the empirical findings, placing the changes observed in teacher education, their gender dynamics, possibilities, and changes within the overall context of educational reform.

Notes

1. During the 1980s and 1990s Hollywood produced several movies about schools and in most of them the main role was a male teacher. The following list does not attempt to be complete but to show the most popular films: *Teachers* (1984), *Stand and Deliver* (1987), *The Principal* (1987), *The Substitute* (1987), *Lean on Me* (1987), *Dead Poets Society* (1989), *Kindergarten Cop* (1990), *Mr. Holland Opus* (1995), *Renaissance Man* (1997), *187* (1997), and *In & Out* (1998). Even in foreign movies we find the same trend, as in the case of the Italian *Ciao Professore* (Hello Teacher, 1994) or the Argentinean *Un Lugar en el Mundo* (A Place in the World, 1995). Without claiming that the previous list is the most complete one about this topic, the only exception to the rule, if the main character is a teacher, thus it must be a man, was the movie *Dangerous Minds* (1995). Granted, to have men as the leading character in movies is the norm in Hollywood, but I want to call the attention to the divergence between most people's personal experience of schooling and how the media portrays the same phenomenon. For an interesting collection of essays about the relationship between media and schools, see Maeroff (1998).

2. The "feminization of teaching" is not a universal phenomenon. Dove (1986) reports that in some African countries elementary education positions are mostly occupied by men. It is important to recall that for centuries teaching was a masculine profession. However, with the development of the modern systems of public schooling in the last 150 years elementary school teaching has indeed become in Europe, South and North America, a feminine profession. For further discussion see Acker (1996); Morgade (1997).

3. In Argentina, during this century, a normative denominated the "3x1" established that for every three female teachers listed in the ranking to have access to positions such as principal or district supervisors, there must be one man included (Morgade, 1992a). In the United States similar policies of male preference were seen during the Depression era (Acker, 1996).

4. In a 1992 study at University of Toronto, Faculty of Education, student teachers were asked about why they wanted to become teachers. Not surprisingly, the most frequently mentioned answer was: "I want to make a difference" (Fullan, 1993: 10).

5. This dialogue was produced in one of the workshops that were held during the field-work for this research. Needless to say, it was repeated with minor variations several times.

6. Based on a number of measures of teacher satisfaction the U.S. Department of Education found out that in 1993–1994 only 40 percent of teachers reported that they would certainly be willing to become teachers again. Clearly economic considerations are an important factor in explaining teachers' burnout. Despite having literacy skills equal to those of most other professionals, teachers' average annual earnings and average weekly wages in 1991 were lower than those of accountants and auditors, private-sector executives and managers, physicians, education administrators, and registered nurses (U.S. Department of Education, 1997: 6).

7. To give only one example of an apocalyptic understanding of the proliferation of images, Susan Sontag (1977), for one, has seen panoptic photographic production as a potentially sinister ally of the late-capitalist state:

> A capitalist society requires a culture based on images. It needs to furnish vast amounts of entertainment in order to stimulate buying and anesthetize the injuries of class, race, and sex. And it needs to gather unlimited amounts of information, the better to exploit natural resources, increase productivity, keep order, make war, give jobs to bureaucrats. The camera's twin capacities, to subjectivize reality and to objectify it, ideally serve these needs and strengthen them. Cameras define reality in the two ways essential to the workings of an advanced industrial society: as a spectacle (for masses) and as an object of surveillance (for rulers). The production of images also furnishes a ruling ideology. Social change is replaced by a change in images. The freedom to consume a plurality of images and goods is equated with freedom itself. The narrowing of free political choice to free economic consumption requires the unlimited production and consumption of images. (57)

8. The use of drawings and other nonlinear interpretative devices is not very common in educational research. Nevertheless, there is a limited but compelling body of literature produced by researchers who have experimented in this area. Regarding the use of drawings, the book edited by Pamela Bolotin Joseph and Gail Burnaford (1994) is an excellent example of the importance of looking at images as crucial texts about teaching, and it includes an article that explores the images of teachers produced by children (Nikola-Lisa and Burnaford, 1994). Brian Matthews (1996) and Catherine Tuckey (1992) also use drawings produced by children in their exploration about images of scientists. The book that is perhaps closest to this research is Sandra Weber's and Claudia Mitchell's (1995) research on the influences of popular culture on teachers' identities. See also, Barman (1997), and Margolis (1994, 1998, 2000).

9. John Berger (1980), one of the most astute observers of art and visuality of the twentieth century, has pointed out that in some of Magritte's paintings there is an intentional use of the two languages (the visual and the verbal), which produces the effect of cancellation of one another.

10. At this stage of globalization of the planet, and given the hegemonic power of the Western scientific and research complex, this should not be a surprise. However, it is important to recall that education is always a local enterprise. In that sense not only my structural living conditions (a Latin American living and working in North America), but also my research experiences, have convinced me that we need to develop research strategies of mapping and locating the changes happening simultaneously at the local and global level using comparative approaches. For a thorough discussion about the changes in different national educational systems in relation to the local-global processes, see among others Arnove (1999), Rhoten (1999), and Samoff (1999).

11. Zizek says that the classical detective "maintains an eccentric position throughout; he is excluded from the exchanges that take place among the group of suspects constituted by the corpse" (Zizek, 1991: 60).

CHAPTER 1

GENDER, IDENTITY, AND POWER:
WHO CARES?

In 1989, a student in one of my seminars on multicultural education included in his final paper a simple, yet compelling, anecdote about his teaching experience:

> Each September I am greeted back to the new school year with the ever-important class list. The other teachers and I immediately scan the list for possible problem kids or an exceptionally bad class. The list could even be given to the seventh grade teachers who would instantly assess each student according to how cooperative and smart they were. After noting possible problems, the teachers begin to count. More than the actual number of students, they count precisely how many boys and how many girls each class contains. This is always the most important statistic of the year. Of course, the lucky ones get the majority of girls, and the others count the year as a loss. (M: age 28)

This anecdote illustrates how gender arrangements and orders permeate our daily life as educators, as they are embodied in the functions, goals, and everyday practices of educational systems. As I thought about these patterns, I began to wonder: How is it that these very visible arrangements are invisible to us that we take them for granted? How can we select or construct a theoretical corpus that fosters our knowledge about gender, schooling, teaching, and teacher education?

With these questions in mind, this chapter presents a series of basic premises, guiding hypotheses, and conceptual discussions organized around four relevant axes: identities and gender, schools as gendered spaces, the concepts of caring and dialogue, and context and power.

My explicit goal is to articulate a coherent, yet hybrid, discourse,[1] which would contribute to the understanding of important dynamics at play during the education of teachers. The hybrid rationale for this chapter rests on the deliberate attempt to borrow from diverse authors, disciplines, and traditions that do not fit easily under one roof: feminisms, cultural studies, critical pedagogies, Foucauldian and Gramscian analyses, and comparative and historical studies, among others. These approaches also contain tensions and represent unique institutional practices. They are infused by hope, skepticism, and simulacra, inevitably caught in the permanent interplay of economy, politics, and culture.

About Identities and Gender

A guiding hypothesis of this book is that there is a permanent influence and crossing of borders among individuals and social structures in processes of identity formation (García Canclini, 1995; Donald, 1992). Following this hypothesis, this study avoids the either/or approaches of emphasizing the influence of external structures on the individual (i.e., class, gender, race, ethnicity) or considering individuals as carriers of self-contained identities (based on socialization or combinations of homogeneous class, gender, race, or ethnic characteristics).

Crossing borders does not imply the existence of a crystalline determined map nor the (conscious) knowledge of the path or the best route to get from point A to point B. Rather, crossing borders points to a constant and unstable passage from one sphere of action to another (Ross, 1988). These processes are expressed as constant oscillations of class, gender, sexual orientation, spiritual, and ethnic-related vectors that induce the deployment of distinctive forms of relationships among individuals, social groups, institutions, and societies in general (Balibar and Wallerstein, 1991; Gutierrez and Larson, 1994).

James Donald (1992) has proposed that the consolidation of any given identity, be it "personal," "national," or "communitarian," is always an "educationally" unfinished project. In these pedagogical and political projects, there is a permanent generative process that creates and reproduces boundaries and borders by means of a recombination and *bricolage* of social and personal structures (Donald, 1992). This permanent interplay produces open-ended identities that cannot be derived from homogeneous collective identities (i.e., race, class, religion, or gender), nor be imposed mechanically.

> For not only are subjectivities always only ever problematically occupied, but they have also to pass through the messy dynamics of desire, fantasy and transgression. This unruly and unresolved 'self' (the gap between what we are supposed to be and what we have in actuality not become) provides the space of individuation and agency. (O'Shea, 1993: 501)

These complex sets of relationships (between class, gender, race; and ethnicity and between individuals and social entities) are conceptualized as the juggling challenges of difference and identity (M. Ferguson, 1991). However, this situation has led some researchers toward a quest to distinguish "true" opinions from "false" ones (Duranti and Goodwin, 1992), or substantive statements from arbitrary ones (Hollan and Wellenkamp, 1994, 1996). Usually, such quests are based on the assumption that a person's *identity* is a self-contained and non-contradictory system, or that "identity" is some sort of stable contextual framework that is waiting to be discovered and described by the researcher (McLaren and Giarelli, 1995; Rust, 1996).

As for the connected issues of identity and identity formation, people do not always present themselves in a single noncontradictory form (Casey, 1995; Delamont, 1990; Giroux, 1990). Identity and sense of self are not innate features of individuals or communities, nor are they fully developed at once and then inscribed in stone (Foucault, 1986; Turner and Bruner, 1986). Rather, they are in permanent tension, re-creating themselves through the hard work of social relations between people and their social, spatial, cultural, emotional, and physical contexts.[2]

One of the most fundamental processes of identity formation is that of achieving a sense of stability and security in our personal modes of being a male or female. Sexual identity is frequently explained by references to genetic configurations (XX/XY) as the biological determinants of the adoption of essentially feminine or masculine behaviors or spheres of action. Robert Connell in his classic book *Gender and Power* (1987) argues that gender is a linking concept between fields of social practice and the nodal practices of childbirth and parenting. Accordingly, perhaps in its simplest form, the concept of gender challenges definitions of what constitutes these identities, by stressing the fact that, biologically speaking, females and males are similar in most ways. They are distinguishable only by a small, although very important, range of differences ultimately manifest in the selective reproductive capacity of the female body. However, biological differences do not explain or give unquestionable evidence

about diverse social, cultural, and sexual behaviors (Giddens, 1993). As Gayle
Rubin ironically comments:

> From the standpoint of nature, men and women are closer to each
> other than either is to anything else—for instance, mountains,
> kangaroos, or coconut palms. . . . [T]he idea that men and women are
> two mutually exclusive categories must arise out of something other
> that a non-existent "natural opposition." (1975: 178)

While biology and physiology play a role, self-identification as a man or as
a woman also rests on complex labeling processes.[3] During childhood, and
reinforced during one's whole life span, individuals are consistently labeled as
"boys" or "girls," and in many cases these labels conform to concordant
biological differences in the chromosomal, hormonal, and morphological
apparatus. The differences at the biological level become a beacon, a signaling
system of organizing expectations rather than the fixed cause of differentiation
between masculine and feminine identities (Giddens, 1993). Accordingly, this
book does not dispute the likelihood that there are biological influences on males
and females. Yet the biological concept of sexual differences in itself cannot
completely account for gender distinctions.

Discussing the topic of sexual differences, Judith Butler challenges the
dominant language of interiority or internalization of fixed identities. She uses
the concept of performativity in which "the gendered body [as] performative
suggests that it has no ontological status apart from the various acts which
constitute its reality" (1993: 136). The advantages of using Butler's performative
concept of gender is that a sense of identity (including sexual, ethnic, or class
identity) is bound to an open-ended set of practices that uncovers the way to
alternative performances, even amidst the most restrictive spaces. In other words,
there are more than two "gender possibilities produced within the repressive and
constraining practices of our compulsory heterosexist culture" (Schrift, 1995a:
96).

Therefore, gender as a conceptual category refers to the historically and
socially rather than biologically constructed distinctions between male and
female, masculine and feminine. In fact, gender appears to be integrally involved
in social organizations and in the construction of knowledges and identities in
such a way that many of those differences seem to be natural and not social
constructions. The challenges created by the opposition between the "natural"
versus the "constructed" perspectives about gender are clearly articulated by
Butler, who argues:

> If gender is a construction, must there be an "I" or a "we" who enacts
> or performs that construction? How can there be an activity, a
> constructing, without presupposing an agent who precedes and
> performs that activity? . . . For if gender is constructed, it is not

necessarily constructed by an "I" or a "we" who stands before that construction in any spatial or temporal sense of before. Indeed, it is unclear that there can be an "I" or a "we" who has not been submitted, subjected to gender, where gendering is, among other things, the differentiating relations by which speaking subjects come into being. Subjected to gender, but subjectivated by gender, the "I" neither precedes nor follows the process of this gendering, but emerges only within and as the matrix of gender relations themselves. (1993: 7)

Following Butler and others (Acker, 1996; Stromquist, 1996a), in this book gender is understood as a sociohistorical construction that affects and is affected by individual and social practices that are consciously and unconsciously exercised. As such, gender is part of a complex system of norms and values that is extremely influential in shaping the relationships between individuals of the same or different sexes, between individuals and society, and between individuals and institutionalized structures of power (Kabeer, 1994; McLaren, 1995; Stromquist, 1996b). The use of gender as a conceptual tool allows the analysis of women's and men's experiences not as isolated categories, but as part of broader social relationships in which women are commonly positioned as a subordinate group in the allocation of resources and responsibilities (Jelin, 1987). As Kabeer notes:

Treating gender as one aspect of social relations reminds us that it is not the only form of inequality in the lives of men and women. While "gender is never absent," it is never present in pure form. It is always interwoven with other social inequalities, such as class and race, and has to be analyzed through an holistic framework if the concrete conditions of life for different groups of women and men are to be understood. (1994: 65)

There is an important distinction between acknowledging differences and accepting the social rules ascribed to a given form and embodying these forms by conforming with the hegemonic form of being a "man" or a "woman" in a given society. International, national, regional, ethnic, and especially class variations, are of enormous importance in mediating sexual differences and producing different patterns of gender relations (Butler and Scott, 1992; hooks, 1994; Mouffe, 1992). Without doubt, there are a number of problems with assuming that all women and men are affected in the same way by historical circumstances:

There is no "women" and no "woman's experience." Masculine and feminine are always categories within every class, race, and culture in the sense that women's and men's experiences, desires, and interests differ within every class, race, and culture. But so, too, are class, race, and culture always categories within gender, since women's

experiences, desires, and interests differ within every class, race, and
culture. (Harding, 1987: 7)

Kabeer, Harding, and other feminist scholars have convincingly suggested
that *experiences* do not have essential meanings outside a particular discursive
context. This point is brilliantly captured by Joan Scott's reflections: "Experience
is at once always already an interpretation *and* is in need of interpretation. What
counts as experience is neither self-evident nor straightforward; it is always
contested, always therefore political" (1992: 36).

Understanding gender regimes as discourses of power and identity implies
the challenge of exploring the connections between what is experienced and how
those experiences are represented. Discourses about gender do not exist detached
from social relations or in a historical vacuum. What is designated under the
category of gender or what is considered a gender issue is not a straightforward
reflection of the social and economic conditions of men and women, but gender
is constructed within these conditions. Moreover, for discourses to have any
impact, they have to resonate and connect to bodies, the subjective feelings and
understandings about their "experiences" by men and women. In other words,
our bodies are the locus of the experiences, but not as simple territory with a
fixed destiny, *tabulas rasa* that will be inscribed by natural and or supernatural
forces, as some biologistic accounts propose. I revisit the concept of the body and
its place and/or displacement in modern pedagogical accounts in later sections of
this chapter, but for now it is important to say that our bodily experiences are
always interrogated by the discourses of power and disciplinary practices, and
for the same reason, they offer the possibility of resisting such practices. Robert
Connell convincingly clarifies this point:

> Bodies, in their own right as bodies, do matter. They age, get sick,
> enjoy, engender, give birth. There is an irreducible bodily dimension
> in experience and practice; the sweat cannot be excluded. . . . The
> bodily process entering into the social process, becomes part of
> history (both personal and collective) and a possible object of politics.
> Yet this does not return us to the idea of bodies as landscape. They
> have various forms of recalcitrance to social symbolism and control.
> (Connell, 1995, in Woodward, 1997: 212)

To conclude this section about the use of the concept of gender, I would like
to point out that it has represented not only theoretical improvements but also has
greatly influenced public policies (Acker, 1994; Connell, 1987; Lather, 1991;
Vare, 1995). Nevertheless, there is a common tendency to treat gender as
synonymous with women's topics, and that is a shortcoming. There are historical
and political reasons behind this tendency. The attempt to preserve patriarchal
and unequal sexual and cultural relationships, or the "invisibility" of women in
most of the social sciences studies for several decades, has been the catalyst of a

strong reaction, mainly among feminist theorists and practitioners, that rightly places "women first" (Stromquist, 1992; Weiler, 1988). However, stressing the role and experiences of women is a required but not sufficient theoretical and political action. In other words, if the emphasis is understood as focusing solely on women, then it can be interpreted that the problem, and hence the solution to it, rests entirely with women, alienating the possibilities of creating meaningful alliances with groups of men.

This book, while dealing with situations and institutions in which the majority of actors are women, takes men into serious consideration as well as discusses the process of construction of masculinities and femininities. Furthermore, as previously discussed, we need to ground our elaborations in their specific historical and geographical coordinates. Following this rationale, the next two sections discuss the "ideology[4] of machismo" and the "ideology of Marianismo and motherhood" as key components in the discourses about gender in Latin America.[5]

About Hegemonic Masculinities and Machismo

Recent research on masculinities (Connell, 1996; Messner, 1997; Mac an Ghaill, 1994) has produced an important body of knowledge that can be summarized in the following points:

- Masculine identities are not fixed, but constantly changing in response to social, historical, geographical, and individual considerations.
- They originate through an individual's interaction within and between gender regimes and gender orders, where the parallel process of construction of femininities is of equal importance.
- Masculine identities are reorganized in multiple traits forming hierarchical relationships within themselves and external to them. In other words, there are scales or poles of maleness in any given society.
- The masculine identity that has acquired hegemonic position in a given society claims its superiority over alternative forms of masculinities and over women in general.[6]
- Hegemonic masculinities depend on cultural, racial, religious, and economic characteristics.

Connell (1995) describes masculinity as a life project involving the production and reproduction of complex and yet fragile—in the sense of being historically mutable—identities. However, without essentializing any type of masculine identity and at the same time recognizing the existence of alternative forms of maleness, in most of the world (granted, there is always an exception) men as a generic group enjoy the privileges of the *patriarchal dividend* (Connell,

1995). This dividend results from the comprehensive situation of disadvantage in which women in general are located. This dividend is shared to a greater or lesser extent by all men, even by those who are oppressed by the structures of the hegemonic masculine regime or who attempt to refuse to model their lives according to the seemingly infinite examples of "normal masculinities." Enjoying the patriarchal dividend does not imply total domination or unchanging forms of domination, as is exemplified by the important changes that occurred during this century regarding the position of women, or the uneasy recognition of homosexuality as another "normal" way of being.

The patriarchal dividend must be seen as an obstacle and not as a given a-historical product, impossible to challenge. In fact, I am arguing the opposite, that the recognition of individual masculinities as life projects, oscillating between different locations in the gender regime, allows for multiple shifts and contestation. Challenges and contestations in this case are not the required result of modern social change, the necessary conclusion of capitalist development. Rather, the changes we are recognizing now are old news. Genderized identities are messy territories, and any attempt to script them to only two "normal positions" has never been achieved; indeed, it seems an impossible option for the present or the future.

Notwithstanding the fluidity of masculinities, Connell's (1995) classification of four main configurations—hegemonic, subordinate, complicitous, and marginal masculinity—seems rather appropriate for this project and is widely accepted.[7] Hegemonic masculinity is associated to the broader structure of power known as "patriarchy," and it is "naturalized" as the flag-bearer of the "normal" label. Under this label, features such as paternal responsibility, imposing order and discipline in both the domestic and public worlds, the provision of economic stability, the maintenance of traditions associated to the rule of the state and national identities provide the broad parameters that allow any male to fit within the normal masculine model.

Conceptually all hegemonic forms—despite the different manifestations in each society—claim to embody the power of reason, the supreme ideals of humanity, the greatest chances of maintaining and improving social order, because the masculine model is proposed as the "natural" carrier of the best interests of the whole society, and not the historical result of material conflicts, available technologies, and discourses (Connell, 1995).

Hegemonic masculinity represses and oppresses the expression of alternative masculinities. In this double bind of oppression and repression, authors like Robert Connell, Deborah Britzman, and Michael Messner locate gay masculinities as subordinate masculine forms. The common assumption of the hegemonic perspective is that male homosexuality is perversely connected to a pathological feminine position and as such must be repressed.

Homosexuality is characterized by "pro-family" representatives as "unnatural," "evil," and psychologically "perverse"; but male homosexuality is even more dangerous than female, in the pro-family view, because it signals a breakdown of "masculinity" itself—or what one right-wing ideologue calls the "male spirit," or the "male principle." (Pettchesky, in E. Martin, 1997: 553)

These stereotypes are also sustained by a combination of economic and political power, potent mass media, and the implicit threat of violence. Jane Kenway and Lindsay Fitzclarence point out that "[h]egemonic masculinity makes its claims and asserts its authority through many cultural and institutional practices, particularly the global image media and the state, and although it does not necessarily involve physical violence it is often underwritten by the threat of such violence (1997: 119).

Various studies have argued that the use of violence, both physical and verbal, acquires some degree of legitimacy when it is related to sports, the playground, the military, and within schools (Connell, 1990; Mac an Ghaill, 1994; Messner, 1992). This relative degree of legitimacy, condensed in phrases such as "boys will be boys" or "blows make men," contains an interesting paradox: In order to develop a true masculine identity, men have to endure very damaging emotional hardships and threatening physical practices.

This paradox becomes more evident in the celebration and normalizing reinforcement of the masculine virility implied in the ideology of machismo. Without doubt, machismo as an ideological construct is the most widely known model of masculinity in Latin America. *Macho*, *machista*, and *machismo* are very common terms in the region, used by men and women to describe people or situations. In and of themselves, they do not necessarily have an a priori negative connotation as do the similar English terms "male chauvinist" or "chauvinistic."[8]

What needs to be stressed is that although common to Latin America, it is important to ground the notion of machismo within particular contexts and after careful analysis of its specific manifestations. In other words, machismo carries significant weight in the construction/definition of masculinity in the region, yet it does not have a single model or pattern of manifestation.

The *Complete Dictionary of Sexology* (Francoeur et al., 1995) defines machismo in the following terms:

Machismo (*adj. macho*) (Sp.) The concept and cultural imperatives associated with masculinity in Latin American cultures; the Latin American word for the mystique of manliness. Machismo stresses male physical aggressiveness, high risk taking, breaking the rules, casual uninvolved sexual relations with women, and elective penile insertion in other men. Though useful to describe an extreme male chauvinism, the term as used by non-Latinos to some extent represents a stereotype with deep-rooted value judgements and

cultural assumptions. The term is said to be derived from *macho* in the
classical Aztecs language, meaning "image," "reflection of myself."

In general terms machismo is often used to stress aggressive behavior and
intransigence in male-male relationships and masculine sexual domination in
male-female interactions (Goldwerth, 1985; Gutmann, 1996). Among others,
Violeta Sara-Lafosse (1998) distinguishes *machismo* from the patriarchal system
by emphasizing the lack of involvement in parenting as the distinctive
characteristic of the machismo. The systematic use of sexual and symbolic
violence against women and homosexuals (both men and women) is often
justified as the defense of traditional family values, religious principles, and a
loosely defined sense of public morality.

What seems rather interesting is that (in Argentina and other parts of Latin
America) the traditional description of the macho and its cult to physical
courage, rudeness, and lack of emotions coexists with other very popular and
also traditional models of masculinity. A brief analysis of the world and words of
tango provides examples of these distinctive ways of being a macho.

About tango, as Julie Taylor comments, "although a major symbol of
national identity, the tango's themes emphasize a painful uncertainty as to the
precise nature of that identity" (1998: 2). This imprecise nature is re-created
through the permanent tension and recognition that the past "lives" in the present
but that life as in the past is already gone. Thus, tangos often sing of nostalgia.
The barrio of the past, the love for and by the mother, broken promises of eternal
love, the purity of ideals and innocence that are lost when the man is seduced by
the lights of downtown and its women.[9]

The tango ostensibly sings of love, but it is not the romantic love that leads
to marriage or conventional arrangements, but to loving relationships that can
only be secured through undying passion and unconditional loyalty. However,
not even in those cases where the protagonists of tango are embraced in passion
and love is there access to a "happily ever after" situation. There are countless
tangos where the lovers, usually the woman, who—by faith, by choice, by
history or simple malice—walk out of the "great love."

Consider the following excerpts, taken from two of the most popular tangos
ever. The first refers to failed love due to the actions of the "bad girl" who
abandons the humble and proud male.

Percanta que me amuraste	You, indecent girl, who left me
en lo mejor de mi vida	at the prime of my life
dejandome el alma herida	leaving my soul wounded
y una espina en el corazón.	and a thorn in my heart.
(Mi noche triste)	(My sad night)
	Music by Samuel Castriota
	Lyrics by Pascual Contursi, 1917

Or consider this second example, in which "luck" which is a mean woman, also abandons the suffering male, suggesting again that romantic love is impossible.

Cuando la suerte que es grela	When lady luck, who is very mean,
fayando y fayando,	failing you and failing you,
te largue parao, [. . .]	leaves you alone, [. . .]
Cuando rajes los tamangos	When you have torn your dancing shoes
buscando ese mango	looking for the money
que te haga morfar . . .	to eat . . .
La indiferencia del mundo	Only then will you feel
—que es sordo y es mudo—	the indifference of the deaf and dumb
recién sentirás!	world!
Verás que todo es mentira,	You'll see that everything is a lie,
verás que nada es amor,	you'll see that nothing is love,
que al mundo nada le importa. . . .	that the world doesn't care. . . .
¡Yira! . . . ¡Yira! . . .	It turns! . . . It turns!
(Yira . . . Yira.)	(It turns . . . it turns.)

Lyrics and music by
Enrique S. Discépolo, 1930
(Author's translation)

What seems quite remarkable about masculine characters in tango is that even though they are predominantly single, middle-aged, and middle-class (Archetti, 1997: 202) there is no uniform archetypal image, but a shifting constellation of fluid characters that allow different images of masculinity and identification. One can be a true *man* and simultaneously a cynical rich man, a humble and loyal worker, a romantic dreamer, an adventurous don, or a strong and rude loser attempting to hide his tears while remembering his mother or lover.

Tangos offer, in their detailed and complex choreography, in their intricated lyrics, to women and men multiple genderized positions, and yet, notwithstanding this multiplicity, the world of tango is still hegemonically masculine and overtly heterosexual.[10]

These multiple configurations of masculinities in tango can also be read as a critical comment, pointing out to the failure in what is often described too uniformly under the machismo label (Mirandé, 1997). These configurations express the anticipated failure to attain not only a true essential identity based on eternal and stable positions promised in the ideal of romantic love and incontrovertible gender identities, but also solid, uniform national identities. Perhaps for these reasons Marta Savigliano says about tangos, "No smiles, Tangos are male confessions of failure and defeat, a recognition that men's sources of empowerment are also the causes of their misery. Women mysteriously have the capacity to use the same things that imprison them—including men—to fight back" (1995: 209).

The connections of masculinity with discipline, public morality, and family values need also to be seen in relation to the development of discourses about femininity. The previous discussion of the examples of tango made clear that in the multilayered and open-ended process of construction of hegemonic models there are also open-ended processes of resistance and alternative knowledges. Savigliano's comments in regard to the case of tango elegantly summarize this point:

> A reading of tango that is oblivious to the strategies of the weak—the active presence of women as resourceful subjects—rushes a continuing battle into frozen images. Women have been victimized by tango ruffians in the most cruel and patronizing ways, but they have given their men a hell of a lot of trouble. And I believe that despite the threatening outcomes of tango plots—overwhelmingly favorable to men—women followers of the tango cult were often heretics when it came to the macho cult rejoicing over the female characters' abilities to make trouble. (1995: 70)

About Emphasized Femininities and Mothering

> The "conquest" of women is considered by men here (in Argentina) to be a duty, and it often implies humiliation and the deliberate inflicting of pain. But though men conquer and humiliate women as lovers, they adore and worship mothers. The relative immunity enjoyed during the years of the *proceso* [military dictatorship 1976–1983] by the group called Mothers of Plaza de Mayo may be a case in point. (Elon, 1986: 287)

If the hegemonic model of masculinity in Latin America is represented by the much propagandized virility of the macho, its correlate has been another powerful image, that of the all-embracing selfless mother. It is important to clarify that the ideology of motherhood cannot be conceptualized as having an hegemonic position vis à vis hegemonic masculinities, but should be understood as a privileged or emphasized form of femininity (Connell, 1995).

The emphasized femininity of motherhood frequently invokes the ideal of a female spirituality which advocates that women are morally superior and emotionally stronger than men. The vision of the woman as the heart of the household, the home ruler within the single traditional family structure, driven by the daily battle to fulfill the needs of children and the desires of the husband, is prevalent. These emphasized feminine structures produce different motherly identities and forms of subjectivity, styles of individual gratification, enjoyment, and sense of worth. By the same token, as an emphasized position, it promotes disapproval of others who do not belong to the group of self-sacrificing mothers.

In addition, the ideology of motherhood is of particular importance in this book, because it has been extremely influential in the development of the teaching profession not only in Latin America but in most of the West (Grumet, 1988; Sugg, 1978).

In Latin America, especially given the relevance of traditional Catholic structures, the figure of the mother is a powerful presence.[11] Exploring the impact of organized religions and popular beliefs embedded in religious and traditional convictions is thus crucial in understanding the ideology of motherhood and women's situation in Latin America (Jelin, 1987; Puiggrós, 1991). Jean Elshtain points out that "a religion that includes a Holy Mother as an object of veneration, devotion, prayer, and yearning offers a much more potent symbolism as part of its repertoire than do religions that have been stripped systematically of any such imagery" (1994: 80). Notwithstanding the recognition that religious discourses are one (albeit powerful) influence among many, the models of womanhood and femininity valued and celebrated by religion establish important boundaries. While sexuality as connected to mothering is emphasized, other forms are seen as deviant and amoral. Chris Weedon is not alone when reflecting, that given the strong influence of Catholicism in the region, "sex is defined as naturally heterosexual and procreative and femininity is implicitly masochistic" (1987: 96).[12]

A complementary, although different, view of the role of religious influences in Latin America can be seen in Sonia Montecino's (1988) study about the influence of *mestizaje* (the forced mixture of white Europeans with indigenous populations) on the region's identity formation. Montecino suggests that the violence exercised by European males against native women, coupled with the blending of Catholicism's adoration of the Virgin Mary and indigenous beliefs in which women are associated with the "mother earth" and are the givers of life, has influenced the development of a double standard for many women. On the one hand, most women are constrained to find their worthiness in the sexual reproductive activities that lead to motherhood; on the other, women as a social group are expected to battle daily to be as unselfish and pure as the Virgin Mary (Medina, 1994).[13] These two premises combined provide the basis for the ideological discourse known as *Marianismo*.

Marianismo and "mothering" as the emphasized models of femininity in the region are often associated with conservatism and passivity. This association is neither surprising nor restricted to Latin America. Carole Pateman (1984) notes that the distinction between public and private spheres is at the base of the founding moment of patriarchy in the United States. This distinction reinforces the conception that mothering (essentially feminine and private) is antithetical to citizenship (historically masculine, and by definition, public). Emphasized femininity is also supported by the superabundance of images and metaphors that confine good women to be good mothers, and good motherhood with caring, passivity, and self-sacrifice.

Notwithstanding the influence of these emphasized models, I would like to argue against taking "mothering" for granted. As previously discussed, hegemonic masculinities and emphasized femininities have not been developed in a historical void nor refined by giving them *essential* characteristics. Along these lines, it might be more useful if we examine some examples of the radicalization of presumed apolitical mothers.

In Latin America, the paradigmatic case of *Madres de la Plaza de Mayo* (a human rights organization formed by mothers of Argentina's "disappeared" during the military dictatorship of 1976–1983) and similar organizations throughout the region has shown that even politically unprepared mothers can cross the apparently fixed boundaries separating the private and public arenas, transgressing norms, values, and mores, and overcoming immobility and fears.

These mothers' identification with their maternal duties (and even with religious beliefs)[14] and lack of political experience did not stop them (and other human rights activists) from crossing all the boundaries of very limited and controlled social and political structures (Hernández, 1997). The *Madres de la Plaza de Mayo* forced the whole country to reconsider what was public and private. As one of the mothers eloquently expressed: "When everyone was terrorized we didn't stay at home crying—we went to the streets to confront them directly. We were mad but it was the only way to stay sane" (quoted in Molyneux, 1992: 188).

Searching for their daughters, sons, and grandchildren undoubtedly causes them *private* pain and sorrow. However, what began as individual suffering by isolated mothers became a powerful catalyst for public demonstrations and for seeking new ways of organizing and doing politics. The ethical ideas and actions of this human rights group gave birth to a potent social movement and were also significant in the creation of a new discourse in which ethical components were the articulating axes of a new political scenario that could no longer exclude mothers and grandmothers from the public sphere. In several cases, precisely because of their appropriation and resignification of Marianismo and mothering, some human rights organizations and social movements have found greater levels of legitimacy and relative autonomy to maneuver, even amidst the most hostile conditions.

As in other important examples such as the most famous Argentinean woman, Eva Perón, the appeal to the emphasized femininity could be resignified. Eva Perón, the childless "spiritual mother of the poor in Argentina," defied almost all the moral principles of the country's hegemonic cultural conservatism of the 1950s, including those of the official Catholic Church. At the same time, however, she exploited the imagery of the dutiful wife who stood behind her husband and proposed traditional roles for women. J. M. Taylor (1979) points out the importance of political and class distinctions in the construction of many of the myths about Evita. For most of the poor and working-class people, Evita was the "Lady of Hope"; for the upper middle class, "the oligarchy" (in Eva Perón's words), she was the "Woman of the Black [sic] Myth," or in simple words, a "prostitute." Later, almost twenty years after her death, Eva Perón became the "Revolutionary Mother," giving birth to countless daughters and sons who fought, in the name of Evita to restore democracy after a long period of dictatorship. Even today, the historical figure of Evita arises great controversy. As with the women in tango, no simple reading about Eva Perón is possible. For some people she was a saint, for others the evil incarnated.[15]

In Argentina, the use of the "mothering ideology" has also appeared in other professional, social, and political movements, including teachers' struggles. Nevertheless, legitimacy and relative autonomy in the use of the mothering ideology do not necessarily imply significant changes in unequal patterns of power, nor do they accomplish the goal of stopping violence against women, or improving the learning conditions of students per se. Indeed, Coomaraswamy (1994) has noted that there has been a permanent criticism, especially by some feminist groups, about these types of strategies. If the mother ideology is accepted as the primary "identity mark" and used as a political tool, there are often very conservative overtones that result in divisions and problems with incorporating other women and likely political allies into these groups' claims and struggles. Moreover, as Paulo Freire (1989; 1993) repeatedly points out, the ideology of motherhood coexists and sometimes reinforces severe discrimination against those who are the supposed beneficiaries of these actions. In order to further explore these topics and how they influence the education of teachers, the next section discusses schools as gender regimes.

About Teacher Education Programs as Gender Regimes

I would like to argue that in order to understand teacher education programs, their achievements and failures, their hopes and ordeals, we have to understand them within the frame of the new financial and technological bases of capitalist production; the global developments; the new cultural maps; the changing class, racial, and the gender patterns of discrimination and exploitation suffered by vast sectors of the population.[16]

In order to do so, we need to anchor our discussion in the recognition of classrooms as workplaces, teachers as workers who are integrated in the local economy, students as prospective workers, parents as workers all immersed in the context of globalization and its current glorification of market-like arrangements as the only possible model of development CCCE (1999).[17]

While it is clear that within capitalist societies there is no term-by-term correspondence between gender and economic actions, we must acknowledge that the appropriation of surplus value constrains, yet does not determine, the possibilities of the emergence of gendered practices and social institutions in direct challenge to the status quo. Nevertheless, when the intrinsic coercive and productive natures of all social relationships are conceptualized as relationships of power, we can see how they affect and are affected by the intended and unintended actions of different social and political actors.

The key assumption here is that classrooms are gendered workplaces, and that more often than not, gender articulates most of the interconnected subject positions that are at stake in schools. The claim that teacher education programs are gendered spaces does not imply that gender dynamics over-determine relationships of class or race, but points to the particular importance of gender in the process of preparing teachers for their work in classrooms and schools.

Robert Connell (1996) argues that four types of relations—power relationships, division of labor, patterns of emotion, and symbolization—interact in the configuration of an educational institution's gender regime.

1. *Power relations* involve relationships of domination, resistance, and control among administrators, teachers, and students. They are commonly expressed in the control of resources and administration of disciplinary actions. Good examples of these relationships are the overrepresentation of men in leadership positions and the use of physical strength among students as means of controlling desirable spaces (cafeterias, playgrounds).

2. *Division of labor* includes the allocation of specific tasks among members of the institution. Teachers teach, students learn, and administrators administer. Division of labor also comprises more subtle allocations such as the stereotypical (and strongly institutionalized practice) of science as a masculine field and literature as a feminine one.

3. *Patterns of emotion* include the patterns of structure that define areas considered to be masculine or feminine, especially in their relations to sexuality. In this regard, research has amply discussed how the prohibition of homosexuality occupies a privileged role in schools' attempts to define masculinities, while the promotion of sexless womanhood plays a similar role in the definition of femininities.

4. *Symbolization* draws much of its strength from the larger cultural structure of society, yet each school creates its own symbolic codes in language conventions, uniforms, and the assignment of feminine or masculine characteristics to certain areas of the curriculum.

There is a relatively open-ended interaction among the relationships of power, labor division, emotions, and meanings. In other words, schools actively create and control their own gender regimes within the confining boundaries of the larger cultural, political, economic, and religious structures. Each regime allows for the creation, re-creation, and repression of femininities and masculinities, and in so doing it also delimits the institutional structure of opportunities, rewards, and punishments embedded in the daily tasks of schools, thus extending the influence of this regime beyond institutional walls.

Connell (1996) points out that gender regimes do not have to be internally coherent or immutable structures. They are presented as "impersonal social facts," and teachers and students participate in gender regimes in variable and active terms. Students actively use these spaces, assuming and constructing gendered identities that cannot be predetermined. More precisely, students may end up constructing identities that do not follow the apparently precise script that parents and teachers may have intentionally created. However, there are masculinities and femininities that occupy the top positions in the normalizing hierarchy of a school's gender regime. Some boys and some girls perform their gender identities in ways closer to the imagined "normal" behaviors. These patterns are sustained by a broad spectrum of social and school-based practices; chief among them is the sustainability of an imagined school population that is entirely heterosexual, has a "normal family" (mother, father, siblings), and conforms to the hegemonic rules of society.

Another way in which schools operate as gender regimes can be seen in how classrooms in particular adapt characteristics of both public and domestic arenas within the framework of the more general gender order of a given society. Thus, it is not surprising that for most of the twentieth century, women working as elementary education teachers in many Latin American countries have commonly been called, described, or equated with other "naturally" proper feminine figures such as "mothers," "aunts," "misses," "girls" or "sisters" and in some cases they are addressed by their first name in the diminutive form (Fischman, 1997; 1998).[18] For instance, Marilia Carvalho's (1996) analysis of the interactions between Brazilian primary school teachers and between them and subordinate personnel (teacher aides, janitors, and cooks) demonstrates that women teachers engaged in those exchanges as a prolongation of their domestic roles (teachers behaved in schools as if they were in their houses managing the tasks of a house employee). Another prolongation of the domestic sphere into the life in schools is the already-mentioned use of the appellation "aunt" for female teachers by the students and their families. Stromquist (1997) points out that this tradition may be seen as a way of creating a friendly and personal relationship between teachers and students but also may reflect a pattern of disrespect for the professional status of the female teachers.

Several studies (Freire, 1993; Morgade, 1997; Stromquist, 1996b) have shown that these names were (and are) not naive constructions, but rather societal ways of shifting attention away from the specific histories and characteristics of women teachers (i.e., professional conditions, civil status, age, and above all, their sexuality). In this way, teachers' concrete characteristics are effectively toned down and substituted with stereotypical features associated with the domestic sphere.

The few men who work as teachers in elementary public schools are mostly addressed as "Mr. X" or "Professor X"—where the last name is de rigueur. These forms of addressing male teachers also conceal their individual characteristics and stress a presumed professionalism that, nevertheless, is coupled with a suspicious gaze. Men working in elementary schools trigger a myriad of contradictory feelings that threaten and, at the same time, appease the community at large (Messner, 1997). Male teachers, especially working with younger children, are often perceived as potential homosexuals and sexual predators, even by some of their female colleagues. At the same time, male teachers, especially those working with older students, are considered conveyors and guarantors of order, practicality, and discipline. Moreover, those men who remain in the teaching profession for more than a few years are subtly but surely "encouraged" to abandon the classroom and become a figure of authority, such as a principal or supervisor (Connell, 1995, 1996).[19]

These distinct ways of seeing and naming have been extremely influential in creating structures of discrimination, as well as in shaping the professional and social status of teachers, both male and female. The former indicates that on the one hand, classrooms allow for controlled interactions between familiar actors (teachers and students) within a well-known and limited space that resembles the "domestic kingdom" with particular "feminine characteristics." On the other hand, classrooms are public spaces, connected and scrutinized by parents, policymakers, researchers, and the media but mediated by the powerful structures of the school's administration. For many female teachers, leaving those semipublic spaces to pursue positions of leadership in the administration that by definition is a public space, implies not only moving to a new territory but also venturing into arenas that are traditionally hostile for women.

One of the reasons for this hostility is that the administration of schools has historically relied on modern ideals of bureaucratic organization. This model has been—and still is—influenced by strong associations with hegemonic masculine ideals. By embracing the goals of rationality, neutrality, and explicit and impersonal norms, this rationale predicts that schools will operate efficiently and will provide transparent and equal opportunities for all. The strong connections of this model and its stated goals with the already described characteristics of hegemonic masculinities are well known (K. Ferguson, 1984).[20]

Both in Europe and the Americas, during the development of public school systems in the late nineteenth and earlier twentieth centuries, women entered massively in teaching positions.[21] The economic, political, and ideological reasons for this phenomenon are discussed in chapter 3, but we should bear in mind that this entrance was in many cases framed within the tradition of the mother-teacher. At the same time, it was established that "teaching is not managing" (Morgade, 1992a; 1992b). Consequently, women teachers were not supposed to pursue positions of leadership.[22]

In a parallel mechanism men were seen as better administrators and moved into the upper echelons of the administration, satisfying the functions that the patriarchal system reserved for them. They embodied the notions of the bureaucratic model, as the "natural" warrantors of discipline and order. Jill Blackmore (1994, 1995) points out to three strong masculine images that were pervasive throughout the development of educational organizations: the patriarch, the bureaucrat, and the multiskilled manager.

Beginning in the 1970s a new figure, that of the multiskilled manager, who is able to lead teams, to manage ever shrinking budgets, to set standards, and is apt for negotiating conflicts and making tough choices, emerged. Schools are complex organizations in increasingly more complex communities. These communities are accustomed to seeing men in control and thus they also expect to see men as principals or administrators. Common beliefs about the practical reasoning, objectivity, and stronger sense of discipline of men were also intervening factors. Even the concept of making a career is crossed by gender considerations (Acker, 1996).

Sara Knopp Biklen's (1995) study of elementary school teachers describes how unappealing the concept of the "administration career" for women teachers was because administrative positions were seen as bureaucratic posts, without real decision-making power, far away from their main interests—the children— and related more to discipline than to teaching. As discussed previously, authority and decision making are frequently conceptualized as connected to domination and violence. In general terms, if a woman wants to move up, out of the semipublic space of the classroom, she is usually perceived as being too ambitious or not caring enough for the children, and this is not ethical for women.[23]

The use of time is also a significant conditionality to women teachers' involvement in positions of leadership (Acker, 1996). Under traditional family and institutional arrangements, many women, as both teachers and mothers/wives, have found little time for the extended school meetings and other time-consuming practices required in those positions of authority. Despite these constraints, women have been increasing their numbers in leadership positions, and perhaps more important this presence has been conceptualized by several scholars who have been putting forward alternative visions not only regarding leadership and authority but also on how to organize schooling practices.

About Gender, Caring, and Dialogue in Schools

Throughout the 1980s and 1990s a multidisciplinary body of literature has exposed and criticized the exclusive use of men's leadership experiences as the model to follow when analyzing issues of administration and leadership (Brown, 1999; Cancian and Oliker, 2000; Gilligan, 1992). One of the best-known contributions to this body is Stanford philosopher Nel Noddings (1984, 1991, 1992, 1995, 1999), who attempts to invert the leadership equation. Her work and proposals about the role of caring in schooling and especially in teacher education (Griffin, 1999) has gained considerable currency, and it deserves careful examination. She begins by theorizing feminine ways in the fields of ethics and education from a perspective that emphasizes relationships, emotions, and an *ethic of care*.[25]

> An ethic of care does not eschew logic and reasoning. When we care, we must employ reasoning to decide what to do and how best to do it. We strive for competence because we want to do our best for those we care for. But reason is not what motivates us. It is feeling with and for the other that motivates us in natural caring. (Noddings, 1995: 138)

Caring is a special relationship between two individuals and it strives to preserve the uniqueness or "otherness" of both participants.[26] Maintaining the sense of otherness is by implication an acknowledgment of differences and unequal positions of the participants in the relation. Noddings searches for a balance in the inequalities of these relationships by proposing a fluid change between carer and cared-for positions (Noddings, 1992). This alternance is possible because the cared-for will engage in other relationships where she or he will assume the position of the carer. In the concrete case of schools, Noddings' goal is that students will develop caring practices with others because of their experiences of being cared for by teachers. Even though caring requires "involvement" it is not constrained or limited to the type of romantic involvement that some critics of Noddings fear.[27] As Noddings expresses, "Feeling is not *all* that is involved in caring, but it is essentially involved" (1984: 32).

Noddings is purposefully clear that the guiding principle of caring is to help others actualize their uniqueness through the creation of singular narratives arising from the dialogue between the carer and the cared-for. In her model, there is a clear recognition that there are collective and social narratives that will shape the dialogue and thus the construction of individual narratives. However, Noddings notes that "caring is not unconcerned with individual rights, the common good or community tradition, but it de-emphasizes these concepts and recasts them in terms of relations" (Noddings, 1991: 45).

For Noddings, dialogue is the most fundamental component of the model of care. True dialogue must be open-ended, in the sense that the participants cannot predict a priori its results: "Both speak; both listen. Dialogue is not just conversation. There must be a topic, but the topic may shift, and either party in a dialogue may divert attention from the original topic, to one more crucial, or less sensitive, or more fundamental" (1995: 140).

The creation of these unique narratives through dialogue is perhaps the most problematic and the most relevant characteristic of Noddings' caring model. It is relevant because (as it is described in chapters 4 and 5) the goal of creating individual narratives through caring dialogue matches, to a great extent, the ideals that many teachers profess, and in those ideals there is an implicit promise of change. Oakes and Lipman (1999) are a good example of this position when they express that caring carries not only a higher moral position but it is in "theoretical and practical terms" a superior pedagogical approach.

Noddings' articulation of the concept of caring is also problematic because it cannot resolve the challenges set forth by the constraints and influences that cultural, political, economic, and religious structures have on the construction of the modern caring citizen—almost exclusively a woman, who looks very much like the image on page 2.

The key point I am trying to convey in this section is that we cannot propose a pedagogy, centered on caring, and dialogue, without being aware of how pedagogy, caring, and dialogue are developed within the particular contexts of signification. Individual, institutional, and social practices of power produce systems of knowledge that assign the value of true to certain concepts, images, and metaphors, such as the belief that male teachers are better administrators and at solving discipline problems or that female teachers should be "caring" motherly figures. In order to understand the who's, what's, and how's of the processes of constructing meanings about teaching, gender, and social relations that have become *true*, it is crucial to discuss the contributions of communication ethnographers, cultural studies scholars, and Michel Foucault on the conceptualization of context, dialogue, and power.

About Context and Dialogue

Taking into consideration the contributions of communication ethnographers, "context" is understood as a "set of discursive procedures and conditions that organize the qualifications and opportunities of speakers to make statements, and that establish conditions under which those statements are heard as authentic or true" (Lindstrom, 1992: 104). Although different contexts—such as socialization, culture, structure, public/private sphere, and orders of discourse— often appear to constrain who can speak, and what can be stated, there are always alternatives to be found. Room is almost always available for people to develop and construct alternative voices and to confront the already established true discourses as they navigate various contextual spaces. Nevertheless, people elaborate discourses, including alternative or oppositional ones, in contexts saturated with conditions that constrain what can be heard, and that translate into "audible" utterances (Goffman, 1981).

In other words, "none may enter in the order of discourse if [she] he does not satisfy certain requirements or if [she] he is not, from the outset, qualified to do so" (Foucault, 1981: 61–62). Further, an order of discourse establishes conditions under which the content is considered or *heard* as true or false. Foucault expands on this point:

> It is always possible that one might speak the truth in the space of a
> wild exteriority, but one is "in the true" only by obeying the rules of
> a discursive "policing" which one has to reactivate in each of one's
> discourses. (Foucault, 1981: 61)

In this view of discourses and contexts, what one says is only validated as
"true" if what is said, and how it is said, obeys the contextual discursive rules that
have been set for each individual (i.e., teacher versus student) and group (i.e.,
native versus immigrant, men versus women, economically privileged versus
working class) within each given social setting (classroom, labor market,
family).

Alessandro Duranti links the construction of social "truths" with the need to
rethink traditional models of communication. Elaborating on this idea he says,
"We cannot simply talk, as the classic model does, about Speaker, Message and
Referent. The potential or actual role played by the audience in constructing a
sequence of interactions is essential for explaining the multifunctionality of . . .
linguistic devices" (1993: 233).

Rethinking the traditional model of communication is especially important
for this project because the ideals of constructing classrooms as caring and
transparent spaces, where open dialogue and fluid communication occur, are
very often cited not only as a desirable goal, but also as the key mechanism that
will solve most of the problems not only within but across classrooms, cultures,
races, and genders.[28]

We hear constantly appeals made by teachers, researchers, and policymakers
about the need to improve dialogue. There is an implicit assumption that through
it the participants (teachers, students, parents) will arrive at mutual
understanding, overcoming imposition, and solving differences. These appeals
offer dialogue as a prime strategy open to democratic deliberations and more
efficient than top-down lectures in the process of constructing meaning,
transmitting knowledge, and teaching values (such as tolerance, participation,
and so on).

There are two related problems with this model. First, it assumes that in
dialogue there are only two participants (speaker-receiver, teacher-student).
Second, it also assumes that there is only one (more or less explicit) goal:
understanding the message. Elizabeth Ellsworth's creative use of Chang's
discussion of Serres ideas about these assumptions will help us in the
understanding of these two points.

> [D]ialogue always depends on a joint effort by the interlocutors to
> fight against "noise," against any third party that threatens the
> reciprocity between the interlocutors . . . in every communicative
> event, participants "must" unite against phenomena of interference
> and confusion, or against individuals with some stake in interrupting
> communication . . . sender and receiver . . . must join forces to expel

> the interference, the evil demon, a "third man," namely, any party that
> may interrupt the sending/receiving of messages. (Chang in
> Ellsworth, 1997: 106)

This model of understanding dialogue works against the most common definitions, and even our own perceptions of everyday communicative practices in schools. Perhaps, what is most troubling of all is that the considerations of Foucault, Chang, and Ellsworth open a way that seems to lead into a very odd space. Through our daily engagements in dialogue, and our own utterances and discursive practices, we are participating in the co-constructions of regimes of truth, even in those that may oppress and damage us. Again, Duranti's observations help in the clarification of this topic.

> Speakers may hint at possible (embarrassing, threatening, unexpected) truths. They may describe a world of a situation that is only half-true, or characters that are only half-real. The audience is often expected to do the rest of the job either by accepting or denouncing the potential descriptions of the world more or less vaguely suggested—but not necessarily asserted—by the speaker. (Duranti, 1993: 237)

This discussion about discourses and context indicates that the common process that we named as dialogue is also a mechanism of social-historical construction that not only expresses explicit political, economic, gender, and racial interests but also responds to implicit rules of power (Schrift, 1995b). This last concept is the focus of the next section.

About Power and Context

Power is traditionally understood in a negative sense, as something that is wielded against other. For example, when power is used, its effects are seen in the form of censorship, interdictions, and ultimately, as punishments. Thus, power is treated as a possession, something that only the "mighty" people in a society benefit from. In this understanding, power is situated in concrete spaces, and is often associated with certain professions and positions in a community.[29]

In contrast to this negative approach to power, late French scholar and activist Michel Foucault proposed a positive and productive consideration of power. His ideas about the multiplicity of power sites, and its presence in all relationships, from the most basic structures of interpersonal relationships to the macrostructures of the distribution of economic production, consumption, and exploitation, have greatly influenced contemporary social sciences. Foucault, and many after him, understood power as fundamentally *productive* and correlative with the production of knowledge and as generating processes of classification and resistance. In *Discipline and Punish: The Birth of the Prison*

(1977), one of his seminal works, Foucault begins his genealogical studies about power by analyzing the mechanisms of interrogation and discipline of the body and then he proceeds toward the study of the discourses that those practices produce. These analytical procedures allowed Foucault to inquire about the constitutive character that "capillary" practices have on the rules of formation of particular ideological and historically situated discourses.

In this line of thought, power is a relational concept because "power is not an institution, and not a structure; neither is it a certain strategic strength we are endowed with; it is the name that one attributes to a complex strategical situation in a particular society" (Foucault, 1990: 93). Therefore, power should not be treated as a commodity that can either be owned or exchanged; the exercise of power is a "classificatory procedure" that objectifies as well as constitutes *subjects* which are understood as both persons and bodies of knowledge (Roth, 1992: 690). It is in light of these elements that Foucault argues for the need to look at "the most immediate, most local power relationships at work" in the production of discourses of truth (Roth, 1992: 97).

James Roth notes that "as a result of power's unfixed location and its oscillation between prohibition and permission, Foucault inferred that 'power relations are both intentional and non-subjective'" (1992: 690).[30] For Foucault, power is always a relation that both suffocates and promotes human actions. Power fluctuates from permission to repression, expressing subjective and collective intentions, institutional needs, and structural conditions. The dissemination of power, accordingly, should not lead to a complacent acceptance of omnipresent and immutable structures of domination, as critics of Foucault often assert. It is pertinent to quote Foucault's remarks at length:

> Relations of power are not something bad in themselves, from which one must free one's self. I don't believe there can be a society without relations of power, if you understand them as means by which individuals try to conduct, to determine the behavior of others. The problem is not of trying to dissolve them in the utopia of a perfectly transparent communication, but to give one's self the rules of law, the techniques of management, and also the ethics, the ethos, the practice of self, which would allow these games of power to be played with a minimum of domination. (1980: 129)

As Thomas Popkewitz observes, power "rests in the complex sets of relations and practices by which individuals construct their subjective experience and assume an identity in social affairs" (Popkewitz, 1991: 14). Also important to this analysis is Foucault's understanding and discussion of knowledge and its relation to power. Perhaps no other paragraph is as well known among his writings on the subject of "power" and "knowledge" as the following:

> Power and knowledge directly imply one another; that there is no power relation without the correlative constitution of a field of

knowledge, nor any knowledge that does not presuppose and constitute
at the same time power relations. (Foucault in Hoskin, 1990: 49)

Drawing on Foucault's analysis, then, it is possible to postulate that both
teachers and administrators, female and male, are engaged in regimes of truth
about themselves and the world around them. Foucault says that regimes of truth
are an "ensemble of rules according to which the true and the false are separated
and specific effects of power attached to the true" (1980: 132). The link between
what is accepted as "true," and the social power that affords the speaker of the
"truth" versus the speaker of "falsehoods," or rather, of *unaccepted* "truths," is
clearly established here.

In the elaboration of the relations between power and knowledge, Foucault
introduces a special type of knowledge that is "subjugated" (Foucault, 1980).
This distinctive type of knowledge is historically designated and defined as
having lesser value, as being naive or uncivilized. The conjuncture of
knowledge, power, and regimes of truth and the idea of subjugated knowledges
have important implications for the study of teachers and gender. In many ways,
the discursive formations developed by teachers (who are mostly women) about
themselves can be seen as subjugated knowledges.

The construction of a particular concept as true (i.e., women are naturally
good teachers) cannot be detached from power-knowledge articulations
(Cherryholmes, 1988). There are four considerations in analyzing power-
knowledge articulations. First, there are particular discursive articulations of
power-knowledge operating in the specific context of a study (be it the large
social structures or a teacher training institution). Second, these discursive
articulations acquire a sense of coherence. Third, these discourses discipline the
subjects that enter in the context in which a particular articulation of power-
knowledge is operating (i.e., this program wants women teachers who will teach
better than men, but the program also needs men who will be the administrators)
(Roth, 1992). Fourth, understanding these articulations and discourses is a
necessary step in bringing together the voices and actions that designate what can
be heard as true discourses at the specific arena of study.

Following this line of reasoning, groups that have traditionally been
included, yet their voices silenced or subjugated in a given context (i.e., children,
students, women, people of color, members of the working class, gays and
lesbians), are also "participants" in the reticular organization of power. Members
of those groups are also participants and subjects (in the Foucauldian sense) in
the elaboration and meaning-making process of the regimes of truth about
themselves as traditionally privileged speakers (adults, teachers, affluent white
men, heterosexuals). However, as Dussel points out, "[t]o talk about the reticular
organization of power does not imply that a fair distribution is taking place. On
the contrary, the notion of asymmetry is central to the Foucauldian notion of
power" (Dussel, 1999: 7).

In order to further investigate this notion of disparate speakers and audiences sharing power, indeed co-constructing "truth" statements, it is of utmost importance to revise what Foucault has termed as techniques or technologies of power.

About Technologies of Power

Foucault devoted considerable attention to different technologies of power. He was interested in exploring not only how these mechanisms are used on and contested by individuals and populations, but also to what extent these technologies serve as manifestations, or visible links, of contemporary relations of power in the genealogy of the modern *soul*, or what Foucault called *normalized individuals*.[31]

In fact, the idea of the normal subject was (and still is) a primary construction that has served as the strongest column of the modernist project par excellence, democracy. Democratic regimes require as a sine qua non an autonomous subject (the modern citizen) who is free, acts independently of the forces of the state police, and yet is self-vigilant and also polices others who are seen as deviant or abnormal subjects (N. Rose, 1990).

Foucault links the genealogy of the modern, disciplined subject with the development of technologies of *production* (related to the organization of space, time, and capacities), of *signification* (assigning true/false meaning), of *domination* (examination and classification, normalization of the deviant), and of the *self* (telling the true about oneself, i.e., confession). Foucault specifies that in order to produce a "genealogy of the subject" one must pay attention to the interactions of all these technologies. The point of articulation between these technologies is provided by the concept and apparatus of "government" (Foucault, 1988).

By *governmentality* or governmental rationality, Foucault (1988) refers to different operations intended to guide or to change the conduct of a given population. Tomaz Tadeus da Silva (1998) describes "government" as the particular historical form of organizing social affairs concerned with maximizing the productive capacities of the population for the welfare of the state. This governing is dependent on precise and measurable knowledge about the population and its individuals.

Governmentality, however, has a double implication; it indicates government on subjects (i.e., individuals and groups subjected by the rule of the state, school authority) as well as self-government. As James D. Marshall points out: "According to Foucault, the arts of government, or reason of state, have troubled us all, so that we are not the free autonomous individuals and choosers of individual projects that the liberal framework, and liberal education, would make us out to be" (1995: 372). Similarly, Ian Hunter (1994) sees the development of modern nation-states and the process of governmentality as intrinsically related to the development of a "pastoral bureaucracy."

The articulation between bureaucratic forms of control of the population during the rise of the nation-states (in which the new science of statistics was key) and religious forms of control of the morality (in which confession was fundamental) constituted the two axes of this pastoral movement. According to da Silva,

> [p]astoralism is defined as mode of personal control which uses techniques of moral problematization and self-examination to produce self-governing and self-controlled individuals, that is, individuals capable of governing themselves. The "autonomous" person is himself/herself a product of this technology. The modern state did not invent this moral technology—it just adapted it to its own ends, that is, ends of government. The modern mass schooling is, thus, a product of this improbable but nonetheless quite convenient combination: the bureaucratic mode of government and the Christian mode of personal conduct. (1998: 23)

Through these processes, nation-states (first in Europe and later throughout the Western Hemisphere) promoted restricted forms of public schooling as one of the main vehicles for the delivery of this enlightened and secular pastoralism. Public schooling—the mass, free and compulsory new form of education— needed to imagine and create not only a new class of client-followers for the pastoral bureaucracy (children-students), and a new group of civil-servant-pastors (public school teachers), but also a new type of knowledge (modern pedagogy). These three reconstructions, students, teachers, and pedagogy, were, and still are, processes of "bio-politics" (Foucault, 1978). In Foucauldian analysis (Popkewitz, 1998a, 1998b; Popkewitz and Brennan, 1998; Ball, 1990a, 1990b) bio-politics are understood as the regulation of the individualized bodies of a society by the application of technologies of the self and disciplinary practices (which were by no means straightforward, or free of struggles and contradictions).

Chapter 3 provides a more detailed historical perspective on these topics, particularly as they relate to teacher education programs in Argentina. Yet, it is worth to note here that since the nineteenth century, these changes in the regulation of students, teachers, and pedagogical *bodies* are, in the words of Thomas Popkewitz, "not only changes in the rules of pedagogical reason but changes in the strategies by which systems of social inclusion/exclusion are constructed" (1998a: 536). Popkewitz reminds us that pedagogies, power, discipline, and discourses are always operating at the level of the body and they are unavoidably political. This political condition is permanently changing, because it is not outside history, power, resistance, class, ethnicity, or gender regimes. It is undoubtedly embodied in the regulatory mechanisms of pedagogical practices.[32]

About Moving Forward

This chapter began with an anecdote of one of my students, and I would like to conclude this rather hybrid framework with a second one. In this case it is a narrative constructed by Veronica, a former Chicana student who is now teaching third grade in a public school in California. I invited her to talk to undergraduate students interested in teaching in a workshop called, "So you want to be a teacher?" and Veronica created a series of fictional/real responses of what some of her third-grade students would like to say to these future teachers. What follows is the imaginary voice of one of them:

> So you wanna be a teacher? That's what Ms. Veronica told me aye [yesterday]. Ahh . . . wait. I haven't introduced myself. My name is D. Actually I better say that my name is Dario cuz Ms. Veronica sometimes gets pissed. Aight, you wanna be a teacher. Well I am here to tell you what's up. First, you wanna be coming into my barrio and teach me that $2 + 2 = 4$, when I know for a damn fact that 2 and 2 is a 22. What you been smokin'? Yeah, I am high right now. So? I go to school like this because the teachers are boring. They are up there all talking about Egypt and those fucking pyramids. Was that have to do with me? Those brothers lived in class compared to my projects. They didn't have to deal with cucarachas, the loud music, and the cops rolling by every 10 minutes. And then when we read, we read all these stupid books that I don't even like. Like "The Indian in the Cupboard." Well, that homie must have been high because he was all chueco talking to a toy indio. Except I remember when Ms. Veronica read her favorite book to us. I think it was called "The Outsiders" or something like that. It was pretty cool aye. So, you wanna be a teacher and deal with mocosos like me? Man, I will rip you off in two seconds and not even care. And then the minute you get close to me and think you have figured me out, I am Audi 5000, that means out. You don't believe me? You wanna see my scars? I tried to kill myself twice already. Nobody cares. I guess that is what I am here to tell you. . . . You wanna be a teacher? Well, like be a teacher that cares. Talk to us. Listen to us. Care about us. You know. Make us feel as if we mean something. Hey, I gotta jet. I told Ms. Veronica that I was going to the bathroom. Shit, she probably called the Coast Guard, huh? Peace.

The words of Diego (as told by Veronica) revisit many of the hybrid topics of this chapter: power, context, identities, masculinities, violence, control, knowledge, authority, schools as gender and class regimes, dialogue, and, of course, caring. But these words have other qualities, too. These are words that hurt. These are words that puzzle. These are words of rage. And these are also words that invite us to reflect and act. I hope that the main concepts presented in this chapter will also have those qualities. Before entering into the realm of data analysis, chapter 2 presents methodological considerations, procedures, and techniques used for this book.

Notes

1. Dussel et al. (2000) have noted that hybridity is a concept that originated in the field of biology and that it has become a fad term for social theorists, denoting the blurring, confusing, and intermixing phenomena of contemporary culture (García Canclini, 1995; Bhabha, 1994).

2. This process of identity construction should also be understood as part of the historical process of creation of the "modern subject" in Foucauldian terms. Michel Foucault (1982, 1986) has linked modern forms of regulatory power with the multilayered processes of subjectivization. There are, however, two meanings of the word subject: Subject to someone else based on control and dependence and tied to her/his sense of self-identity, or consciousness of the self or self-knowledge. Both meanings suggest a "power which subjugates and makes subject to" (Foucault, 1982: 212).

3. It should be noted that "labeling" in this case does not imply that there is a "true-inner identity" that the label is going to cover. Labeling processes are also technologies of the self, thus operating in the intertwining of the social and individual.

4. In this book I use the concept of ideology in the sense presented by Stuart Hall and James Donald, which is closely influenced by Antonio Gramsci's proposals. For them ideology is: "the framework of thought which is used in society to explain, figure out, make sense of or give meaning to the social and political world . . . Without these frame-works, we could not make sense of the world at all. But with them, our perceptions are inevitably structured in particular directions by the very concepts we are using" (1986: ix–x).

5. Even though these discussions focus on femininities and masculinities in Latin America, I would argue that the most general descriptors transcend the geopolitical borders of the region, especially due to the important migratory movement of millions of Latin Americans throughout the so-called developed world.

6. Following Gramsci's ideas, social scientists such as Best and Kellner (1991) and Laclau and Mouffe (1985) have come up with an understanding of the concept of hegemony as an ever-evolving political, economical, ideological, and cultural set of processes by which the dominant social sectors (hegemonic bloc) elicit consent from the popular sectors. And yet, hegemony is inseparable from conflicts and struggles over it. Moreover, in any hegemonic process the struggle for control over the symbolic and economic means of a given society and the role the state plays in such struggles cannot be diminished. Cultural, political, and pedagogical aspects in the construction of hegemonic orders are undoubtedly important. However, Gramsci, as a Marxist intellectual, never ceased to stress the importance of economic factors, because he insisted that the *economy* determines, in the last instance, the extent of the compromises and agreements that can be achieved between the dominant groups and the popular sectors. He further clarified this point in the following excerpt: "Undoubtedly the fact that hegemony presupposes that account be taken of the interests and the tendencies of the groups over which hegemony is to be exercised, and that a certain compromise equilibrium should be formed—in other words that the leading group should make sacrifices of an economic corporate kind. But there is also no doubt that such sacrifices and such a compromise cannot touch the

essential; for though hegemony is ethical-political, it must also be economic, must necessarily be based on the decisive function exercised by the leading group in the decisive nucleus of economic activity" (1971: 161).

7. These other forms of masculinities, according to Connell, cannot be as clearly defined—particularly because achieving a hegemonic position involves in preventing alternatives to gain currency, restricting the circulation of those alternative forms to marginal spaces.

8. Alfredo Mirandé (1997) observes that *macho* has entered in the North American popular culture and is being used in a double way. When it is applied to male athletes or popular figures it acquires a positive value associated to sex appeal, virility, and strength; however, when used in relation to the Latino population it is often associated to domestic violence and authoritarianism.

9. Julie M. Taylor humorously describes this situation: "So many tangos sing of betrayal by a woman that, according to the Argentineans themselves, other Latin Americans call the tango 'the lament of the cuckold'" (1998: 7).

10. This imagined masculinity appears to diverge from the model of paternal responsibility, the protection of the family, physical discipline and strength, solemnity, and responsibility in the labor market associated with nationalistic ideologies. This association between masculinity and nationalism is seconded by the studies of George L. Mosse (1984, 1985) and Benedict Anderson (1983). Andrew Parker and his colleagues (Parker et al., 1992) also argue that "nationalism favors a distinctly homosocial form of male bonding. . . . Typically represented as a passionate brotherhood, the nation finds itself compelled to distinguish its 'proper' homosociality from more explicitly sexualized male-male relationships, a compulsion that requires the identification, isolation and containment of male homosexuality" (1992: 6).

11. Affirming that *mothering* is the emphasized ideology for women does not mean that there is only one single model of *mothering* or that women who are not mothers are necessarily seen as outcasts. Given the changes in demographic growth in most of the West, it is easy to assess that womanhood is no longer "exclusively" defined by motherhood. Nevertheless, mothering is perhaps the single most powerful characteristic in the definition of a *normal identity* as a woman. Needless to say, fatherhood does not operate in the same way for men.

12. The main difficulty with this argument is that it makes a general claim about the influence of one stream of Catholic thought, the traditional or conservative Catholicism, not paying attention to other voices, such as Liberation Theology, which also operates within the Catholic tradition.

13. Ximena Bunster-Bunalto has shown that even in those regimes that systematically used female sexual torture, the idealization of the figure of the mother played an important role. In those cases where women-mothers were in captivity they had to go through tremendous transformations. Soldiers needed to degrade those women, and a constant practice was to deny those women's motherhood. "The combination of culturally defined moral debasement and physical battering is the demented scenario whereby the prisoner is to undergo a rapid metamorphosis from Madonna—'respectable woman and/or mother'—to whore" (Bunster-Bunalto, 1993: 253).

14. It should be noted that religiosity or spirituality were important aspects for this heterogeneous group of mothers. During the first weekly march held by a small group of mostly middle-aged women with almost no prior political experience, each participant wore a nail attached to her jacket, to remember the sacrifice of Christ, nailed to the cross.

One of these mothers of the disappeared explained that they also had their share of Christian suffering and relived Mary's grief (Mellibovsky, 1997).

15. What were the unique characteristics of this woman that provoked such heated and enduring emotions? Julie M. Taylor (1979) develops the idea that Evita was extremely skillful at using socially and culturally accepted female attributes in manners and styles that interposed, challenged, and gave comfort to both men and women. This author explains that images of the feminine nature in mainstream Argentinean culture, as in many other societies, are linked to mystical power. The magic that Eva was able to produce was similar to the romanticized aspects of revolutionary figures. A long paragraph by Elshtain uncovers many controversial topics about the fascinating figure of Evita, as well as the topic of gendered ideologies. Do not expect a tidy picture. What one finds consistently linked in the many, even antipodal, Eva images is a vision of femininity, of mystical or spiritual power, and revolutionary leadership, and all these elements put a person or a group at the margins of established society and at the limits of institutionalized authority. The most powerful woman in Argentinean history, a spellbinding rhetorician who cried out to rapt assemblies of tens of thousands, held no office. Beyond or outside of institutional arrangements, she was paradoxically free to inhabit many roles, to play many parts, and to be imagined by others in fantastically at-odd ways. This freedom, of course, had built-in limits; she always claimed she was but the poor mouthpiece of Perón: "I do not have in these moments more than one ambition, a single and great personal ambition: that of me it shall be said . . . that there was at the side of Perón a woman who dedicated herself to carrying the hopes of the people to the President, and that people affectionately called this woman Evita. That is what I want to be" (Elshtain, 1994: 80).

The poor, and especially poor women, still cherish Eva Perón's memory even as others condemn her influence, her evil seductions, her cruel treatment of any who stood in her way. For them, Evita was a divine intermediary, allowing dialogue and exchange between the people and the president. At the same time, Mr. Perón claimed that she was instrumental to his plans; in sum, for him, Evita was his creation. "Her work was extraordinary," he added. God himself operated through her; hers were tasks arranged with the help of divine guidance. Evita did not object to such claims, nor did the poor, who asserted that she was a saint.

It is possible to speculate that the successful style of leadership of the Peróns was intentionally adopted to appeal to elements of traditional stability (i.e., family authority, religious values) in a particularly tense historical period. But the question remains as to why this cultural context that intentionally voiced and promoted traditional and even awkward feminine images led to the development of images of very powerful "public" women instead of submissive ones. Even though the well-known gender ideology of Latin American machismo appears in the mythology of Eva Perón, it is not exclusively or precisely a case of a dominant father (Mr. Perón) versus a dominated mother (Mrs. Perón).

16. In this section I draw mostly from the research works of Robert Connell (1987, 1990, 1992, 1995, 1996), who has provided one of the most extensive and persuasive body of arguments about schools as gender regimes.

17. These comments may sound as some sort of outlandish infection in a book about gender, almost as if the virus of old Marxism has infected the author. On the contrary, this preoccupation with the political economy of teaching is an expression of concern and not a nostalgic call for the past glory of a unified agent of change. It is an expression of concern about the lack of interest in the political economy of schools on the part of many educational scholars.

18. This tradition of using the first name in the diminutive form is also seen in the case of very important political figures. In Argentina, the first wife of President Juan Domingo Perón was popularly known as Evita. His second wife, Isabel Martinez de Perón, was known as Isabelita. In Nicaragua, President Violeta Chamorro was commonly referred to as Doña Violeta.

19. I am not suggesting that sexual fears are the main reason for the abandonment of the profession by men, but that it is a contributing factor that is often overlooked. According to the U.S. Department of Education, National Center for Education Statistics, among new teachers, 81 percent of women expected to be teaching in two years, compared with 62 percent of men. Women were also more likely than men to expect to teach in the long term (69 percent compared with 52 percent) (Connell, 1996: 14).

20. In this framework, bureaucracy is not only a rational structure, it is also a physical structure of power, whereas the higher the person ascends in the bureaucratic structure, he (more often than she) has more formal authority. Even the more contemporaneous discourses about organizations that appear to challenge traditional hierarchical structures insist in the promotion of emotionally neutral leadership in order to secure objective decision-making processes.

21. The massive entrance of women requires some qualification. As previously discussed, not all women have the same experiences and possibilities, and in order to understand the dynamics of gender it is imperative to pay attention to race, and class formation. What follows is a large and thorough passage of Jacqueline Jones in reference to the difficulties of black women to access to schools. Her comments are a good example of the need of not obliterating differences or essentializing "women experiences" while analyzing the topic of the feminization of teaching: "By the early twentieth century, the small black public teaching force had been feminized; at the national level, women in the profession outnumbered men by a ratio of above five to one. This ratio was true for the North as well as for the South, though the number of black women involved rarely totaled more than a handful in any area. In Chicago in 1929, for example, there were only 134 black female teachers. It is difficult to generalize about these teachers, though they were probably young, single, confined to the lower grades and paid less than whites performing the same jobs. As black school attendance and political power gradually increased in neighborhoods like Harlem and Chicago South Side, a few black teachers were appointed by a highly politicized citywide school board. Still, most of these positions in predominantly black schools would continue to go to white teachers, who show little sensitivity to the special needs of their students and quickly label them inferior in mental aptitude" (1995: 180).

22. This limited participation in positions of leadership was also extensive to women's participation in the teacher's union. See Cortina, 1992; Bonder, 1992; Braslavsky, 1992.

23. A similar point should be made regarding gay and lesbian teachers. In this case, they are a priori perceived as unethical beings ill-suited to pursue positions of leadership.

24. For instance Jeannie Oakes and Martin Lipman side with Noddings in their support of an ethics of care in order to improve educational systems. Asking their readers what is the best option between approaching discipline problems, using Noddings' model or an alternative called assertive discipline, they express that building "a caring classroom community" is our best alternative. This is because "substantial research evidence reveals how caring classrooms support high-achieving, socially just, intrinsically motivated teaching and learning and reduces unproductive student behavior. Assertive discipline, on

the other hand, is a commercially hawked scheme to control behavior, and it practices and motivates an authoritarian, anticommunity, and less intellectually challenging classroom. Furthermore, it has no support in sound educational research" (1999: xix).

25. Noddings uses "feminine" in the classical sense. In that regards she comments that if particular approaches or expressions (such as to begin searching for answers to a problem from a moral perspective) are more commonly used by women than men, it is a matter of empirical investigation and she does not want to pursue that road (Noddings, 1991; 1992).

26. Noddings is clear that she is referring to a relationship between two individuals and that it is impossible to bring more than a single cared-for into it. In that sense, she points out that we cannot care for whole groups but only for individuals and only one at a time (in Schutz, 1998: 384).

27. Noddings continuously asserts that care implies a permanent search for social and scientific competence, challenging students with questions that are at the core of human existence. Therefore, caring in the classroom will have implications beyond the realm of schools. Caring must provide the opportunities for students to acquire the knowledge and skills necessary to make a positive contribution in whatever field of study or work they might choose.

28. I resume the discussion of this model of dialogue and its role in a pedagogy of care in the last chapter of this book.

29. This understanding is typical of Structural-Functionalists (Alexander, 1989; Parsons, 1956), who generally follow Max Weber's classical definition of power as "the capacity to exercise one's will even in the face of opposition" (Weber, cited in Grabb, 1990: 118). Similar understandings are reflected in the works of Marxist thinkers, although the focus is on the class and economic overtones of this concept. A case in point is Nicholas Poulantzas, who refers to power as the capacity of a "class to realize its specific interests in a relation of opposition to another class" (1978: 36). Even though Poulantzas concedes that power relations go beyond class structures and include race and gender, economic power is central because it determines the structures (of power) in the last instance; "class power is the cornerstone of power" (1978: 44).

30. Although, Foucault did not regard individuals as mere victims of "power," he also did not believe that they were aware of the broader consequences of their actions. He commented, "People know what they do; but what they don't know is what what they do does" (Foucault, in R. Jones, 1990: 93).

31. Alan D. Schrift notes that "Foucault addresses this soul most explicitly in the discussion of the construction of the delinquent as a responsible subject, arguing that there is a subtle transformation in the exercise of power when punishment no longer is directed at the delinquent's actions, but at his very person, his 'being' as (a) delinquent" (1995b: 32).

32. Inés Dussel presents one example of these regulatory mechanisms in her analysis of the famous *Dictionnaire Pédagogique* by Férdinand Buisson, published in 1911. "[This is] an encyclopedic textbook which was distributed to all schools, many pages are devoted to regulating the appearance of teachers and children and their daily rituals. Teachers should make sure that children appear properly dressed and cleaned when arriving to class, as well as establish regulated movements for entering and exiting schools. It also prescribed general movements for the children, such as the following: 'students should march on line, their bodies straight, their arms uniformly positioned, be it crossed over the school desk or behind their backs with their hands shaken'" (Dussel, forthcoming).

CHAPTER 2

METHODS, IMAGES, AND METAPHORS

About the Development of a Methodological Framework

If there is no history, except though language, and if language is elementally metaphorical, Borges is correct: "Perhaps universal history is but the history of several metaphors." Light is only one example of these "several" fundamental "metaphors," but what an example! Who will ever dominate it. Who will ever pronounce its meaning without first being pronounced by it? What language will ever escape it? . . . If all languages combat within it, *modifying only* the same metaphor and choosing the *best* light, Borges . . . is correct again; "Perhaps universal history is but the history of the diverse *intonations* of several metaphors." (Jacques Derrida, in Hartley, 1992: 140)

General Considerations

In this chapter I argue that the improvement of educational research demands the elaboration of frameworks able to contemplate the relationships and contradictions developed between the demands of the current global context, the organization, direction, and intentions of the state (accounting for both national and local forms of government), and the rational and emotional discourses of the social actors implicated in the process of research.

In chapter 1, I begin to delineate a hybrid framework for the understanding of gender dynamics in teacher education. This chapter continues the development of this framework by presenting a "toolbox" (Ball, 1994) containing the rationale, methods, and techniques used in the process of gathering data for this book.[1] The creation of this toolbox is justified in the overall intention of this project of becoming a substantial contribution to the current knowledge in the fields of teacher education, gender, and comparative education.

Consequent with these ideas in this research, while paying attention to the structures that simultaneously pressure, restrict, and promote the actions of institutional actors at distinct levels of the educational system, I have tried to avoid essentialist positions and categories by recognizing difference, multiplicity, and contingency as constitutive factors in human relationships without collapsing into forms of "anything goes" in the name of preserving pluralism and particularity (Eisner, 1998).

This book, following the innovative and strong methodological proposals about the use of "portraiture research" developed by and Sara Lawrence Lightfoot (1983, 1997) and Jessica Hoffman-Davis strongly argue that contexts do matter. As these two authors contend:

> Human experience has meaning in a particular social, cultural, and historical context—a context where relationships are real, where the actors are familiar with the setting, where activity has purpose, where nothing is contriver (except for the somewhat intrusive presence of the researcher). The context not only offers clues for the researcher's interpretation of the actor's behavior (the outsider's view), it also helps understand the *actors'* perspective—how they perceive and experience social reality (the insider's view). In addition, it allows the actors to express themselves more fully, more naturally. Surrounded by the familiar, they can reveal their knowledge, their insights, and their wisdom through action, reflection, and interpretation. It is also true, of course, that the actors' natural environment will inevitably present constraints, restrictions and barriers—but they will be familiar ones and the researcher will be able to observe the ways actors negotiate these points of resistance. (Lightfoot and Hoffman-Davis, 1997: 43)

In order to make sense of the complex web of articulating senses and meanings about teaching and gender discourses encountered during and after the period of data collection, a set of methodological guidelines was applied in this research. First, the researcher strove to respect the reconstruction of the perspective of the actors in their daily environments. This has involved the use of special forms of description in which the social categories that the subjects use to define their world are combined with the investigator's theoretical categories of interpretation.

Second, research sites were considered as singular social, cultural, and pedagogic ambits: concrete institutional and ecological instances where the subjects materialize, reproduce, charge with significance, and actively produce activities, while at the same time they are subjected to regulatory discourses of power. In other words, one of the goals was to consider the institutional practices of teacher education as conflictive arenas in which models and strategies of teacher training reflect institutional norms as well as social, political, ideological, and cultural characteristics of the larger contexts in which teacher training programs operate.

Third, this research understands (and advances) a change in the conception of the field site, particularly in relation to the collection of data through observations, ethnographic interviews, and the recollection of images and their discussion by participants. These acts ostensibly lead to improved data quality because all the instances of fieldwork are considered as scenarios in which the researcher and informants/respondents perform different acts, displaying as well as concealing their embodiment of theoretical, ideological, and emotional discourses in a particular context (McLaren, 1995).

Fourth, this research has relied on the extensive use of open-ended interviews, following the patterns and leading role of the respondents and informants, as developed by practitioners of person-centered ethnographies (Hollan and Wellenkamp, 1994). In person-centered ethnographies, the distinction between being an informant or a respondent is noteworthy. When individuals are viewed as informants, the data gathered is of a seemingly objective nature. Informants communicate and report their experiences, understandings, and beliefs as members of a social group in a more or less accurate or "objective" way. In contrast, understanding the individuals as respondents requires looking at the particular (verbal and nonverbal) forms that the subjects' communication take, as well as systematically examining their discursive content, because such a study will indicate something about the emotional organization of the subject (Hollan, 1994).

In this approach, the underlying assumption is that the idiosyncratic ways a respondent/informant organizes themes, the way certain issues and topics are presented or omitted, and her/his repetitions and emphasis may reveal configurations with a double level of significance. Thus, while the respondent's developments indicate his or her personal understanding of his or her own history, these individual discourses are also a rich source of cultural and social information.

In this research, some of the people interviewed were considered respondents and others informants. Specifically, respondents were interviewed one or two times for approximately forty-five to sixty minutes. Informants were interviewed at least four to five times for sixty to ninety minutes. As an informant, the subject was queried about information related to structures, social norms, values, and ideologies that support, restrict, or enhance teacher education programs and about gender dynamics in those programs or education in general. When investigating the same topics with a respondent, the inquiry was directed to: What does being a teacher mean for you (as a female or male; homosexual or heterosexual; mother/father; and so on)?

Following all the previous methodological considerations and the contentions of the broad spectrum of qualitative-interpretative (Eisner, 1998; Lincoln and Guba, 1985) and critical investigation agendas about teachers' education, I have developed eight general criteria that guided the process collection, reduction, and organization of data:

1. To give special attention to the interactions between teachers, administrators, students and their environment, emphasizing the reciprocal effect of these actors and their interactions rather than the simple directional causality of one on the other.
2. To consider teaching and learning as continuous, interactive processes, instead of isolating a few factors of the system of teacher training and branding them as "cause" and "effect."
3. To regard the context of the classroom as an inclusive space in interaction with other environments such as the school, the community, the family, media, and other social institutions.
4. To pay attention to factors that are not easily observable and/or quantifiable, such as social representations, perceptions, thoughts, attitudes, or feelings of the participants, as important and complementary sources of information.
5. To acknowledge the possibility of producing multifaceted descriptions by using a variety of methodological tools that examine not only verbal interactions, but also the production of silence, written documents, and the spatial and temporal organization of schooling, images, metaphors, and allegories.
6. To take into account the heterogeneity of interacting meanings in the historic, economic, political, cultural, social, individual, and institutional aspects of teacher education.

7. To seek meanings that resituate the pedagogic subjects of a research project in the center of the school scene and in the formative experiences that take place there, rather than seeking to establish laws that apply to all situations and actors (Geertz, 1983).

8. To inquire about the relationships between historical and contemporary regimes of truth about teacher education and gender dynamics as they are manifested over time in changing institutional practices (Popkewitz, 1991).

To sum up, this project has employed ethnographic and sociohistorical perspectives as well as tools from image-based research that incorporated not only the speaking voice of the subjects involved in the institutional situations under study, but also alternative forms of expressing those voices. The next section presents the collection of tools and techniques used for the process of data collection.

About the Tools and Techniques Used during Fieldwork

The combination of procedures used in this study has permitted both an in-depth study of competing policy visions, and ideologies about gender, and an analysis of the interactions between students and the individuals that teach them in teacher education programs. The ethnographic character of this research was complemented with the collection of statistical data concerning general education indicators and gender issues. I reviewed secondary data sources, making a comparative analysis of international and national data on education in the region to identify trends and point to areas where more research is needed.

Because the data collection and analysis is also part of a narrative practice that is institutionally bound, and discursively and geopolitically situated, I gathered data and organized it into macro and micro contextual levels.

Macro Level

At the macro level, this project focused on historical and contemporary processes related to the institutional and cultural organization of teacher education. The use of historical sources was oriented to trace changes in the institutional patterns of teacher education programs as well as to incorporate significant dynamics happening in other areas: changes in the conception of femininity, masculinity, theories of development, theories of education, social and economic pressures (at the local and international levels), and in the discourses and orientations about teaching in Argentina. This level includes data that ranges from the origins and evolution of teacher training institutions in Argentina to the most recent changes in federal educational policies, particularly those affecting gender issues within teacher training programs. I paid special attention to recent public responses of teachers to the policy changes and to interactions among public officials, researchers, teachers' associations, teachers' unions, and women's organizations in the city of Buenos Aires. The instruments and data collection categories include the following:

Historical data: A bibliographical search related to the historical development of the teacher training institutions and on the social representations about teaching and teachers from the 1860s to the 1990s was carried out.

Statistical data: A careful comparison was made of national, municipal, and international sources focusing on general educational indicators of elementary school performance during the last twenty years (e.g., enrollment, expenditures, repetition rates); general indicators of teachers' working conditions (e.g., salaries, work hours, accreditation); and general indicators of gender-related issues (e.g., salary disparities, mortality, paid and unpaid work).

Document analysis: Content analysis was performed on: (a) the General Law of Education, curricula, teacher training programs, and didactic materials; (b) documents produced by the Ministry of Education, teachers' organizations, universities and research centers, women's organizations, and international organizations; and (c) coverage of related topics in the media.

Interviews: A series of open-ended and semistructured interviews were carried out with selected informants about the policymaking process in relation to teacher education programs, including government functionaries, policymakers, teachers, administrators, union members, researchers, and participants in women's organizations.

Micro Level

At this level, I conducted observations, interviews, and focus groups in six teacher education institutions and one workshop for adult educators. Two teacher education programs were selected for more in-depth data collection for several reasons. The first location is one of the most prestigious teacher training programs in the city of Buenos Aires and has a relatively large number of male students and faculty. The second is also a well-known institute for teacher training, and it is an almost all-female institution. This last institution was selected because its directors and administrators pride themselves for training the best teachers for poor areas. These two institutes also differ in size and in the socioeconomic status of the students. The following instruments were used for data collection:

Person-centered ethnographies: Respondents from the two selected teacher education programs were chosen using the following criteria: (a) one woman and one man working as the director of a teacher-training institution; (b) two women and one man working as instructors in a teacher-training institution; (c) four female and two male students in a teacher education program; and (d) two female alumnae of the selected institutions currently working as teachers. In order to have as much variety among the subgroups of informants as possible, additional criteria, such as parental and marital status, age, social and economic background, and political experiences, were taken into consideration.

Questionnaire: A general open-ended questionnaire was administered to all the students (178 students) in the six teacher training programs and representing approximately 10 percent of all students enrolled in teacher education programs in the city of Buenos Aires. The questions related to the following areas: (a) student's socioeconomic and cultural background; (b) student's decision to become a teacher; (c) student's opinions and expectations about salaries, labor conditions, and occupational futures; and (d) student's metaphors for the teaching profession and feelings about the image of the teacher as a second mother.

Observations: During the eight-month period of fieldwork, biweekly non-participatory observations were carried out at the two selected teacher training institutions. In addition, three full days of observations in four other teacher training programs were conducted. In all cases, classroom and school activities (ceremonies, informal gatherings, and so on) and students' and teachers' activities outside schools (political demonstrations, field trips, and so on) were included in the fieldwork observations.

Production of images and focus groups: I conducted seven workshops during which images about teaching were produced by the students. In each of these workshops an average of twenty to twenty-five students participated in activities that lasted for approximately two hours. These workshops were conducted at the end of the period of fieldwork observations in each teacher education program so that the students would be familiar and comfortable with the presence of the researcher in the institution. Each workshop was audiotaped and notes were taken by the researcher.

The central focus of these workshops was the production and analysis of images through a technique specially designed and developed in this research. This technique used drawings as an interpretative activity, involving groups of students working to demonstrate their understanding of *real* pedagogical and *ideal* pedagogical situations. It should be noted that because in Spanish some nouns like *Maestro/Maestra* (male/female teacher) are not gender neutral, the directions for this first part of the drawing exercise used exclusively gender neutral nouns, such as *situación educativa real o ideal* (real or ideal school situation).

The directions for this activity were quite open. "On this sheet of paper, please make a drawing/s representing a real or ideal (or both) situation/s related to education." The drawings were complemented with written explanations of the purposes and meaning of the representations, and when necessary, clarifications of certain aspects of the images (i.e., gender, ethnicity, age) were requested. In broad terms, these steps were followed.

- Students were told the purposes of the activity and assured confidentiality.
- Participants were provided with white sheets of paper, colored markers and pencils.
- Students discussed for ten to fifteen minutes in small groups, reflecting on (the characteristics or what would be) the elements to incorporate in the real/ideal images.
- Students chose to work individually or in pairs, and work for fifteen to thirty minutes in the production of the drawings.
- After producing the drawings, the students wrote the rationale for the images (i.e., why their image/s had certain characteristics).
- Once all the students finished with the drawings and explanations, all the drawings were displayed allowing the whole group of students to see each image in detail. Once the images were freely examined, the researcher showed each image individually and read the explanations provided by the author of the image.
- After the students were familiar with all the drawings and their explanations, the group selected one or two images for an in-depth discussion and analysis. This final part of the workshop lasted approximately between forty and sixty minutes.

While the students were working in small groups and producing the drawings, the role of the researcher was as unobtrusive as possible, taking notes and observing the process. During the group discussion, the researcher hung all the images on the blackboard or a wall and asked the students to look at them. The researcher coordinated the whole group discussion, took notes, and recorded the opinions and exchanges between the students.

It is important to state that the workshops devoted to the production of images were used as a complementary tool and not as an isolated effort of obtaining personal narratives. These workshops have offered spaces for reflection for all their participants, while providing new elements related to theoretical debates on issues such as social reproduction and social change and the connections among personal life, social institutions, and social structure.

The data produced in these workshops were analyzed in two successive and complementary forms. First, all the drawings were coded and grouped according to the presence or absence of specific features such as gender of teachers, gender of students, depictions of particular situations (poverty, violence, boredom, discipline, caring, and so on). Following William J. Mitchell's (1992) reflections about visual truth, the presence or absence of specific features was understood as a representational commitment to express a specific feature. First:

> Image-production processes make certain representational commitments: they record certain kinds of things and not others, and they record some kinds of things more completely and accurately than others. These representational commitments determine in a very obvious way the limits of a resulting image's potential uses in an act of communication. . . . Secondly, a picture used in an act of communication must have the correct type of intentional relationship to its subject matter. (In other words, it must be about the right sort of thing.) (Mitchell, 1992: 221)

Second, the presence of representational commitments was understood as evidence of data, and thus allowing for quantification and establishing frequencies of distribution of specific features (i.e., percentage of female/male in drawings about real teachers). These tendencies, discussed in chapter 5, constitute part of the "evidence" that this research used in the understanding of gender dynamics in teacher education. Yet these visual representations were understood as mediated by the heterogeneous cultural constructions of the students who participated in this research. Therefore, understanding these representations requires to see them in their context of production. To do so, the analysis of the images is cross-referenced with their written rationale, the data obtained from the application of questionnaires, and the discussion and examination produced during the workshops.

Final Notes on Methodological Issues

The data obtained via the production of images, interviews, observations, open-ended questionnaires, and other procedures produced a permanent interplay of tensions. Sometimes written statements coincided, while others contradicted information obtained through direct observation, or that denoted in images. These tensions and contradictions became thematic axes that guided the analysis of this project instead of being discarded as unruly variables. Accepting tensions and contradictions as thematic axes was central to this researcher's efforts to respect the participants' voices and rationale without forcing their systematization and analysis by using previously developed external categories.

Accepting that cultural and social elements of a given society are always present in individual or group story(ies) does not imply that the researcher should assume that culture and society predetermine the scope or content of an individual's understanding of culture and history.[2] How cultural beliefs and practices may or may not influence the individual's development is an issue that needs to be actively investigated and not taken for granted (Hollan and Wellenkamp, 1994). In addition, the fact that there may be some issues and characteristics of a culture that affect a particular individual in a certain fashion may give us clues about how differently these cultural aspects influence a person's experiences and his or her perception of those experiences. Therefore, this research has attempted to elude countless details and anecdotes and to avoid appropriating *differences* into essentialistic identities of the Other (McLaren, 1995; Rust, 1996).

However, the relationships established between researcher and her or his interviewees are not neutral as understood by traditional anthropological approaches (McLaren, 1993, 1995). For these reasons, it is obvious that the field sites, as well as the related interview situations selected in this research, are not "natural" places in which natural events occur. The impossibility of considering the field site as simply a spatial location of the research, uncontaminated by social, cultural, and economic tendencies of a given society, requires seeing the field site as the arena in which multiple patterns of power are developed, constructed, and challenged.

Each of the tools used in this project, historical analysis, questionnaires, interpretative activities, interviews, and observations has contributed to the difficult task of understanding teacher education programs, their histories, structures, and especially their dynamics around issues of gender. As distinct and partial tools they allowed for different modes of analysis that nevertheless need to be taken in conjunction with each other, in explicit recognition that educational research needs to go beyond either/or tendencies manifested in the exclusive use of quantitative versus qualitative or top-down/bottom-up approaches. In other words, the hybrid character of the methodologies used in this research responded to the need to understand that in teacher education there are no single causes and universal patterns, but as the words of Borges and Derrida indicate in the opening of this chapter, "diverse intonations of several metaphors."

Notes

1. Stephen Ball (1994) has described the use of a "toolbox" in educational research as encompassing diverse concepts, methods, and theories that would serve as the foundations for the task at hand.

2. This does not imply, however, that a research project should be developed from a nontheoretical point or from an intellectual void that would lead to a closed empiricism. See Kohli (1995) and Kincheloe (1991).

CHAPTER 3

A BRIEF HISTORY OF ELEMENTARY TEACHER EDUCATION IN ARGENTINA: INSTITUTIONS AND SOCIAL REPRESENTATIONS

This chapter has two intertwined goals. First, it will present three historical-institutional models of teacher training in Argentina: the "Normal School;" the "Professorship"; and what I have termed, for lack of a better term, the "Adjusted Teacher Training Model."[1] Second, it will discuss the social representations of teaching advanced by these three institutional models of teacher education.

In historical terms, the development of these three models was mainly articulated around two distinctive axes. Historical, political, and institutional arenas have constituted the first axis, whereas the second axis centers in the demands created at the interior of the pedagogical field of teacher education.

The first axis provides the contextual parameters of functioning for the institutions of teacher education. Thus, analyzing this axis allows for a better consideration of social and educational conflicts and tensions, principally between the state and different sectors of the population. These tensions are manifested in struggles, reforms, and political negotiations mainly located at the level of the provision of educational services.

The second axis is revealed in the conflicts for the development of hegemonic representations about what an elementary education teacher ought to be. The social representations about teachers are constructed, paradigmatic images of teaching that overlap with more general regimes of truth. Social representations are in a sense archetypical images of teachers—indicating a "tendency to form representations of a motif—representations that can vary a great deal in detail without losing their basic pattern" (Jung, 1964: 58).

The overall objective of this chapter is to provide the required social and historical contexts for the understanding of gender dynamics in contemporary institutions for the training of elementary education teachers in the city of Buenos Aires, which is the focus of chapters 4 and 5.

Origins and Trajectory of Argentina's System of Teacher Training

The Normal Schools (1870–1969)

In 1870, President Domingo Faustino Sarmiento—who is today remembered as the "schoolteacher of the nation"—established the first Normal School,[2] after the French model of the same name. The Normal Schools were specialized institutions at the secondary level that focused mainly on pedagogical and didactical training of elementary education teachers, rather than on the traditional liberal and encyclopedic curriculum of the national secondary schools.[3] Another contrasting characteristic between this model and other secondary education options was that the Normal School did not allow students to go to the university after completing the second level of schooling.[4]

Between 1870 and 1895, thirty-eight Normal Schools were created throughout the country. Among the initial problems that these schools faced were the high rate of dropouts and "job desertion" among their male students. The figures are quite dramatic. For example, between 1888 and 1890, 60 percent of the male students had deserted their jobs. In 1892, out of a total of 1,704 teachers with a teaching degree, only 1,235 were working in schools (Terigi and Dicker, 1997).

While the tendency toward "job desertion" among males in favor of other work options and college studies was on the rise,[5] a larger number of women enrolled and completed their studies at the Normal Schools. Several hypotheses have been suggested to explain this phenomenon. First, there were clear economic reasons. The state made it an official policy to recruit women as teachers because it was a common practice to pay them smaller salaries than males.[6] In 1858 D. F. Sarmiento, whose ideas about education profoundly shaped Argentina's education, stated, "Women's education has been a topic of choice for the philanthropist; however, the education of women for the noble profession of teaching is also a matter of economy and industry. Public education will be less expensive with women's help" (Sarmiento, 1858, quoted in Birgin, 1999: 41).

Second, at that particular historical juncture (and for a good part of the next century), teaching was considered one of the few chances for women to "decently" make a living and if married of complementing her husband's wages.[7] Because education was looked upon as an almost altruistic offering to the community, middle-class women were offered a limited participation in the public space. At the same time, women and authorities needed a way to avoid stigmatizing teachers as "unruly public women" (in Argentinean parlance, the concept of "public women" means prostitutes). Although these topics will be explored in greater detail in the next section, it is important to advance the notion that one of the keys for the understanding of teaching during this period is that schooling was invested with sacred virtues: teachers became lay apostles and schools became second homes.

Gender differences in enrollment were rather important. In 1909 there were 4,189 female students and only 885 male students in the Normal Schools.[8] Given this scenario, it is fairly accurate to say that in Argentina, the Normal School and teaching as a career were "feminine" and family-oriented from the beginning of the profession.[9]

In addition to the gender differences, it is worthy to note that, contrary to the higher social and economic status of the (mostly male) students in other secondary education institutions at that time (i.e., the national schools that led to university studies and public administration jobs), students in Normal Schools were recruited from the middle-class and lower-middle-class sectors. The only requirements to be accepted into a Normal School were to have an elementary school degree, a "good moral" certificate, and a physical capacity certificate given by a doctor (Dicker and Terigi, 1994).

To summarize this brief historical presentation, it is worth to stress that from its origins, the Argentinean educational system had special schools for teacher training, independent from the rest of the educational system. Likewise, teaching careers were organized in different programs according to the level these teachers were intended to teach (i.e., preschool, elementary, and secondary). This structure remained mostly unchanged until the 1960s, when after important debates, the system of "professorship" for teacher training was created. However, before discussing this change, it is important to present the oldest and most important social representation about teachers transmitted by the Normal School.

The Normal School Teacher: Apostles and Second Mothers

The hegemonic social representation of teachers supported by the Normal School was the figure of the educator as a sort of lay missionary who devoted her or his life to nurturing new generations. The religious overtones of the Normal School movement were related in part to what Durkheim (1903) described as the acceptance of the Catholic liturgy of teaching, in the sense that schools became a new temple, the "temple of knowledge," and teachers became the lay apostles of the state in a quest for enlightenment in the civilizing crusade of educating the people (Hunter, 1994; Popkewitz, 1993).

In Argentina, as in many Western countries, these ideas soon became standard qualifying factors for teachers. Thus, teachers, but especially women teachers, had to have the right moral character and vocation to be teachers. Vocation was often expressed as closer to the ideals of maternal love, caring, dedication, and giving of one's self to the children in the name of patriotic—and frequently religious—principles (Weimberg, 1983). Silvia Yannoulas (1996), among other researchers who have studied the development of the Normal School in Brazil and Argentina, has pointed out that the convergence of teachers as surrogate parents (more likely mothers) and as lay apostles for the new missionary actions of the state was initially developed by Pestalozzi (1747–1824) and perfected by his disciple, Herbert Froebbel.[10]

The dissemination of "scientific theories" that saw women as "natural teachers" coupled with an incipient yet strong cult to motherhood (still very much in place in the present) were extremely popular in Argentina, particularly among the incipient middle class and newly arrived immigrants (Morgade, 1992a, 1992b). Shari L. Thurer, commenting on the cult of motherhood in this historical period, states:

> In her late nineteenth-century heyday, the clergy, poets, politicians, and just about everyone put mother on a pedestal. She was a balm for every wound inflicted by the hostile outside world. Within the walls of her garden, mother taught virtue to children who would grow up and say, "All that I am, I owe to my angel mother." (1994: 186)

The poetic, philosophical, and scientific exaltation of the teacher-mother proved powerful in the Argentinean context to the extent that these ideas were reflected in the educational policy recommendations of the Pedagogical Conference of 1882.[11] The recommendations of the Pedagogical Conference were put in practice by Educational Law No. 1420. Article 10 of this law stated that only female teachers could be assigned to the lower grades because "having equal knowledge, women, without a doubt, have a better capacity for teaching than men." However, it is important to reiterate that at a less idealistic level, these recommendations and rules sought, on one hand, to produce a teaching corps willing to accept very low salaries, and on the other hand, to avoid job desertion, more frequently seen in men than women (Tedesco, 1980).

In order to understand the development of this particular social representation about teachers, it is worth to point out two other intervening factors. First, during this historical period, the state made enormous efforts to build a national system of education and such a task required more teachers than ever before. This project required enormous amounts of public money, particularly for a state budget exhausted after almost forty years of civil war. Thus, there were limited resources for public education, and female teachers were presumably less costly than male teachers (Tedesco, 1982; Yannoulas, 1996). Second, and at a very concrete level, professional or career opportunities and universities were closed to women at this time. Thus, even for those women who may have wanted to choose a different path, they did not have other "decent" choices or viable options, and perhaps to a large extent teaching was seen for many of those pioneer women teachers as a liberating personal experience. Sarah Chamberlain Eccleston,[12] one of the sixty-five North American teachers hired by the national government to help in the daunting task of creating a mass system of public education, wrote in her memoirs thoughts that may have very likely resonated with many women teachers during that period:

> In the summer of 1876 I resolved to carry out my desire to prepare for a teacher of kindergarten, although bitterly opposed by mother, brothers and relatives. I wanted to be independent, to no longer be supported by them, willing as they appeared to be to maintain me and my children. (Pat Parker, 1997–1999: 2)

Within the imaginary boundaries of this representation, newly trained teachers learned that it was not valid to ask for better salaries or working conditions: mothers as well as apostles are not worried about material gains. Instead, teachers as mothers or apostles had high social prestige. That is, they were perceived as "naturally unselfish" and giving. As one may guess from this situation, teachers were neither seen as workers nor as true professionals by the community or even by themselves. In that sense, women teachers shared similar status with housewives who were expected to happily perform various tasks all day long, supposedly fulfilling their most intimate desires of raising healthy families.

This representation of teachers was greatly influenced by positivism, nationalism, and Catholic thought (Alliaud, 1993; Puiggrós, 1990).[13] In this hegemonic scheme, as long as the Normal School reigned supreme in teacher training, it was "natural," even "scientific," that women should teach under the command and supervisory gaze of male administrators and with lower salaries than their male peers (Bonder, 1992; Schmukler, 1992). Religious ideas and constant references to more elevated models of motherhood, such as religious references to the Virgin Mary or Argentina's patron saint, the Virgin of Luján, were brought in to establish the sense of abnegation that was expected from teachers. By the same token, these concepts transmitted a particular sense of the model of women that teachers were expected to be and of the moral standards they were supposed to have.

The emphasis in the moral aspects of education should not be understood as a total dismissal of math and sciences. Among Normalists (such as Pablo Pizzurno and Ernesto Nelson), education was considered a science and serious matter. The emphasis in science and rigor was not only part of the Normal ethos but a credo used for battling against the lack of "official credentials" and supposedly lack of preparation of thousands of practicing teachers. Accordingly, for many who taught and learned in the Normal Schools were struggling to impose their cultural capital as the only one that guaranteed the moral, scientific, and methodological unity required for the development of universal principles for education. Within the Normal movement the teachings of Herbart and other positivist thinkers were uneasily combined with more spiritualist principles developed after Froebbel and Pestalozzi. Years later this combined positivistic and spiritual cultural capital was coupled with the ideas and proposals of pragmatist philosophers James Dewey and Henry James.

As previously mentioned, Froebbelian ideas about organizing the schooling process as an extension of the household were also key in organizing gender-oriented traditions and rituals in the Normal School. Providing a "homelike" environment for the younger generations was a priority. Not surprisingly, one of the first pedagogical metaphors of the Normal School was to equate learning with eating (feeding is the first interaction between mother and child). Therefore the main role of the mother teacher was to "feed literacy, values, and civic virtues" to the students. However, given the influence of Catholic ideas and rituals, under this ideological construction, teachers (mothers/apostles) had to deliver other types of nourishment, considered far superior than the strictly material food.[14] As was commonly expressed among teachers, they were to provide the food for the spirit of those who suffer the hunger for enlightenment.

This social representation of teachers cannot be underestimated. Not only was it hegemonic during the long period of time in which the Normal School was the only institution that certified teachers, but it was also part of a stronger symbolic web that has proven to be very difficult to challenge and even more difficult to resist and transform. Nevertheless, teaching did provide a narrow route for some women who actively pursued working in schools as perhaps the only avenue to legitimately participating in the world outside the home. Yet, at the same time, they were also participating in the construction of regimes of truth about the "proper place for women" in society. In sum, the Normal School and the ideology of the second motherhood fertilized the grounds for the early feminization in Argentina's classrooms and duplicated the sentimental discourse of prioritizing child nurturing and good motherhood as in Pestalozzi or Rousseau's archetypal mothers.

All of the above elements do not imply that this model was unique or that it was not challenged during this long period (see Birgin, 1995; Davini, 1995; Suarez, 1994). However, it was only at the end of the 1960s, in the social and historical context of a military dictatorship, that the educational authorities launched what became a successful institutional challenge and promoted new state-sponsored social representations of teachers. The main instrument for this challenge took the form of a direct attack on the institutional roots of the "vocational teacher," the Normal School, which will now be discussed.

Professionalization Is an Order: The Tertiarization of Teacher Training (1969–1988)

In 1969, by executive decree of a military dictatorship, the training of elementary and preschool teachers was made into a third (nonuniversity) level degree. This reform established the creation of teacher education programs (preschool and elementary) organized in a two-year course study and a half-year residency. With this reform in order to be a teacher, students had to have a secondary education diploma granted by a Normal School.[15] Other secondary education diplomas required an equivalency test.

None of these changes directly linked the training of teachers with university studies or with schools of education in universities. However, in some areas of the country, a few universities did open teacher education units. Even in those cases, the students who opted for teacher education were not allowed to transfer units or credits to future university level studies.

The change from secondary to a tertiary level was accompanied by important discussions about the professional status of teachers and teaching. The critics of this reform focused their attention on the length of time spent in training teachers because the change to the third level shortened teaching studies. This reform made teacher training a two-and-a-half-year major. In contrast, the defendants of the reform saw tertiarization as the beginning of the process of professionalization by lengthening the time of teacher training. For them, the reform meant that in order to be a teacher, it was necessary to spend seven and a half years in classrooms (five in secondary education plus two and half in a teacher training institution).

The 1969 reform ended the Normal Schools' monopoly on teaching accreditation. At the same time, Normal Schools were able to diversify the careers they offered by incorporating teacher training for secondary schools and even technical careers. This diversification ended the close relationships of elementary schools and teacher training programs within the Normal Schools, and led to a very complex system of training and certification.

This reform was attacked on many grounds. Amongst the most important points was the lack of academic resources to support the tertiarization of teachers' training at a massive level and the absence of research to sustain the claimed advantages. It was also pointed out that "the new proposal tried to limit the formation of many teachers that, supposedly, would have no jobs" (Braslavsky and Birgin, 1995: 78).

In the formative aspect, the tertiarization attempted to make teacher training more professional and less vocational, first, by increasing the requirements to become a teacher (i.e., tertiarization) and by an attempted adaptation of the curricula to the scientific standards of the new developments in psychology and pedagogy. As previously mentioned the Normalist model had a strong positivistic ingredient, which this reform tried to place as the defining component for teacher education. Nevertheless, some authors (Terigi and Dicker, 1997; Suarez, 1995) point out that tertiarization, in spite of producing a change in the institutional structure, did not generate a substantive change in the general orientation of the curricula, and the much searched-after scientific preparation of elementary teachers was never fully developed or implemented.

In addition, the persistence of severe criticisms to the performance of elementary schools was also seen as proof that tertiarization was not the right path to professional life nor to improve the quality of preschool and elementary education. For those who were opposed to this model, the new graduates of teacher education programs, far from mastering the techniques and instrumental knowledge that could guarantee a more "efficient" schooling (the expected result according to the theoretical principles of tertiarization), actually had more difficulties in their school performance compared to the "old" graduates from the Normal Schools (Braslavsky and Birgin, 1995).

The Normal School had helped to create and sustain the representation of teachers as mothers or apostles of education. The subsequent model of professorship required a distinctive representation of teachers, one that would match the dominant ideas about development and scientific progress. The defendants of the professorship model looked for its paradigm in the figure of the "technician."

The Argentinean Teacher as a Technician

During the period 1940–1970 the national state had adopted a strong interventionist stance toward planning and commanding the economy. State-sponsored industrial policies, toward the creation of a strong national market based on import-substitution strategies, were implemented at the same time that large sectors of the population were incorporated to those activities. Through this process of economic and industrial development, workers' rights were expanded, incorporating important numbers of previously excluded sectors (including women). All the while in the 1960s the diffusion of "developmental theories" (including behavioral and conductist psychological and pedagogical approaches), educational planning and measuring following clear standards (such as Bloom's famous "Taxonomy of Objectives"), in tandem with the social and economic "modernization" paradigm of development, were the most important elements influencing the elaboration of the social representation of teaching as technical work (Krawczyc, 1993; Puiggrós, 1991; Suarez, 1995).

Studies about this period (Davini, 1995; Suarez, 1993) have indicated that for the supporters of this new representation of what teachers ought to be, the Normal School with its emphasis on caring and vocation was an obstacle to the improvement of the quality of education. In addition to those elements, it is important to recognize the effects of the first wave of feminist discourses that also began to question the stereotypical and idealized images of the "good mother" and by extension, the ideology of teaching as an extension of motherhood (Thurer, 1994).

A radical measure was needed. Instead of apostles, the country required professional workers, skilled technicians of education able to follow detailed curricula. The model of reform strongly relied (and gambled) on the benefits of changing teacher education from the secondary level to the tertiary level and massive efforts to train teachers in the educational technologies of planning and measurement (Suarez, 1994). This process of reform was also conceptualized as a process of "proletarization" of teachers.[16] The proletarization of teachers has implied that "teachers are not merely made more like other workers in economic terms, i.e., less economically advantaged, more vulnerable to redundancy and pressure toward increased workload. It also involves a loss of control over the work process, a loss of definition by the worker of the essential elements of the task" (Guinsburg, 1992: 431).

It is clear that the old model of the teacher-mother relied heavily on gender stereotypes and imagery. The same was true for the technician model. Several studies (Davini 1995; Puiggrós, 1987; Suarez, 1993, 1994) have shown that for teachers, the process of becoming technicians has relied on important dynamics based on gender stereotypes. Those stereotypes determined that in the educational field there are some "specialists" that produce, plan, and efficiently evaluate the knowledge that other "technicians" (teachers, mainly females) have to transmit according to the rules, schedules, and procedures devised by the "specialists." In this case, teaching becomes know-how, limited to following rules, goals, and content produced by others. Everything is divided into the smallest units to be measured by the supervisor. Those specialists were not all men; however, many were, and this system was articulated following a masculine gender order. Once again, it is apparent that the main function of female teachers is reduced to the most "reproductive" aspects of teaching.

These efforts were highly resisted, not only within the Normal Schools but also by many social and political actors that saw these reforms as contrary to their social, economic, and educational interests of establishing a new form of dependency. It is worth remembering that those were the prime years of the Cuban Revolution and Cardoso and Faletto's "Dependence Theory." Also, Ivan Illich's and Paulo Freire's (earlier, later revised) ideas about the oppressive functions of formal education had started to gain currency. Nevertheless, from 1955 to 1983, the country was very rarely ruled by democratically elected governments, and the successive military dictatorships made a great deal of efforts to spread the image of teachers as technicians. This model presumed and promoted the political neutrality of pedagogical endeavors, which fit not only the needs but perhaps (in light of the students' revolts of the 1960s) mostly the fears of the military rulers.

The process of tertiarization, coupled with the teacher as technician model, resulted in several conflicts within teacher training institutions that were often connected to civil protests and unrest, in a context of a quasi-permanent state of political uneasiness of the country. Such conflictive processes, however, did not have any substantial results in terms of changing the structures of teacher training. Only after the process of democratic transition, which started in 1984, was somehow consolidated, were educational authorities able to devote energy and time to a renewed effort to changing teacher training.

The Context for the Adjusted Model
of Teacher Training (1984–1996)

Despite the criticisms and signs of alarm that arose about the quality of the training of teachers, the system of teacher training initiated in 1969 remained unchanged until the late 1980s. The society in general had to wait until the horror and terror imposed by several military dictatorships were over to start thinking about the role of education in the development of the country.

The context of democratic transition initially had a positive impact on schools and teachers. After experiencing an extremely cruel dictatorship that especially targeted teachers and intellectuals and closely controlled the daily functioning of schools, universities, and cultural spaces, the restoration of democratic rule opened the space for a much-needed positive evaluation of "education." Linked with this evaluation one expectation was clearly echoed in educational debates: all social sectors voiced the demand to make teachers professionals through the updating and bettering of their training. However, this demand was complicated by a severe economic crisis, and the application of economic packages of structural adjustment that affected public spending in social services dramatically (Samoff, 1994). Consequently, teachers' salaries (as the salaries of all other state employees) lost substantial ground compared to those of industrial workers and other professions.

Although it would be inappropriate at this time to thoroughly discuss the many elements involved in these processes (the final section of this chapter resumes this point), a brief summary provides the required historical context in which the latest attempts to reform teacher education programs occurred.

During the previous periods of authoritarian rule, unions adopted in some cases survival defensive strategies, and in others the leadership of the unions directly collaborated with the government. By the late 1980s, however, with the democratic transition in place, workers' organizations and teachers' unions in particular adopted more proactive policies that shocked the nation. In 1988, after seven smaller strikes, the National Confederation of Teachers launched a forty-seven day strike that ended in a massive demonstration called La Marcha Blanca (the White March) demanding better salaries and working conditions. Despite popular support for this labor protest, Argentinean teachers did not fare very well in the defense of their salaries and working conditions (Carnoy and Moura Castro, 1996). By the same token, public criticisms and direct attacks on teachers were also on the rise. Given this critical situation, it is not surprising that enrollment in teacher education programs manifested a noticeable decrease and teachers were targeted as directly responsible for the poor performance of public schools.[17] In a thorough report about the latest educational reforms in Latin America, Martin Carnoy and Claudio de Moura Castro reflect on the changing positions of teachers and their unions:

> The problem for teachers' unions (and for all public service unions) in opposing reforms is that teachers provide educational services not to the government that employs them but directly to the public—in this case, parents and their children who want to receive the greatest return on their tax dollars. The reforms promise to increase educational efficiency, and if teachers oppose they can be easily characterized by reformers as self-serving, not interested in the education of children but only in their own salaries and well-being. Indeed, teachers' unions in Latin American countries have generally done poorly in getting the public to identify with their position, in part because teachers have rarely fought for reforms that increase educational performance of children. And whereas individual teachers have often been admired for their fine efforts on behalf of improving pupils' learning, teachers' unions have, as a collective of teachers, rarely helped to initiate change that would make schools more effective. In essence, while demanding that teachers be treated as professionals, unions have usually interpreted their role as representing teachers only as employed workers. (Carnoy and Moura Castro, 1996: 40)

This quote resumes some of the complexities of the relationships between teachers, their organizations, the state, and the society during this period. Notwithstanding the basic accuracy of Carnoy's and Moura Castro's points, it should be noted that in Latin America the "taxpayer" subject is not a social subject as well established as in the United States or Europe. For that reason, the idea that "parents and their children who want to receive the greatest return on their tax-dollars" needs to be taken somewhat skeptically. Similarly, some teachers' unions are creating new instances for the study of pedagogical alternatives, searching for the improvement of the educational system without losing track in the struggle to improve teaching working conditions. Some of the unions' new strategies are the gathering of national and international educational scholars, creation of research institutes, teachers' reflection workshops, and public campaigns, explaining the situation of schools.

Adjusting Teacher Training (1984–1996)

In 1988, the same year of the *Marcha Blanca*, the most popular and massive demonstration launched by Argentinean teachers, the first important attempt to change teacher training was initiated. That year, an experimental project was implemented in more than twenty Normal Schools, and in 1989 it was extended to seventy more. It was called the "Curriculum of Teachers of Elementary Schools," or the Majistiaris de Educación Básaca (MEB) plan. The MEB plan returned the responsibility for the initial training of teachers to the high school level, which meant that the first two years of the teaching major were undertaken during the last two years of high school, and then students continued for two more years (in the same institution), completing a total of four years for their teaching credential. This, of course, meant a restructuring of the teaching-oriented high school curriculum and combining it with the tertiary-level curriculum into an integrated educational structure.

Considered by its critics as a "step backwards" from the tertiarization and as an attempt to reduce "the professional status of teachers," the MEB plan sought to resolve the dilemma between the need to prolong the training time to achieve the educational level desired and the need to shorten the length of time that students at the tertiary level needed to invest to obtain a degree with such low salary expectations. The MEB was implemented in 1988 and was discontinued in 1990, having produced only two classes of graduates.[18]

Under the government of President Carlos Menem (1989–1999), the modifications proposed for education focused on legal and administrative aspects rather than curricular or institutional ones. There were two important changes for teacher training set out in various laws, resolutions, and decrees.[19] First, the definition of teacher training as a continuous process that "is initiated when the individual starts her/his training, but continues throughout his/her career, as a response to the needs arising from the work process, for which she/he must continuously prepare" (CFCyE, Recommendation 25/92).

The second most important regulation put into place in this period was the executive decision by which all teaching majors are at the level of higher education. This decision is in tune with an (almost) worldwide tendency to lengthen teacher training through tertiarization, and in some cases by transferring it to universities.[20]

The rationale behind the adoption of these lines of action in the training of teachers is that they would solve persistent problems, such as the lack of articulation between teacher training and research, outdated curricula, and the diminishing social prestige of the teaching profession, among many others. To achieve these goals, the new legal framework points to certain conditions that must be achieved:

- Institutional continuity between initial training and continuing education. However, the initial training must offer a complete and thorough preparation for the practice of the teaching profession.
- Introduction of the formation of the teachers into the realm of adult pedagogy.
- Combination of theory and practical training, in order to prepare teachers to solve curricular and institutional problems.
- Development of practical mechanisms by which regular attendance in continuous post-initial training courses will be guaranteed.

The old Normal Schools, originally established exclusively for teacher training, now have four educational levels relatively independent of each other: preschool, elementary school, secondary school, and teacher education programs. In addition, one Normal School can host a single or several programs of teacher training: preschool, elementary education, special education, secondary education, technical education, and art education. However, it is important to note that this multiplicity of teacher training alternatives in a single establishment is due more to historical and institutional factors that affected the creation and subsequent evolution of individual institutions, rather than to strategic planning focused on the improvement of teachers' education.

The analysis of the current structure of the system of teaching accreditation indicates that elementary school teachers are not only trained at Normal Schools. At the present, elementary school teachers are trained by many different organizations in various programs: Normal Schools, provincial institutes, higher educational technical institutes, private institutes (including lay and religious institutions), and universities. More important, it is interesting to point out that not everyone who teaches in an elementary school (particularly men) has been formally trained within the teacher training system. The lack of fully accredited teachers has important implications for the structure of the teaching corps and the special characteristics that it displays.

Currently, there is no total clarity as to the future structure of teacher training. The experiences and criticisms accumulated since the tertiarization of teacher training in the late 1960s clearly indicate the need for substantial changes in the academic and institutional organization of the training and accreditation of teachers. However, it is still unclear if the changes that are under revision today would favor the process of making the training of teachers a "professional" option or if they would reproduce an antiquated and exhausted educational structure.

Finally, any attempt to reform teacher education carries an implicit or explicit rejection or acceptance of previous social representations about the teaching profession. In that regard, the proposals undertaken during the period of 1984 to 1996 are not an exception. However, the new representations of teachers are not only heatedly contested but also less clearly defined than the previous ones. The next and final section of this chapter presents the most important characteristics of these conflicting representations.

Conflicting Representations (1984–1996)

The proposed changes of the 1984 to 1996 period resulted in several conflicts and consequently brought up disagreements and serious tensions throughout the teacher education institutions. Such conflictive processes, to which neither teachers and their organizations nor the society as a whole were accustomed, represented a critical challenge to the former situation. Particularly, many women teachers began to question the stereotypical ideology of teaching as an extension of motherhood. Moreover, the ideas of teaching as professional work and schools as workplaces were and still are controversial. What Acker sharply states for the North American context is strikingly similar to the Argentinean situation:

> It would not be necessary to belabor the obvious, were it not for the pervasive conceptions of teaching as a calling and of teachers as adults who do what they do mostly because they care deeply about children. The association of these images with women is important in shaping the occupational culture and the approaches of the scholars. Thus, an emphasis of teaching as a work not only highlights the tension between "work" and "profession" but speaks to a difference between work and non-work, the latter associated with the notion of women engaged in natural, quasi-maternal caring. (1996: 102)

However, during the peak years of the development of the Argentinean model of the welfare state (1940s to 1980s), corporatist political behaviors were favored.[21] The origins of the welfare state have been associated with state policies of industrial and financial recovery during the post-Depression era in the United States, based on a "social pact" (New Deal). In addition to the financial and industrial measures, a key feature of the welfare state was the promotion of concertation policies between employers and organized workers through their unions. It is this last aspect of political concertation between unions, the private sector, and the state that has secured a place for teachers' unions in the discussion of public educational policies. In Argentina, the participation of teachers' unions in the process of educational policymaking was prompted by the social and political developments that followed a corporatist model. This model required the legalization and institutionalization of the organized labor movements and industrial relations that were in many cases controlled by the state. In that context, the simultaneous appreciation of teachers, and an increase in their professional status—due in part to the process of unionization and the supposed benefits of the tertiarization of teacher education—gave teachers and their organizations a great deal of legitimacy that yielded opportunities to participate in and influence the formulation of educational policy and curricula (Torres and Puiggrós, 1995).

Blaming Teachers—Blaming Women

At the same time, due to the severe economic restrictions already mentioned, this period witnessed important changes in the working conditions of teachers and, thus, the learning conditions for students (Ezpeleta, 1991; Isuani et al., 1991; Narodowski and Narodowski, 1988). A research study conducted with 1,700 teachers by the city of Buenos Aires secretary of education (Almandoz de Claus and Hirschberg de Cigliutti, 1992) showed that contrary to the popular belief that women go into teaching due to the shortness of the workday, 60 percent of these women teachers work two shifts (not with the same group of students), and 70 percent would prefer to teach full-time to the same group instead of part-time to different groups in order to focus on the pedagogical work instead of social tasks not directly related to teaching, such as general health care, vaccination, the provision of food, and the like, which for many teachers in poor areas take as much as 50 percent of their daily tasks. Moreover, 17 percent of all teachers are separated or widowed with children, and they have more than two jobs in order to meet their living expenses.[22] Indeed, only 36 percent are tenured in their positions, and 30 percent have university degrees, a condition that is not acknowledged in terms of adequate salary compensation or in promotions.

Another important feature to take into consideration is that enrollment in teacher training institutions decreased dramatically between 1992 and 1995, and if that trend resumes, the country may face a shortage of teachers (Dicker and Terigi, 1994). Perhaps changes in the social representation and responsibilities of being a teacher have influenced this trend. As a female teacher describing her everyday working conditions—not very different from many of her colleagues—claims:

> I call the roll, I collect students' monetary contributions to the school (cooperadora escolar), I check for lice, I fill in the daily folder, I plan classes, I watch the ones who come in or leave, I prepare a snack, I listen to the children's problems and sometimes to the parents, I meet with the principal, I stand in the playground and prevent the children from climbing the walls: there isn't any time left to teach the subjects I had planned. (F, age 32)

Undoubtedly, several of the tasks described by this teacher resemble traditionally ascribed "homemaker" tasks. As Acker (1996: 122) states, "Just as we forget that the home is a workplace for homemakers, teaching's image as a natural nurturing encourages us to forget, that the classroom, too, is a workplace." This example shows that the above quoted teacher does not have a "natural inclination" for caring; instead, she is doing what she considers vitally urgent, and not what she may find pedagogically important.

Situations like these are linked to the overall decline of the educational quality of Argentina's public system of education and to the emergence of a new social class: the new poor. The application of programs of economic stabilization has resulted in a notable reduction of inflation and also an outstanding increase in the levels of poverty and in widening the gap between rich and poor. In Argentina during the last fifteen years, the top one third of the population (in terms of income) increased its earnings by 26.2 percent. The traditional middle class lost 9.2 percent of its income, while the bottom third of the population's income fell 14.9 percent (Boron, 1995). These few features appear to indicate the presence of a new social scenario represented by an increasingly complex and heterogeneous new poverty (Coraggio, 1992).[23]

One of the distinctive characteristics of the new poor is that the class position of this intriguing emerging social group is a very complex analytical subject. Among the main traits of the "new poor" is the group's relatively high educational credentials (i.e., secondary or higher education completed) and the relatively small number of children per family. In that sense, the new poor share some sociocultural characteristics with the non-poor population. On the other hand, they are like the structurally poor, mainly because their access to secure and well-paid jobs is quite limited, and despite having achieved higher levels of education, these educational credentials do not lead to better or more secure economic positions.[24]

Some analysts (Tedesco, 1991) have claimed that the diminishing value of educational credentials is due to the massification of education. For others (Paviglianitti, 1991; Boron and Torres, 1996), the decline in the value of educational credentials is related to the implementation of programs of structural adjustment that have deeply affected the quality of education. The last national measurements of the quality of education have indicated that almost 60 percent of high school students have failed the language and math exams and that many university students lack the required knowledge expected in university graduates (Braslavsky, 1993b).

Several works about education and economy (Reimers and Tiburcio, 1993; Samoff, 1994; Teitel, 1992) have linked declining educational expenditures, dropout and repetition rates, and the erosion in living and working conditions of teachers in Latin America to the economic austerity measures associated with external debt reduction and structural adjustment programs (SAPs).[25] The SAP's discourse has been theoretically and ideologically oriented by the rhetoric of the (quasi-magic) benefits of the free market. This rhetoric, which is articulated as a neoconservative discourse (Carnoy and Torres, 1995; Gentili, 1994a, 1994b), has taken a powerful hold on Latin American societies, particularly affecting state-sponsored programs such as public schools. These actions are taking place in a context in which there has been a vicious offensive on the social and personal rights of minorities (including the majority of poor women) and the social, political, and economic infrastructures that have traditionally supported them.[26]

These policies of social and economic restructuring have implied great changes and profound implications in the size and functions of the state (Fischman, 1998; Rhoten, 1999). In educational terms, restructuring the public education sector has basically involved the application of tighter systems of accountability in the context of de-skilling, standardization, and changing rationales of the teaching profession (Gentili, 1994a, 1994b; Popkewitz, 1993; Tenti Fanfani, 1993). Pressure to do more work in the same amount of time or more work for less money or with more students is a clear manifestation of what has been termed the "intensification of the teaching" (Apple, 1986). Both de-skilling and intensification are phenomena well known to Argentinean teachers. This situation should not be a surprise, given the fact that in Latin America "the education sector suffered disproportionately the adjustment burden and that the promises of the seventies were dashed in the eighties. Changes in the structure of the education budget, that are not justified on efficiency and equity grounds, accompanied these reductions" (Reimers, 1991: 8).

Perhaps one of the best examples of these changes can be found in the way in which teachers have subsidized the system of public and private education with their daily work. One of the most pressing issues, and certainly an area of highly heated debate, is that of the state of the efficiency of Argentina's public education system after the application of several changes contained in socioeconomic programs of structural adjustment. What seems to constitute a big surprise for many of the most critical voices of these structural adjustment programs (Carnoy and Torres, 1995; Samoff, 1994) is the fact that despite all the spending reductions and other restrictive measures, the percentage of dropouts, repetition rates, and even levels of enrollment have not changed as dramatically as the decline of educational budgets.

In Argentina official statistics demonstrate that basic schooling currently covers 93.5 percent of the relevant school-age population (6 to 12 years old) and there is a dropout rate of 13.1 percent. The problem with these indicators is that they do not explain the important imbalances in terms of quality among the different social sectors or regional imbalances. Similarly, Braslavsky (1993a) and Almandoz de Claus and Hirschberg de Cigliutti (1992) point out that the quantitative growth of the system has surpassed the qualitative possibilities of an educational system that was programmed to have only a limited coverage. Moreover, these authors observe that the same quantitative growth has implied impoverishment of the educational system rationale: overcrowded classrooms, less hours of instruction, infrastructure deficits, and increased working tasks for teachers. All of the above has influenced the recent characterization of teaching as a risky and unattractive profession.

In sum, it is clear that the reduction in public funding affected the quality of education and to a lesser extent the quantitative expansion of the system. Yet, how is it possible to educate more students with smaller amounts of money? Carlos A. Torres and Adriana Puiggrós (1995) have provided one compelling argument explaining this phenomenon. For these authors, the reduction of teachers' salaries has provided the much needed resources to keep schools open in the context of severe cuts in educational budgets under the application of structural adjustment programs. In that regard, it is suggested that teachers were one of the main subsidizers of public schooling through the intensification and speedup of the teaching profession.

In Argentina, given the fact that salaries represent almost 90 percent of educational budgets, any increase in student enrollments, accompanied by any decrease in school budgets, suggests at least two possible explanations that are not mutually exclusive: (a) it could be presumed that there is a decrease in teachers' salaries and the savings are used to pay for more teachers; or (b) there is a large increase in the number of students per teacher accompanied by the worsening of school conditions (overcrowded classrooms and schools). The combination of these two hypotheses seems to be the case in Argentina. For instance, between 1970 and 1995, teachers' salaries decreased by more than 25 percent (accounting for inflation at 1987 consumer prices) (Birgin, 1995).[27] Nowadays, teachers' salaries are less than those of ten years before (Tenti Fanfani, 1993; Torres and Puiggrós, 1995).[28]

There are, however, other interpretations to consider in this discussion. An influential World Bank paper that contains several policy recommendations for "improving" the country's educational system subscribes to the idea that elementary teachers receive low salaries because they work fewer hours by choice, without considering the extra hours that every teacher has to spend in planning and evaluation.[29] This report also points to the low moral and motivational aspects of the teaching workforce, as well as organizational issues, as reason for the lack of educational improvement:

> Managing teacher staff and their career is an especially complex issue. Low teacher morale, reduced time teachers spend in the classroom, and slowness in adopting more modern teaching techniques are cited as the main causes of deterioration or stagnation in the quality of primary education. Teachers' salaries are low, a factor that is related to the shortness of the class day. Teachers usually work 3-1/4 hours net (and as low as 2 hours in some cases); perhaps the lowest workload in the world. Although Argentina has a widely recognized capacity for research in pedagogy, it is only in exceptional cases that teachers actually apply curriculum updates and new methodologies. (Kugler, 1991:11)

Intensification and de-skilling are also mixed with increasing public criticisms for the performance of public schools. These criticisms are often directed at teachers, creating new tensions in the relationships between teachers and educational authorities. Even where there is less focus on blaming teachers, there is a good deal of attention to issues around improving the quality of teachers, such as competency testing, certification, and national exams, which have been perceived by teachers and their unions as attempts to increase control over them. In short, diverse attempts are being made to improve those aspects of teachers' activities deemed crucial to improving the quality and excellence of teaching and learning. However, in this context, excellence becomes almost exclusively linked to attempts to reduce expenses of financially overburdened school districts and to make the systems more cost-effective, which usually involves layoffs and substitution of fully trained, more expensive teachers for lower paid instructional personnel (ECLAC, 1992; IDB, 1991).

Another aspect that has influenced and fueled criticism about elementary education teachers, and especially about the work of the teacher training institutes, is the legacy of educational functionalism and reproduction theories (Narodowski, 1996). These two schools of thought argue, on the one hand, that schools reproduce social stratification and, on the other, that social ills are due to bad learning habits and/or poor teaching—consequently, teachers should be held accountable for the lack of educational success. Criticisms of teachers are also related to the undeniable impact of the mass media, especially television, which has become a major challenge to school and teacher knowledge, points of view, and methodologies. These changes have reduced not only the political influence of teachers, but also their social esteem. Notwithstanding, social esteem of teachers is not a homogeneous construction; it varies among and within different social groups. Yet it is fair to say that the old representation of teachers as enlightened and heroic people has been replaced by one in which bureaucratic and mediocre characteristics prevail. Several comedy shows, comic strips, and popular television commercials present women teachers who are the exact opposite of the stereotypical teacher-mother. Today, teachers are portrayed as lazy, lousy, dirty, authoritarian, and corrupt, in need of "adjustment."

Finally, elementary education teachers, being mostly women, are also challenged by the social constructions of gender. The following two anecdotal episodes seem to condense part of the challenges ahead.

One of the most powerful persons in Argentina is the country's former minister of economy (1990–1995), Domingo Cavallo. A Harvard University alumnus, often regarded as a brilliant economist in both local and international financial circles, his voice and opinions are always material for national attention. Doubtless, commanding the economic policies that decreased annual inflation from four digits to less than 5 percent has given Cavallo an important platform. However, the decrease in inflation was also accompanied by a dramatic increase in the rate of unemployment, which in 1998 was officially recognized as close to 18.5 percent and is affecting more women than men. It is in this context that the minister's voice has to be understood. In a public speech, broadly printed and broadcasted he used a "gender-based" argument to explain the reasons for such dramatic unemployment figures and their relationships to the welfare crisis:

> You (women) are the cause of the crisis of the Argentinean state! Don't you see the number of homeless kids, drug-addicts and the elderly in public parks? These things happen because women are out looking for jobs, and thus, producing the crisis of the state. Now the state has to take care of the homeless kids and the elderly. Don't you understand what you do, what you cause? (Cavallo, 1995: 15)

Two years later, in May 1997, I witnessed a variation of Cavallo's ideas. Twenty-five teachers, females and males, were on hunger strike in front of Argentina's congress. They were protesting the closing of educational facilities, low salaries, and abominable working and learning conditions, mainly the result of economic restructuring and neoconservative social and cultural policies. For them, the protest measures were necessary in order to call attention to the dismal situation of the country's educational system and the perilous future facing Argentinean children. The media, government, and even some teachers were criticizing the strikers for not fulfilling their "duties" as teachers inside the classrooms, betraying their students—their children. The strikers responded that they loved the children and that the strike was defending the children and the system of public education. Numerous letters to the editors, articles and editorials in newspapers, magazines, and television shows were immediately engaged in the discussion about "the real vocation of the teachers," and in not a few cases, the second mother figure was evoked. Clearly, the gender overtones of the arguments are familiar to the topics and themes discussed in this and previous chapters: power, identity, sex, gender, teaching, learning, resistance, and struggle.

Despite all the blaming, problems, and challenges, it seems that teachers, especially female elementary teachers, who face such a disadvantageous situation are still managing their classrooms. They are also demanding training and sometimes getting together with their students and students' parents to defend their working conditions and children's learning opportunities.[30]

Nevertheless, teacher education programs are facing a pressing dilemma. Many teachers have expressed the need to recover some of the early features of the mother-teacher model so as to avoid conflict with the state by attempting to remain politically neutral, to rise above materialistic concerns (such as salaries), and by focusing on building national identity and instilling moral values.[31] Yet at the same time, given the current educational crisis, harsh public criticisms, and declining working conditions, other teachers point to the need to develop political and pedagogical actions that challenge their current diminishing status, not only as teachers but also as women. In any event, what seems clear is that one particularly acute axis of conflict between teachers and the state, and also among teachers themselves, revolves around gender issues. In other words: Is it possible, within this context, to retain one symbol of good teaching—that is, the loving and caring associated with the figure of the "teacher-mother"—and at the same time obtain social and material recognition that is currently denied in part due to the displaying of these same symbolic features? Michael Apple poignantly describes this dilemma:

> It is absolutely crucial to say, however, that at the same time, commitments to environments that embody an ethic of caring and connectedness—commitments that are often so much a part of women's daily experiences and are so critical in an education worthy of its name—may actually provide the resources for countering such rationalized curricular models. (1993: 141)

The previous historical presentation of programs of teacher education was developed in order to provide an appropriate background knowledge about this field in Argentina. Although such background is rather important, it is insufficient for the understanding of this problematic field. In order to imagine better teacher education programs and to make them more effective, it is also important to observe and listen closely to the voices, memories, narratives, metaphors, and actions of students, teachers, policymakers, and administrators, and develop more subtle frameworks of analysis, critique, and action in order to alter the current hegemonic arrangements. Thus, with these goals in mind, the next chapters present and analyze those voices, images, and narratives of contemporary teacher educators and students from Argentina.

Notes

1. While the Normal and Professorship historical models are names that also describe a particular type of institution of teacher training, the third model, named as "Adjusted Teacher Training," does not. This name was selected given the impact and prevalence over all aspects of education that programs of social and economic adjustment had during this period. There were, of course, alternative social representations such as "a-moral teachers" or "anarchist teachers." However, several studies (Davini, 1995; Suarez, 1994) agree that since the origins of the teaching profession until the present, the Normal and Professorship models are the two main archetypal paragons presented to the new generations of teachers during their formal training. The apostle/second mother and technician representations have proven to be, if not totally resistant to changing times, reforms, governments (and desires to change), at least very powerful in providing the dominant metaphors and images informing the social expectations about teachers. Indeed,

they still resonate in the current debates about reforming teacher education and among teacher education faculty and students.

2. Even though there were previous attempts to develop Normal Schools, such as one created in 1819 in the province of Buenos Aires by James Thompson, a Lancasterian teacher (Narodowski, 1996), the definite institutionalization of the system of Normal Schools was achieved under the influence of Sarmiento's efforts. One of the first directors of the Normal School, located in the city of Paraná, was Professor Jorge A. Stearns, a North American pedagogue highly recommended by Mary Peabody Mann (Horace Mann's wife). Alice Houston Luiggi wrote the book *65 Valiants* documenting the stories of sixty-five "Yankee schoolteachers" who traveled to Argentina between 1869 and 1898. These teachers were part of a program initiated under the direction of Domingo Faustino Sarmiento (first as minister of education and later as president of the republic from 1868 to 1874). Sarmiento, who had traveled in Europe and the Untied States studying those early systems of public education, befriended Horace Mann and other politicians and educators. He was particularly impressed by the educational experiences he observed in the state of Massachusetts. Those experiences, and his appreciation for the North American model of development, inspired Sarmiento to develop a plan to bring a thousand North American teachers to Argentina to start schools and train local teachers. Only sixty-five teachers are known to have made the journey.

3. In order to attract male students, the Normal Schools offered scholarships to them. This situation was a clear attraction for students coming from poor families.

4. This limitation of the Normal School was suppressed in 1945.

5. "Job desertion" includes teachers with a degree who never actually worked as such and those who did so for a very short time. For a thorough discussion of this topic, see Braslavsky and Birgin, 1995; Terigi and Dicker, 1997.

6. In Argentina, lower salaries for women were and still are generally accepted and, as will be discussed later, in some cases even justified. This fact is sustained by a common belief that women's salaries should "complement" their husbands' incomes. This income subalternity is coupled with the idealization of teaching as a natural extension of motherhood, which stresses the "traditional feminine values" of child care rather than the transmission of content/knowledge (K. Weiler, 1988). These ideologies and metaphors that associated teaching with women and woman with mothering have a long history that requires attention.

7. The idea that the Normal Schools of teaching were *decent* alternatives for women, defended by Sarmiento and thousands of women that pursued the profession, was not always easily accepted, particularly in the case of those who defended the thesis that the "lay system of education" represented a terrible danger for the moral future of the country. Another prominent Argentinean intellectual, Manuel Galvez, wrote in 1914 that those women in Normal Schools were trapped in places of lust because they were not teaching the Catholic moral. See also Beatriz Sarlo (1998).

8. There was a greater proportion of male students in the provinces than in the capital of the country, perhaps due to the lack of other educational options and that a high school diploma was a great advantage to obtain positions in the public administration.

9. In addition to references to schools as second homes, or schools as families, there was also a disproportionate large number of male principals and supervisors, directing and evaluating the large number of female teachers. Just as the father provided discipline in the family, the male principal dominated the "second home." Before the 1930s in the

province of Buenos Aires not a single woman was appointed for the position of district supervisor (Pineau, 1997).

10. Froebbel, an early champion for the establishment of kindergartens, was also an adamant defender and promulgator of the idea that women have a natural tendency to act as spiritual guides, thus, converting them into naturally good teachers. According to this representation, teachers had an almost sacred mission and they were regarded as the "second mothers" or "mother-teachers" of the young students (Alliaud, 1993; Morgade, 1992a).

11. This conference established the basis for the country's educational system, and it was the legal referent for the system of elementary education until its replacement in 1993 by a new federal law.

12. Sarah Chamberlain Eccleston graduated in 1858 from the Bucknell's Female Institute. She moved to Argentina in 1876 with her 7-year-old-son after the death of her husband. While in Argentina she spent a good deal of her energies helping to found kindergartens and train kindergarten teachers.

13. Adriana Puiggrós (1990, 1991) and many of her colleagues at the APPEAL institute for the study of the history of education in Argentina and Latin America have forcefully argued that despite the "official defeat" of antistate Catholic forces in the educational debate that led to the configuration of the national system of elementary public education as a lay structure, such downfall did not imply the absence of religion within the curriculum. Alejandra Birgin (1999) further comments that religion and morality were not incompatible terms because even the lay forces within the Normal movement saw religion as a powerful tool in their civilizing quest.

14. This vision is what Paulo Freire called the nutritionist view of knowledge, in which "[i]lliterates are considered 'undernourished,' not in the literal sense in which many of them really are, but because they lack the 'bread of the spirit'" (Freire, 1985: 45). Consistent with the concept of knowledge as food, illiteracy is conceived of as a "poison herb."

15. Those new programs were mostly attached to Normal Schools. In other words, with these reforms Normal Schools offered three or four levels of education to their students: preschool, elementary, secondary, and a tertiary level.

16. For a discussion of similar trends in the United States, see Apple (1986).

17. The decrease in the enrollment in teacher education programs was also influenced by the universities' new admission policies and changes in the university programs that were savagely damaged by the 1976–1983 dictatorship. Also, a deep deterioration in teachers' salaries may have played an important role in discouraging future students.

18. It should be noted that in several interviews with faculty in teacher education programs and educational researchers involved in this program and despite its short period of existence, the MEB was well remembered and regarded as one of the best executed reforms in teacher education.

19. The list of those legal instruments is as follows: the Transference Law N-24.049/91 and Presidential Decree N-954/92; the Federal Law of Education N-24.195/93; Resolution 32/93 of the Federal Council of Culture and Education (CFCyE), "Alternatives for the formation, perfecting and training of teachers," Decree 36/94 of the CFCyE, Federal Network of Continuous Teacher Education, Law of Higher Education N-24.521/95.

20. However, there are important institutional players such as the World Bank, that claim that the best investment is in-service training and not preservice training.

21. Although the welfare state is considered a distinctive form of the democratic liberal state in advanced capitalist industrialized societies, many of its characteristics were adopted in Latin America. A conspicuous feature of the welfare state is the required interventionist role of the state in the economy and massive public expenditure in both productive and nonproductive sectors of the economy. The most typical welfare polices are defined as government protection of minimum standards of income, different forms of social security (such as unemployment benefits and state-sponsored pension plans for the elderly), nutrition, health, housing, and education (Popkewitz, 1991; Wilensky, 1975, 1976).

22. Gender dynamics seem to be influential at this respect. At first glance, a small percentage of male teachers (less than 8 percent) seems to have higher hierarchical positions than their female counterparts (Morgade, 1992b).

23. Often we find the terms "pauper" or "impoverished" identifying these new poor. In that regard, I follow Alberto Minujin's distinction. For this researcher, the "structural poor" is the poor population defined by a historically negative measurement of the national Basic Needs' Index. In that index, measures of income (above or below the poverty line) and a series of basic needs such as housing, water, electricity, health and food access, and sanitary deficits are combined. Conversely, the new poor may have had better basic life conditions in the past. Even though they may still own their homes and do not have water or sanitary emergencies, these basic needs have seriously deteriorated. For further discussion, see Minujin (1992) and Barbeito and Lo Vuolo (1992).

24. Taxi-drivers with degrees in architecture or sociologists working as waiters in the city of Buenos Aires are fairly common examples of this new situation.

25. Moreover, several studies have asserted that structural adjustment programs were particularly pernicious to women in general, showing the following trends: (a) The total burden of women's work has increased under recessionary conditions. SAPs have reduced social expenditures, rather than increasing them to offset these pressures; (b) Employment creation is weak under SAPs, especially for women; (c) SAPs have done little to address institutional gender inequality in the formal and informal sectors of national economies (Cook, 1994: 15).

26. Recognizing and criticizing these attacks is by no means intended to suggest that the old structures of the welfare state were always successful in promoting more egalitarian societies. Nevertheless, it would be a mistake not to look at the history of personal and collective struggle that has contributed and benefited from the welfare state. In other words, it is very difficult to dismiss the fact that with contradictions, advances, and steps backwards, the actions of public schools as a key component of the welfare state did improve—in relative ways—the social conditions of the most economically disenfranchised groups of the Argentinean society.

27. This loss is more pronounced in years of acute economic crisis (1981, 1982, 1985, 1989, and 1991).

28. Compared to salaries in the private (noneducational) sector of the economy, the salary of a teacher with fifteen years of service is, on average, only 64 percent that of a secretary employed in the private sector, and only 75 percent of the salary of a taxi-driver. At the top of the scale, an elementary school teacher with twenty-four years of experience received a salary that, on average, represented only 11 percent of the salary of a manager

in the private sector, and 76 percent of the salary of a secretary in the private sector (Torres, 1994).

29. In fact, this paper is part of the World Bank sector country study in which there are guidelines for restructuring education in Argentina. These guidelines have oriented most of the government policies (Fischman, 1998; Paviglianitti, 1991).

30. It is worth noting that during several teachers' strikes and demonstrations, teachers rallied around the slogan "in defense of the public school and for our kids."

31. There are several teachers' organizations that have expressed such a position. In fact, "teaching as a calling" is perhaps the cornerstone of the ideological position of the Normal Schools, the national teacher training institutions. Some teachers' unions have struggled against state policies and have strengthened their public position by defending these characteristics. For a detailed analysis of this situation, see Krawczyc (1993) and Morgade (1995).

CHAPTER 4

TEACHER TANGO:
CARING, SUFFERING, AND SMILING

> Tango is a strategy with multiple faces: music, dance, lyrics, performance, philosophy. . . . None of these aspects exactly reproduces or reinforces the others. The dance stops when the music pulls; the lyrics challenge the dance; the male and female of the couple follow and resist each other's movements; the music, syncopated, surprisingly halts. Starts again. Tango is recognizable in these contrasts and in the tension that they generate. And the tension itself is dramatized in a melodramatic way, a melodrama of stereotypes on the move, unstable stereotypes, stereotypes of the unpredictable. (Savigliano, 1995: 16)

Since the classic study entitled *Pygmalion in the Classroom,* by Rosenthal and Jacobson (1968), it is well known that the way teachers (as well as media, communities, researchers, and others) perceive and construct a particular profile of students influences the actions and expectations about the future performance of these students. In turn, students will react (accept, negotiate, resist, or challenge) those definitions about themselves constructed by their teachers (or the media, communities, researchers, and so on). Thus, this chapter's main goals are to present and discuss the perceived profiles, characteristics, and categories manifested by faculty and students in Teacher Education Programs (TEPs) in the city of Buenos Aires. It also attempts to recognize the diversity of the subjects of this research and the complexities of this area of inquiry.

To do so, it is essential to comprehend and scrutinize how past trends are manifested in the present, locating breaks and permanencies, ruptures and stable traditions in the institutional life of TEPs. In this chapter, it is contended that the analysis of patterns and variations in enrollment trends in TEPs, and the explanations for them advanced by teachers, researchers, and the media, represent an important step into this type of inquiry. These trends not only give much needed information about the perception of social and economic circumstances in which the TEPs are located, they are perhaps the prime area that illustrates the contradictions between the perceptions of TEP faculty and students. Thus, the initial section of this chapter presents the changes in TEP enrollment and how fluctuations in matriculation are perceived by faculty and researchers and used to advance semisociological conclusions about the future of teaching. The discussion of those trends intertwined with other sources of data (interviews, institutional observations, analysis of the news) will contribute to a reconstruction of the general profile of how current TEP students are perceived.

In the second section of this chapter I present and discuss the information obtained through the application of a qualitative questionnaire given to 178 students enrolled in TEPs in the city of Buenos Aires (1995–1996). The main goal of this section is to characterize TEP students as a social group, discussing their perceptions about teachers and teaching and paying special attention to their responses with respect to the image of the teacher-mother and technician models in schools. The third and last section of this chapter presents the information obtained through a collection of drawings produced by the students and the results of two focus groups that followed the creation of the drawings.

Enrollment Trends in Teacher Education Programs (TEPs): Fear and Relief

During the period of 1982 to 1994, enrollment in teacher education programs decreased dramatically nationwide (see table 4.1). The decline for the city of Buenos Aires was approximately 40 percent (Braslavsky and Birgin, 1995). This figure was repeatedly reported in the media and catalyzed a sense of crisis and somber diagnostics pointing to a future lack of educators (Narodowski, 1996; Tedesco, 1991). Indeed, through interviews with authorities in the Ministry of Education and in TEPs, this research was able to establish a high degree of concern regarding a future dramatic shortage of teachers.[1]

Table 4.1. Enrollment in Teacher Education Programs,
City of Buenos Aires (1982–1996)

Year	1982	1984	1986	1990	1992	1994	1996
Total	3,194	2,161	2,116	1,887	1,302	1,472	1,938
%	100%	-32.4%	-33.8%	-40.9%	-59.2%	-53.9%	-39.4%

Note: The percentages show the percent change from the baseline year (1982).

Low enrollment has been one of the major reasons to close TEPs in several provincial states (Birgin, 1996). Throughout all the interviews with faculty of TEPs located in the city of Buenos Aires, it was clear that there is an extended fearful perception that a somber future is looming over TEPs. Those fears are not without bases; as described in chapter 3, in 1997 the Ministry of Education laid out plans for change in teacher education, and two of the main indicators for evaluating the "functionality" of teacher education programs are enrollment and the ratio of graduation. Moreover, in several interviews with officials in the Ministry of Education and educational researchers, when inquiring about the situation of TEPs in general, this researcher registered statements such as "Those places are sick," and "Sometimes we wonder if we would be better off by closing all of them."[2]

In this context it is not surprising that one of the informants of this study, and the principal of one of the TEPs observed, María (55),[3] used very somber terms to described the circumstances and future possibilities of TEPs in general:

> The situation couldn't be worse. I understand that the whole country is in crisis, and that schools are falling apart as a result of very old programs, political battles and salaries that are a joke. We used to have more than twice the number of students we have now. It seems that nobody wants to be a teacher anymore. Have you read the newspapers? Do you see what is going on? Who can live with $300? [she pauses] I know all of that [in reference to the problems], but we need schools to be open no matter what, and for that we need teachers. If politicians and society don't get the message, we will be in serious trouble.
> Question: Who will be in trouble?
> For starters, us, the Normal Schools. No, I'm joking [she laughs], I mean seriously, the country, the future, everything. . . . [She lowers her voice] It is so depressing, I'm old, I don't have energy for this anymore. . . .

María was generally distressed about the situation of education in the country. Her feelings were also shared by many respondents and informants in this study. However, when she "jokingly" refers to the trouble of the Normal Schools, she was also expressing that the critical situation of TEPs was not only a matter of the number of students enrolled but also about who *are the students wanting to be teachers*.

Researchers in the area of teacher education (Birgin, 1995; Davini and Alliaud, 1995) have explained the variation in enrollments as by-products of societal changes. For them, changes in enrollment are strongly related to "external" conditions to the professional field itself. For instance, besides the discouraging effects of economic crises, decreases in enrollment during the 1984–1987 period are explained by changes in university admissions policies.[4] These researchers have also noted that large decreases in TEP students have been coincidental with the most acute periods of economic restructuring (1989 and 1991).

The persistence of severe economic problems, especially unemployment, which during the period of 1994 to 1996 was more than 17.5 percent (INDEC, 1996), was seen as one of the main causes for the 1994 rebound of TEP enrollments.[5] By 1995, a 20 percent increase in the number of students was noticeable compared to 1992. However, the difference between the number of students in 1982 and 1996 was still substantial to maintain a skeptical vision.[6] The main assumption is that a good deal of the 1994 and 1995 increases can be explained as a "job-searching strategy" because of high unemployment rates. Alejandra Birgin, a noted researcher in the area of teachers' education, notes:

> For some sectors of the population, despite the meager salaries, teaching is a secure job. So, contrary to what happened at the beginning of the 1990s when we witnessed lack of interest for teaching because there were other opportunities, today we see the opposite tendency, which *is basically a result of the unemployment levels*. The myth of *vocational choice* has not appeared as an explanation of this phenomenon. (Birgin, 1996: 5. Emphasis in the original)

The increase in the number of TEP students was accompanied by signs of relief as well as concern in the educational field. There was relief because higher enrollment meant that TEPs would remain open. There was also concern because there was a widespread perception that the new, incoming TEP students were inadequately prepared for the tasks of teaching. Several respondents and informants (especially among TEP faculty) voiced their preoccupations related to the lack of basic academic skills of the new TEP students. Those preoccupations were also combined with suspicious comments about the level of commitment to the teaching profession.[7] Those concerns not only pointed to academic aspects, but also to the social background of the incoming students.

Another informant, Silvia (52), director of the second TEP program, stated the following:

> Yes, there is a change in the element. We have to make up for what the high school and the family background did not provide. These [new] students are poorer than the ones we used to get. Most, if not all of them, are working, and many are single mothers. I'm not sure if they will be good teachers.

It is important to clarify that in Argentina the use of the phrase *change in the element* has very negative connotations. The *element* in general is a colloquial reference to social class, as well as a somewhat more diffuse allusion to the ethnic or cultural backgrounds of a given population. In Silvia's testimony, as well as in many others, there is an explicit assumption that poor students won't be good teachers. Even among some TEP students, strong prejudices against the "poor" are noticeable, as indicated by Claudia, a twenty-two-year-old TEP student.

> I'm really concerned with the level, you see? I don't want to discriminate, but I have classmates that come from the *villas miseria* (shantytowns). They are unable to talk, much less to read or write. They shouldn't be here. I'm sorry, but this is the truth.

Before further exploring this topic it is important to present other important actors in the educational arena of Argentina and highlight other points. As the next testimony illustrates, this skepticism or lack of confidence about future teachers is also shared by some researchers, such as Kristin (43), a university researcher.

> I don't have any doubt that there is a change in the composition of students in TEPs. The country is poorer, and those who traditionally went to TEPs now go to the university. TEPs are a second option; thus, you get second class teachers.

Many questions arise about the lack of optimism regarding the quality of the future teachers. So far, there is no clear empirical evidence that the perceived change in the socioeconomic composition of the students is as important as the previous testimonies indicate.

The results of this research coincide with several Argentinean studies on teacher training (Davini and Alliaud, 1995; Terigi and Dicker, 1997) that show that approximately 10 percent of students seem to come from poor families. Thus, if there is a change, it is small. Davini and Alliaud (1995) emphatically state, "From a strict social and economic point of view, the poor students are a clear minority, less than 10 percent. . . . However, looking at other dimensions, perhaps we should talk about "school impoverished students" (101).

Possibly, one of the signs of the school impoverishment is the lack of good command of basic skills. In the last few years, the media and several research reports have voiced caustic complaints about the increase of spelling problems, basic grammar mistakes, and difficulties with oral expression and mathematical proficiency among many students and teachers. Mediocre spelling and mistakes in numerical skills could be considered as manifestations of the decay of the previous school experiences and, in that sense, the above appears to give some "empirical" support to the fears of the diminishing quality of the future professional teaching workforce.

However, besides having more or less knowledge about Spanish or mathematics, there are at least two other ghosts fueling TEP instructors' fears. As seen in previous testimonies, some among TEP staff perceived that the new TEP students lack "vocation." This deficit appears to be ascribed to two groups: poor students and male students. As explained in the following section, related to the topic of teacher's vocation (or lack of it) is the ghost of a frightening homosexuality embodied by an apparent increase in the number of TEP male students and, needless to say, established sexist prejudices.

How to Show Your Vocation

Poor students are clearly a cause of concern for faculty in TEPs, but there is another new group of students that produces suspicious feelings among faculty: in this case the sign of danger comes from some male students. Contrary to the well-known tendency toward the feminization of teaching, in recent years more males have been entering into the teaching profession.[8] However, among TEP faculty there are contradictory positions about the increase in the numbers of men in TEPs.[9] On the other hand, male teachers have a clear position of privilege not only in schools but also in the administrative and political structures of the educational system.

In the city of Buenos Aires men are 10.8 percent of all teachers in primary schools, but they are 31.6 percent of all the principals and 57.2 percent of the district supervisors (Morgade, 1997). The disproportion in the representation of males in higher echelons of the school bureaucracy responds in part to the traditional assumption that they are better suited to have those positions, but also to school district's norms and practices that give them preferential treatment.[10]

In ten of the twelve open-ended interviews with TEP faculty, the larger number of male students was seen as a suspicious sign, rather than as an encouraging element. The next interview fragments with Mirta (43), a TEP instructor, reveal two distinctive rationales, which are similar in their distrust of male students.

> The problem with these students, compared to past years, is that they
> don't understand how hard and important it is to be a teacher and to

get the degree. They think that because it is a short-term program, it is easier, but they are wrong, completely wrong.
Question: All the students are wrong?
No, but many, too many in my opinion. . . . and you know what, . . . the worst are those three guys [three male students]. I know, I'm sure that they don't have the vocation to be teachers. They don't study, don't turn in the lesson plans on time, they are looking for a quick solution, they think this (program) is easy and they will get a job soon. Maybe . . . maybe, they will get the job, but I'm afraid they won't last long.

There are two elements worth discussing in this interview fragment. First, it is clear that for this teacher the current students are not only different from but less committed than past ones. Moreover, there are "too many students" who should not be in a TEP program. Among them "the worst" are three male students. Second, in this statement Mirta implies that "vocation" is a natural disposition to act, born from "superior" (i.e., spiritual) values and not from bodily desires or pragmatic speculations (getting a job). Such a natural disposition seems to be more important for women than for men.

For this TEP instructor, vocation is an internal "calling," and her mission as a TEP educator will be to add the technical and didactic tools that will complement a preexistent unselfish "vocation" that constitutes the essential quality of a good teacher.[11] This understanding of "vocation" as an innate characteristic of a good teacher seems to come into play not only in this suspicion toward (the apparent increase of) men entering into TEP, but also in relation to the fears about (the also apparent increase of) poor women and the possibilities they have of performing well as teachers.

The next interview fragment also demonstrates concern about men as teachers. It coincides with the previous statement in terms of expressing doubts about men being able to be real "teachers." Specifically, the interviewee wonders about the real motive for seven males to become teachers. However, this TEP teacher shows a great deal of concern about issues related to males' hidden homosexuality. Teresa (52), a TEP faculty member, points out (and echoes the media) the possible dangers of having gay men as teachers.[12]

I always like to have more men in my class. They give balance to the classroom. You know, the girls talk like chicken [sic] and men tend to go to the point. I like that. The problem is that they don't have what it takes. At the beginning of the year we had seven [male] students, and now we have only two. The other five came not because they wanted to be "real teachers," they were looking for a job or . . . other reasons too.
Question: I have two questions. What does it mean to be a "real teacher"? and what are the "other reasons"?
Oh, . . . you know the first one. It means love for kids, patience, dedication and [she pauses and laughs] and a good dose of masochism!
Question: And the second question?

> This is more delicate. Have you seen the news about those teachers? [Teresa is referring to two separate incidents of male teachers accused of child molestation that happened that week and were front page in newspapers and prime time television shows.] Yes, everybody is talking about this and it worries me a lot. You have to understand, for ten years we have only had one or two male students, at the most. Suddenly, you have ten. Isn't that strange? We don't discriminate [pause] but I also want to be clear. Not all men should be accepted, only those who have a clear identity [pause]. Don't you agree?
> Question: I'm not sure what you mean.
> You know . . . men that are men. Otherwise, they get the children confused or worse you have these kind of teachers [in reference to the two cases of child abuse]. Kids cannot understand when the messages are mixed. There are some teachers that look, well, very affected. See, now that we have more men here [in the TEP] we should be more selective.

The rampant homophobic discrimination is explicit ("Not all men should be accepted, only those who have a clear identity") even when the teacher attempts to make her opinion "objective" through a "concrete example" from the media ("Have you seen the news about those teachers"). Teresa's panic reaches paranoid extremes when she suspects that the increase in the number of male students is directly linked to sexual molestation, which is equated with homosexuality.

At the same time, a parallel devaluation of women's voices is introduced in this testimony ("girls talk like chicken [*sic*] and men tend to go to the point"). This TEP instructor also reproduces the vocational discourse and in her special way recovers the figure of the suffering apostle-teacher, when she lists the qualities of a good teacher, including masochism as a feature. However, the underlying logic of this testimony is the sense of distrust regarding these "new students."

These testimonies show how different phenomena, such as fears about lack of knowledge, fears about increased homosexuality, and panic about morality, can be subsumed and coalesced under the concept of "vocation." It is evident that for these teachers, vocation should always be VOCATION, a capitalized concept, an innate characteristic. Either you have it or not. Yet, given this hyper-valorization of vocation, it should be noted that these TEP teachers do not associate the idea of "vocation as a calling" with the model of teachers as second mothers. This departure from the earlier model is perhaps a limited manifestation of the limits and decreased value of the social representation of teachers as lay apostles or second mothers.[13]

However, what remains uncritically examined is why there is such a strong disbelief about the possibilities of training good teachers. Why is there such a strong disbelief about the vocational choice of these students? More specifically, why are the "poor" students blamed a priori for future problems?

One possible answer is considered by Guillermina Tiramonti who expresses that "teaching in Argentina is deteriorating, not only materially but in symbolic terms. Teachers have lost legitimacy in the eyes of the society, and such delegitimation goes hand in hand with a delegitimation of the whole educational system. Therefore, only those who were rejected from other options get into teaching" (1996: 5). If Tiramonti is right in her diagnosis, the presence of this small group of nontraditional TEP students is perceived (by some educational authorities, teachers, and researchers) as a threat not only to the future quality of school services but to their own identity.

Two hypotheses can be advanced at this point. If TEP faculty evaluate the current students as being from or having an "inferior/deviant" status, it is possible that such ascribed "inferiority" is acting as a threat to the faculty sense of identity (as middle class, enlightened, and so on). Could it not be that deep discriminatory structures, hidden under the oppressive structures of mandatory heterosexuality and idealized racial, cultural, and religious homogeneities of the Argentinean population, are operating as the habitus of the TEP? These fears about the change in the students' "element," the anxiety over "the poor" taking over the schools, and the menace of homosexuality seem to be connected with desperate attempts by TEP faculty to maintain structures of distinction (Bourdieu, 1984).[14]

These hypotheses gain plausibility when they are placed in the larger social and economic context, not only of the so-called "educational impoverishment" but in the contemporary phenomenon of the new poverty that is presented in chapter 3. In order to begin answering the multifaceted questions surrounding these issues, it is important to provide a more complete characterization of who these future teachers are as well as to pay attention to their explanations. The next section in this chapter provides such a description.

Who Are the Current Teacher Education Students?

The data presented in this section were obtained from 178 questionnaires administered to students in six different TEPs in the city of Buenos Aires. All the questions in the questionnaires were open-ended; thus, the responses were coded and categorized afterwards. This type of qualitative questionnaire was developed in order to identify some patterns of responses without resorting to the use of preestablished units of analysis. Therefore, the questionnaire responses have been qualitatively coded and analyzed in a quasi-quantitative mode. In other words, no specific statistical analysis of the responses will be performed beyond looking for general tendencies as expressed in the frequency of responses. This combination of analytical tools allows the identification of patterns of responses in their proportion relative to the other type of responses, both within each of the TEPs observed, and among different TEPs.

All the questionnaires were administered after the researcher was somewhat familiar with the students, either through prior observations or class discussions. In all cases, the students had to complete a ninety to one hundred twenty minute activity (discuss and draw different educational situations) before completing the questionnaire. This technique proved to be very useful, not only in terms of increasing the rate of responses, but also in the students' involvement and commitment to the task. A discussion of these aspects is the focus of the last section of this chapter.

Main Characteristics of the Teacher Education Students

As noted before, the majority (83.8 percent) of TEP students in this study, following the tradition of the profession, are women. In terms of the civil status, 73.6 percent are single, 23.6 percent married, and 2.8 percent divorced. Most of the male students are single (93.1 percent). If gender and civil status are homogenous trends, age reveals less similarities. Table 4.2 exemplifies this point.

Table 4.2. Age of Female and Male Students in TEPs

Ages	18-21	22-25	26-30	31-35	36-40	Total (N: 178)
All	39.9%	28.1%	15.7%	12.9%	3.4%	100%
Male	55.2%	27.6%	17.2%	0.0%	0.0%	100%
Female	36.9%	28.2%	15.4%	15.4%	0.0%	100%

At first, all the current TEP students appear to share similar characteristics to past TEP students in terms of their socioeconomic background. Based on their parents' education, employment, and self-ascription, these students can be considered middle class, and in a smaller proportion, poor. However, as noted before, what has changed are the conditions and economic possibilities of the "middle class." If, in the past, TEP students devoted most of their time to study, nowadays they divide their time between study and work, including household work (primarily female students).[15] It is important to note that the 20 percent of students over thirty years of age are all women.[16] This group of women in their thirties is in its majority married, with one or two children.

The responses to the questionnaire indicate that 66.9 percent of TEP students are currently employed (see table 4.3). Male students tend to be employed in larger numbers (86.2 percent) compared to 63.1 percent of the female students.[17]

Table 4.3. Percentage of Teacher Education Students Currently Working

Work	Yes	No	Total
All	66.9%	33.1%	100%
Male	86.2%	13.8%	100%
Female	63.1%	36.9%	100%

It is relevant to report that forty-three students (23.8 percent) are currently working in schools or in school-related jobs. Another sixty students (33.7 percent) work in commerce (grocery stores, bookstores, retail) and nineteen (10.7 percent) work as maids or janitors. In fact, 12.8 percent of all the women in this sample fall into this last category.

The fact that almost a quarter of these TEP students are already working in schools reinforces the hypothesis that for many, the Argentinean system of teacher training is acting as a placement office by providing early access to employment, in particular for men. Dicker and Terigi (1994) have reported that it is a frequent phenomenon that many of those students who are granted early access to teaching positions do not finish their teacher education studies. These noncertified students are perceived very critically, both within the TEP and by educational researchers, and it is considered that they do "not have the right vocation" and/or that they "use the system to get a job."

However, the main reasons why those students do not finish their studies remain unclear. Clearly, early entrance to the job market is a strong factor, but it is not the only one. Among other elements that should be taken into consideration are the poor quality of many of the TEPs and the discredited place of the theoretical aspects of teaching, coupled with the strong tradition that teachers learn more (or exclusively) from practical experiences. I resume this point when discussing the responses of the TEP students about their reasons for studying teacher education.

Why Do They Study? Social Mobility, Vocation, and Beyond

When looking at the educational level of the parents of these 178 students, there is a clear pattern. The vast majority of these students' parents (89 percent) did not pursue higher education studies. In that sense, despite the low salaries and poor working conditions associated with teaching, obtaining a degree through a TEP could be considered as a means of social and educational mobility. In other words, getting a higher education diploma could be a powerful motivation to get into a TEP. Nevertheless, there are other elements that should be contemplated,

especially given the fact that for almost all the students in this research, teaching
is their second career choice.

In this group of students, only 64 (36 percent) did not undertake any other
postsecondary studies before starting a TEP. The common element among these
64 students is age. They are the youngest and the oldest (fifty-five females and
three males are between ages eighteen to twenty-one; six females are thirty-three
or older). Accordingly, the rest of the students in this sample (64 percent) have
chosen teaching only after attempting other studies, and many plan to return to
these studies at a later point.[18]

Only 7.9 percent of all the students do not plan to pursue further studies. A
significant group (48.9 percent) wants to pursue a university degree, and 28.7
percent plan to have a second degree in teaching (see table 4.4). In this group,
many plan to have a secondary education diploma (particularly male students),
or specialization that will allow them to work with students who have special
needs (predominantly female students).

Table 4.4. Future Study Plans of Teacher Education Students (Total and %)

Students	University	Other Teaching	Other (No University)	No	Total
All	87	51	26	14	178
%	48.9%	28.7%	14.6%	7.9%	
Male	13	9	4	3	29
%	44.8%	31.0%	14.8%	10.3%	
Female	74	42	22	11	149
%	49.7%	28.2%	13.8%	7.4%	

The social prestige and the economic promise of the university compared to
the lack of prestige of TEPs and meager salaries of teachers are perhaps the two
main reasons that many opt for teacher education as a second option. However,
there are other elements to consider.

First, as noted in a recent study (Dussel, Tiramonti, and Birgin, 2000),
Argentina is witnessing a trend that is contrary to the worldwide observed
feminization of teaching (Acker, 1996). Each year the number of males entering
into the profession increases. Some of them enter into the system through TEPs,
yet many others are using their university credentials as a platform for starting
their careers in schools, particularly at the secondary level.

Second, the initial higher education and career alternative choices of these students reflect traditional gender stereotypes. Among 80 percent of all male students the first preferences were traditional professions such as medicine, law, economics, and natural sciences and engineering. Among females, traditional humanistic studies in literature, education, and arts were important (40 percent), together with psychology (10 percent) and social sciences, including social work (15 percent). These results are not entirely unexpected. As Nelly Stromquist describes, "In some economically advanced Latin American countries, such as Brazil and Argentina . . . science and technology are often selected by men while women tend to select studies in humanities and letters and in teaching" (1996a: 7).[19]

Third, the fact that most of the current TEP students choose teaching after abandoning other studies, mostly at the university level, is seen as a critical issue. In a similar fashion, Justa Ezpeleta (1991) points out that those students who choose TEPs after trying other studies do so in order to avoid further frustration. The following testimonies give support to the description of TEPs as a second choice.

> I tried several careers. First it was law, then computer sciences and finally teaching. I wasn't happy; these choices were too difficult and I had to work. (M 100: age 26)

> I started literature, but I couldn't stand the coldness of the university. I didn't like the way they [professors] treated us. Besides, I always wanted to work with kids, so the right place for me was here. (F 79: age 23)

Apparently, the issue at stake for TEP faculty and researchers is that TEPs seem to be for these students a less valid choice as it is made after having tried other studies. Surprisingly enough, however, these students' main reason for dropping their first choice was a lack of vocation, which, as was discussed in detail in previous sections, seems to be one of the preeminent values in TEPs.

The reasons given by these students for not completing their first higher education choices both illuminate and conflict with their stated rationale for becoming teachers. When the students were consulted about the reasons for choosing a TEP, less than 16 percent saw the TEP as a means of social mobility or as an employment strategy. The majority of the students emphasized vocational reasons and love for kids. These two groups comprised 69.4 percent of all the responses. However, it is important to remember that only 21.9 percent of these students have abandoned their first (mostly university) choices and that most of them have very pragmatic reasons (such as economic or job problems and pregnancies) for not completing their first choice. Table 4.5 summarizes this information.

Table 4.5. Reasons for Not Finishing First Higher Education Choice

Students	Economic	Lack of Time	Marriage	Not my Vocation	Too Difficult	Credential	Total
All	18.4%	20.1%	7.9%	22.1%	28.9%	2.6%	100% N=114*
Male	4.7%	28.6%	0.0%	28.6%	38.1%	0.0%	100% N=21
Female	21.6%	18.3%	9.7%	20.5%	26.7%	3.2%	100% N=93

* The sixty-four students who did not have a prior choice of studies are not included in this table.

A small but significant number of students expressed their intentions of using schools to promote social change. Even those who responded that pursuing a teaching credential was in part motivated by the need for getting a secure job also added that vocational reasons were similarly important. Only three male students pointed exclusively to more pragmatic reasons (short studies and securing a job) as their rationale. Table 4.6 summarizes these trends.

Table 4.6. Reasons to Pursue a Career in Teaching (Total and %)

Students	Vocation	Love For Kids	Social Change	Finding a Job/ Vocation	Short Studies/ Secure Job
All	71	53	26	25	3
%	39.6%	29.8%	14.6%	14.0%	1.7%
Male	9	6	6	5	3
%	31.0%	20.7%	20.7%	17.2%	10.3 %
Female	62	47	20	20	0
%	41.6%	31.5 %	13.4 %	13.4 %	0.0 %

As noted before, twenty-six students (14.6 percent) responded that the main motivation for choosing a TEP was their desire to promote social change. In response to the question, "Why did you chose a TEP?" two of those students explained:

I like to teach and I like to learn. But the most important reason is my need to channel my desires and commitment of helping at a social level to change things. I want, or at least I attempt, to change from the classroom what the government does not do; teach people to feel more safe and committed to the society. (F 108: age 34).

I believe that in this way I will help, perhaps in small ways, to secure the right to education and information. I believe that knowledge makes you free. (F 162: age 29)

Testimonies 108 and 162 show that some of the students in TEPs have a commitment to social change and want to become what Henry Giroux refers to as transformative intellectuals.

Acting as a transformative intellectual means helping students to acquire critical knowledge about basic societal structures, such as the economy, the state, the workplace, and mass culture, so that such institutions can be open to potential transformation. (Giroux, 1988: 138–39)

Looking at the same typology of answers given by males, there is an interesting reversal. In this case, the male students still see themselves as willing to have an active role as social activists, yet their answers show some concern with the need of securing their livelihood. For instance, M 57 wants to promote social change, but at the same time recognizes the need to secure his income and solve the pressures of low salaries. For him, as well as for others outside the teaching profession, one solution is a second and more profitable professional career.

In any society you must have a role. I want to be a teacher, despite the low salaries and other issues. The social aspect, teaching for change, is important, I want to be an active part. I want to change things and not wait for things to happen. Besides, I have another job, I'm a lifeguard and teach swimming. (M 57: age 22)

Similarly, one female student who is currently working as an hourly housekeeper explains her strategy to cope with economic problems as well as her particular understanding of "vocation":

I don't think I will be a full-time teacher. I would love to do so, but I have a strong sense of reality. I have to feed my girl. Right now I'm planning to teach during the morning and do this (housekeeping) in the afternoons, maybe the other way around, depending on the possibil-ities. And who knows, if things get better maybe full-time teacher, but I doubt it . . . [she smiles as if something funny is happening]. Question: Why are you smiling?

> It is because of my classmates. It is funny, how these . . . ah, uhh, hm
> [she hesitates] "blondies" in the TEP talk about the people like me
> (housekeepers), they are so . . . I don't want to . . . [long pause] well,
> in my opinion they are [lowers her voice] kind of . . . stupid, they are
> not bad, but sometimes . . . sometimes, I feel . . . I want to say to them:
> I don't understand why you look down on us, if I make more money
> cleaning houses than I will make as a teacher. Anyway, nobody wants
> to be a housekeeper and for me teaching is what I want to do. I
> discovered that teaching is my vocation. (F 37: age 26)

Testimony 37 is relevant because it problematizes many areas in TEPs. First, as in prior responses, the harsh economic realities are incorporated into the analysis and future expectations of this student. Second, it points to class and cultural differences (i.e., how difficult it is for this particular student to openly criticize her classmates). Third, F 37 presents her desire to be a teacher using the figure of vocation but without romanticizing it. In this case, "vocation" is something to be discovered after other experiences. In this sense, it is possible to wonder to what extent similar processes of "discovery" happened for many other TEP students.

In sum, these students seem to be aware of the limitations of teaching but they are also keenly aware of the limitations of other activities, including the much coveted university studies. It is important to recall that the recent increase in TEP enrollment has been explained by researchers as a result of changes in the socioeconomic conditions of the country. Without disregarding the findings of those studies, the results of this research seem to indicate the need to pay closer attention to the importance of emotional and vocational aspects. Choosing a professional career involves many aspects, from financial or monetary compensation to less tangible and measurable emotional reasons.

This trend could be explained as an attempt to hide the "real" reasons (i.e., obtain a secure yet poorly paid job) but it may also be well rooted in the tradition of "service" and deeply gendered structures of expectations. Bolotin Joseph and Burnaford note that two decades ago, Lortie noted the following:

> The culture of teachers and the structure of rewards do not emphasize
> the acquisition of extrinsic rewards. The tradition of teaching makes
> people who seek money, prestige, or power somewhat suspect; the
> characteristic style in public education is to mute personal ambition.
> The service ideal has extolled the virtue of giving more than one
> receives; the model teacher has been "dedicated." (Lortie, 1977, in
> Bolotin Joseph and Burnaford, 1994: 110)

To conclude this section, there are a series of preliminary findings that point to complex articulations that need to be recalled.

First, the majority of the new TEP students can be considered "new poor" or members of a recently impoverished middle class. Such conditions appear to strongly affect their education. Second, most of these TEP students have started and abandoned university-level studies not related to education. These choices reflect traditional "gendered" options. Third, most of these students plan to continue studying. Some want to pursue a second degree in teaching and/or to get a university degree.

Overall (77.9 percent), the main reasons presented by these students for not completing the first higher education choices were very pragmatic: economic, lack of time, family obligations (such as marriages or pregnancies). Vocational issues had a relative high frequency (22.1 percent) but these issues are less important compared to the pragmatic reasons.

In addition, the explicit rationale for choosing TEPs stresses vocational and emotional aspects rather than economic ones. Nevertheless, all of the students are aware of the economic problems and in some cases, these future teachers plan to combine teaching with other nonteaching activities.

Moreover, issues of job stability and security seem to be relevant for these students. In other words, although elementary teaching has a very low starting salary, it provides some social benefits that appear to compensate for the low income to some degree, especially in a scenario of high job instability.

All the above elements do not easily fit in one explanatory model. For some students, love for children and vocational aspects are used to explain the decision of becoming teachers. Yet for others, teaching is a "second option" (perhaps an intermediate stage) after the much-valued and more difficult university degree. This odd articulation, between vocation for teaching and the apparently simultaneous lack of valorization for teaching, appears to be rooted in the persistence of ideal models of teachers. The next section begins to explore those models in the form of metaphors, analogies, and images presented by TEP students.

Metaphors and Models of Teachers

When answering the question "What other activities are similar to teaching?" many students did not identify other professional activities with teaching. Less than 22 percent of the students related teaching with "prestigious professions," like medicine or journalism. For 37.5 percent of the female students, teaching is like motherhood, and their second choice (28.9 percent) was that no other activity is like teaching. This last answer was the most frequent one among males (38.0 percent). Priesthood was the second choice (24.3 percent) among male students. In 11.9 percent of the responses of the female students, teaching was also compared to nursing and social work (which are typically considered feminine professions).

Table 4.7. Teacher Education Students (%)
What Other Activity Is Like Teaching?

Students	Mother/ Father	Nurse/ Social Worker	Priest/ Nun	Doctor	Farmer*	Other**	None	Total
All	33.2	11.9	8.5	3.9	6.4	5.7	30.4	100
Male	13.8	10.3	24.3	6.8	3.4	3.4	38.0	100
Female	37.5	12.0	5.4	3.4	6.8	6.0	28.9	100

* "Farmer" includes gardener and handicraft person.
** "Other" includes journalist, president, psychologist, historian.

When the students had to explain why teaching was similar to other activities, the variety of answers was remarkable. Responses ranged from issues of time and responsibilities to the low salaries. However, two types of responses were the most frequent. Following the rationale of expressing that teaching is not like any other work, almost 30 percent justified their answer by saying that teaching is a unique activity not comparable to any other.

> You cannot compare teaching with any other activity. Why? To be a teacher you have to be very responsible, not only in what you teach, but your vocation also has to be clear and you have to be serious as an educator. (F 27: age 26)

> Teachers are teachers, this is something unique. (M 156: age 21)

Those students who previously associated teaching with activities that emphasize an idealized "caring" style such as motherhood, priesthood, and social work evoked concepts of vocation, love for kids, and the time dedicated to their jobs in their answers. This group comprised more than 43 percent of the sample (similar figures for males and females).

Students in this group also tended to give answers related to children's welfare.

> Teaching is like being a social worker or a mother. Why? If a kid is not feeling well or gets hurt playing, you have to take care of him [sic]. If he has lice, you have to look for it. If he is aggressive, you have to use psychology to discover what is going on. (F 170: age 35)

> Teaching is like parenting. Why? Because teaching is much more than teaching numbers or letters. You have to constantly put children's welfare first, and that is what parents do all the time. (F 29: age 19)

As repeatedly stated in this book, in Argentina like in many other countries, the perceived link between teaching and mothering has old roots. Consider, for instance, the following statement made by a North American teacher who is regarded as "extremely effective" in preventing and dealing with violent situations in classrooms:

> I would say that it is more like parenting. I talk to them [the students]. I don't keep my distance. I do not keep professionalism between us. I say what I really think, how I really feel. I break all of the rules. I touch them. If they are hungry, I feed them. If they need clothes, I bring them clothes. If they need a ride home, I give them a ride home. I break all of the rules. (Female teacher quoted in Astor, Meyer, and Behre, 1999: 25)

Work with young children is seen as a caring activity that primarily fulfills emotional and custodial needs and secondly other (more) intellectual ones. Perhaps the most notorious trend among these TEP students is one that conjures up an image of a "teacher who selflessly does what s/he does for the sake of the children rather from any desire for personal monetary gain or worldly satisfaction" (Duncan, 1996: 163).

The questionnaires administered to students of TEPs reveal that the idealization of the figure of "the teacher as a parent" is important: seventy-six students (42.7 percent) answered that they feel pride or love when they are considered the "second mother/father" of the students, sixty-six students (37.1 percent) reported (from a sympathetic position) that they understand when other people make that comparison between teaching and parenting. Only 20.2 percent have straightforward negative feelings.

One key fact that needs to be highlighted is that the students' responses clearly contrast with the answers of the fifteen faculty of TEP and the twelve experienced teachers interviewed in this study. These people expressed very negative feelings about the figure of the second mother/father. Thus, before continuing the analysis of the students' responses, it is necessary to have a closer look at the opinions of experienced teachers and faculty.

Experienced Teachers and the Ideology of Second Motherhood

One of the guiding hypotheses of this research is that conceptions about teachers' work simultaneously question and reinforce the figure of the teacher-mother (Morgade, 1992a). As shown before, perspectives that emphasized a restricted vision about "caring" and the presumed "natural" educational tendencies in women also portrayed schools as public extensions of domestic activities. As such, these tendencies have attempted to reinforce the reproductive character of teaching with its socializing mission of "forming" citizens, workers, and/or good persons rather than merely focusing on "teaching academic content." In that sense, teaching is understood as a pastoral activity (Foucault, 1979) that deploys a set of discursive operations that attempt to hide other missions or rationales (political, economical, and cultural) of schooling behind the curtains of neutral socialization processes.

In Argentina, the economic, social, and cultural changes of the last decades have strongly challenged the presumed "domesticity" of schooling. Schools are no longer the "second home." They have become workplaces. The rise of unionism, combined with the heavy discourse of "professionalism," and the undeniable impact of feminist discourses are in part informing the change in traditional perceptions. Paulo Freire (1993) entered into the discussion of this identification between teachers and "foster relatives"[20] of the students, advancing a very critical view. He emphatically states that

> to accept the "aunt" identification does not provide any positive value. It means, on the contrary, the taking away of something fundamental to the *teacher*: her professional responsibility . . . [it] is almost like saying that *female* teachers like *good aunts*, must not fight, must not rebel, must not got on strike. (Freire, in Carvalho, 1996: 79. Emphasis in the original)

In the context of this research, it appears that experienced educators agree with Paulo Freire. They do not consider the ideology of "second motherhood" to be positive, nor is it considered as informing their teaching practices. In several interviews with experienced teachers and faculty of TEPs, there was an overwhelming disagreement with the positive image of teachers as second mothers/fathers. Such discord ranged from complete rejection of this figure (using phrases such as "I hate it") to manifestations of opposition combined with expressions that showed different levels of understanding for those who use that simile to describe teachers' roles.

> I have been teaching for the last ten years, from first grade to sixth grade, and that gives me some authority, doesn't it? Well, let me tell you, if one of my students by mistake calls me mom, that's OK, but . . . I will explain to him [*sic*], "Mom is not here; she must be cooking at home or working, I love you, and I care about you, but I am Ms. Rosa, your teacher."
> Researcher: Why do you . . . ?
> Because this thing of the second mom is old and wrong. It is important to set the limits very clearly and to not send the wrong message. (Rosa, age 28)

One male instructor of TEP shares the general orientation of this group, yet he highlights a different perspective:

The idea of teachers being second mothers was very functional in the past. It worked fine, but that was a long time ago. Therefore, only those who are . . . well, kind of nostalgic and are looking at schools with old eyes, but now . . . now, no. I don't believe our students have anything in common with that model. Maybe some older parents and of course the kindergarten teachers, but that is more an age issue. Definitely, no!!! If someone says that, it is because they still have a romantic idea about teaching and about the kids. (Juan, age 43)

The results of these interviews seem to indicate that there is ample consensus among teachers and TEP faculty regarding the diminishing significance of the ideology of the "second motherhood" for the teaching profession. As such, one should expect that new and alternative models (and metaphors) would replace the old and fatigued model of teachers as apostles of education or second mothers.

However, diminishing significance does not mean disappearance or lack of influence in the gendered dimensions of teaching. As Graciela Morgade has pointed out,

[l]ow salaries, relationships of subordination in bureaucratic jobs, relative power within the realm of the classroom, and above all, the exclusion from the process of knowledge production to favor transmission of social values are conditioning factors which reproduce an ideologically-charged "feminine condition." This limited understanding of the feminine is an active agent in the reproduction of these conditioning factors (Morgade, 1992b: 54).

TEP Students and the Second Motherhood Ideology

Turning again to the responses of the students in TEPs will illustrate the discrepancy of opinions between them, experienced teachers, and TEP faculty. As noted before, seventy-six students (42.7 percent) answered that they feel pride or love when they are considered the "second mother/father" of the students. Sixty-six students (37.1 percent) expressed understanding but not criticisms in regard to the use of this figure. Therefore, this group of responses is closer to a positive valorization (what is clearly seen in the written explanations) than to a negative attitude toward the second-mother figure. Only thirty-six students (20.2 percent) clearly stated their disagreement. However, it should be pointed out that these perceptions differed by gender. In percentages, only 31.1 percent of the men had positive feelings, whereas positive responses were given by 45 percent of the women. Table 4.8 summarizes the responses of the students.

Looking at the distribution of these responses by age, there is an interesting phenomenon. Young students (eighteen to twenty-one years old) and older

Table 4.8. Teacher Education Students
What Do You Feel When Someone Refers to Teachers
as the Second Mother/Father of the Students?

Feelings	Love, pride	Understanding	Disagreement
All	42.7%	31.1%	45.0%
Males	37.1%	41.3%	36.2%
Females	20.2%	27.6%	18.8%
Total	100%	100%	100%

students (thirty-one to forty years old) tend to have more positive feelings about the figure of teachers as second parents than those in the middle age groups. For both the youngest and the oldest, 60 percent had positive feelings (similar distribution for males and females). Additionally, there were not notable variations between those students who are mothers or fathers themselves and those who are not.

Examples of positive answers are the following:

> I like it because it reflects strong links between children, teachers and society. However, parents shouldn't evade their unique responsibilities. I like the idea of the second mother, working together with parents, not as a substitute for them. (F 178, age 22)

> Enormous satisfaction. There are many families that do not care for their children and they [the children] look upon teachers with love, sometimes even with more love for the teachers than for their own parents. (M 65, age 23)

> Personally, I am the happiest person in the world. In two years I will have twenty foster kids. I will teach them, educate them. I will know what they need and they will learn from me. I will be TEACHER. (F 68, age 32. Capitalized in the original.)

The following are typical answers of understanding or mixed feelings:

> On the one hand I feel good, because it shows strong affectionate/loving bonds between teachers and students, besides merely teaching. On the other hand, bad because nowadays children are lacking those bonds (with their families) and that is not good for the kids. (F 89, age 19)

> I feel proud because I am useful to them, yet I feel bad because it shows that everybody needs parental love, and how for many that is missing. In my own experience, there is nothing like love, attention and caring, thus, family. (M 94, age 25)

The following are typical examples of negative feelings:

> I don't like it because parents assign to teachers a responsibility that is not for teachers to take, in some cases to avoid their parental duties. I think that teachers should guide, open students' minds, as independent thinkers, like researchers, for the children to come to their own conclusions. (F 162, age 31)

> I don't like it; however, those who say it are not totally wrong. It is a pity but many times teachers have to fulfill the parental role, even though I don't think it is the right thing to do. (F 167, age 27)

> I think that teaching is very important, but sometimes parents do not understand the limitations and they assign teachers their own (parental) responsibilities. The real problem is that there is an important crisis in the model of the family. (F 116, age 21)

> There are not second parents! Parents could be biological or not, yet nobody earns the title of father/parent only for procreation! However, a teacher is only a teacher. It doesn't mean not being friendly, a counselor and a companion, etc. . . . That is OK, but second father/parent, NO—Impossible—. (M 19, age 20. Emphasis in the original.)

The response of F 167 shows that in some cases in which the answer expressed disappointment or dislike of the "second motherhood" model, there was an implicit acknowledgment of how pervasive such a figure is among these students and others. Other negative responses were also very sympathetic with the figure of the "mother." In those cases, the typical answer pointed to the importance and almost sacred role of the mother (interestingly enough, none of the responses mentioned fathers). Sentences such as "nobody can equal a mother's love" and "there is only one mother, it is nonsense to say second or third mother" were repeatedly written by the students.

Among the students who responded with negative feelings to the figure of the second mother, there was one group of responses (mainly from one particular school that is regarded as the most academic TEP in the city of Buenos Aires) that established a different pattern in their responses. These students blamed those who use or accept the second motherhood figure for diminishing the professional value of teaching.

I think that is an old-fashioned statement and not very useful.
Teachers are professionals [who] work with people, not with "raw
materials." Teachers teach, they try to create valuable people for
themselves and for the society. (F 2, age 29)

I believe that the idea of teachers as second mothers is very extended
and has diminished the opportunities for elementary education
teachers to become professionals. (F 164, age 36)

These testimonies closely resemble the ideas of many educational
researchers in the region, who echo another critical voice coming from Brazil.

When we don't know what to do, we love. I am not denying the
affective dimension in teaching. Like any activity which involves
human relationships, teaching will always include this dimension.
However, when this dimension is absolute, it is very likely that it is
being used as a way to avoid, via feelings, problems which require the
competence of a specialist. (Guiomar Namo de Mello, 1987, in
Carvalho, 1996: 80)

To summarize this section, at first glance, the 178 students in training to
become teachers who participated in this research appear to be a homogeneous
group in terms of the following characteristics: gender, civil status, working
conditions, and explicit rationales for choosing teaching as a career.

This group of students is predominantly feminine (83.8 percent) and single
(73.6 percent). Most of these students are also working (66.9 percent), and many
of them (64 percent) have tried and abandoned other studies before deciding to
enter into a TEP. The students describe themselves as from the middle classes
and state that "vocation and love for kids" are the two main reasons that explain
their decision to become teachers.[21] Not surprisingly, most of them also see
teaching as a feminine activity.

If the previous characteristics indicated homogenous traits for this group of
TEP students, there are also other elements that permit us to see its heterogeneity:
age, future study aspirations, images, and metaphors that TEP students used to
describe teaching.

These areas of homogeneity and heterogeneity not only show plurality of
backgrounds and styles among students, but they also highlight a permanent
tension between expectations and discourses mainly among the TEP students and
their teachers. In general, while students see themselves in terms of positive
dispositions (being committed teachers, antiauthoritarian and caring people),
faculty of TEPs have developed a slightly negative construction of these
students' identities.

Thus, two interconnected topics need to be highlighted. First, there is a gap
between students and the faculty of TEPs regarding the perception of the figure

of teachers as second mothers. This gap indicates that this is a problematic area that is not understood or is underestimated by TEP faculty. This lack of consideration may have negative effects on the training of those students. Such a gap seems to be closely related to different perceptions about gender and class aspects, in terms of what is the habitus of teaching as a professional activity in Argentina. Second, based on the partial findings of this section (and previous ones) it appears that the figure of the second mother does not have a singular definition or meaning. In other words, its quick dismissal as an antiquity, or ideological barrier to the improvement of the professional status of teachers, should be discussed and not taken for granted. In this scenario, what is considered to be good teaching requires a full exploration of the gendered dimensions of what teaching means and what is required to be accepted as a professional of education.

As Linda Darling-Hammond points out, "Teachers teach from what they know. If policymakers want to change teaching, they must pay attention to teacher knowledge [and make] investments in those things that allow teachers to grapple with transformations of ideas and behaviors" (1990: 339). Taking Darling-Hammond's words seriously implies making an effort to capture ideas and images that cannot be presented exclusively by written texts, questionnaires, and interviews. The next section is a step toward that direction.

Thinking Visually

In order to motivate students to think about schooling issues in a less traditional way, I asked different groups of students to make photograph-like drawings about education and afterwards select one or two of the drawings to engage in a whole group analysis.[22]

This technique was used on seven occasions, six times with students of TEPs and once within the framework of a "nonformal education" workshop conducted by the researcher.[23] In general when performing this activity, the researcher took advantage of the "failures" of the system. In all the opportunities but one, this activity took place when the students had a couple of free hours (which is "normal" for them because almost as a rule, faculty in TEPs miss quite a few classes a week). Students were informed of the characteristics of the research and assured absolute confidentiality.

The sequence of events for this activity was the following: the researcher proposed that the TEP students draw either a real or an ideal situation, moment, or character related to education. The students were not given additional directions or indications, except for the following: before making the drawings they had to have small-group discussions (two or three participants) to define the situation chosen by each individual and, after completing each picture, write an explanation of it. Next, the researcher hung all the drawings on the blackboard and read the explanations. After that, the group selected one or two images, and the students discussed them with the coordination of the researcher. The sessions were audiotaped, and notes were taken by the researcher.

Main Trends in Real and Ideal Images of Teachers

During the fieldwork a total of 178 students produced 195 images. One hundred thirty-five (69.2 percent) of these images represent real situations and sixty (30.8 percent) images represent ideal situations. Three styles of representation appeared in these images (stick figures, representational images, and abstract images), which showed representational commitments about teachers, students, and classrooms. A summary of the types of drawings is given in table 4.9.

Table 4.9. Types of Drawings

Female Students (N = 149)	Male Students (N = 29)
112 drawings representing real situations • 110 instances where the teacher was a woman (80 images of teachers without students) • 2 instances where the teacher was a man (in both cases with students)	**23 drawings representing real situations** • 18 instances where the teacher was a woman (3 images of teachers without students) • 5 instances where the teacher was a male (all with students)
49 drawings representing ideal situations • 41 female teachers (6 images without students) • 8 male teachers (all with students)	**11 drawings representing ideal situations** • 10 male teachers (all cases with students) • 1 female teacher (without students)
Overall, female students drew the following: • 30 stick-figure images • 2 abstract representations • 129 representational images (cartoon-like or expressive)	**Overall, male students drew the following:** • 12 stick-figure images • 24 representational images (cartoon-like or expressive)

Figures 4.1 through 4.3 are examples of the three styles of representations used by the students: stick figure, representational, and abstract images.

Figure 4.1. Stick Figure

Real Teacher   Ideal Teacher
"Female Octopus Teacher"   "Happy Female/Male Teacher"

"I wanted to express how *las maestras* [female teachers] deal with multiple tasks. Today they are octopuses. In the ideal case teachers, THEIR SEX DOES NOT MATTER [capitalized in the original] they are simply teachers. Because it is such a great joy to be working with children, they are happy." (F 100, age 22)

Figures 4.2 and 4.3 configure one unified example in which there is a combination of styles. These two drawings were produced by a 35-year-old female student.

Figures 4.2. Representational Image

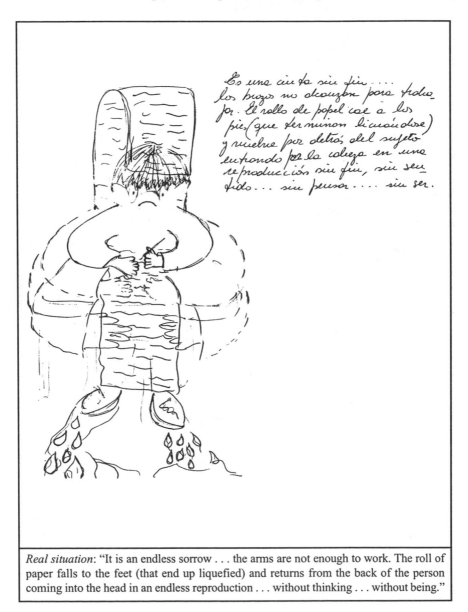

Real situation: "It is an endless sorrow . . . the arms are not enough to work. The roll of paper falls to the feet (that end up liquefied) and returns from the back of the person coming into the head in an endless reproduction . . . without thinking . . . without being."

Figures 4.3. Abstract Image

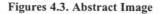

Ideal situation: "In order to learn one has to question and to question and doubt you have to know something . . . To be able to question oneself and ask (questions) is the base of reflexive thought. And he who questions never errs?"

Table 4.10. TEP Students' Real and Ideal Images about Teachers
Features Indicating Representational Commitments (and %)

"Real" Teachers (N = 135)		"Ideal" Teachers (N = 60)	
• White female	(128 = 94.1%)	• Young person	(60 = 100%)
• Frowning	(95 = 70.3%)	• Caring person	(50 = 83.3%)
• Old and stern	(55 = 40.7%)	• White female	(40 = 66.6%)
• Controlling/disciplining	(43 = 67.1%)*	• Smiling	(32 = 53.3%)
students		• Playing with the	(21 = 35%)
• Young and stern	(40 = 29.6%)	students	
• Poor	(30 = 22.2%)	• White male	(18 = 30%)
• Cannot control the	(23 = 45.9%)*	• Knowledgeable about	(12 = 20%)
students		the content	
• Young and caring	(20 = 14.8%)	• White gender neutral	(2 = 3.33%)
• Nervous/desperate/	(20 = 14.8%)		
stressed			
• Knowledgeable about	(20 = 14.8%)		
the content			
• Being disorganized	(16 = 11.8%)		
• Indifferent to the	(10 = 15.6%)*		
students			
• White male	(7 = 5.9%)		

* Percentages based on the 64 images that show teachers interacting with students.

Table 4.11. TEP Students' Real and Ideal Images about Students
Features Indicating Representational Commitments (N and %)

"Real" Students (N = 75)		"Ideal" Students (N = 54)	
• Obedient and passive	(52 = 69.3%)	• Obedient and receptive	(54 = 100%)
• Poor	(32 = 42.6%)	to the teacher's	
• Unruly and active	(23 = 30.6%)	instructions	
• Tired or bored	(16 = 21.3%)	• Orderly and interacting	(54 = 100%)
• Not knowing the	(15 = 11.2%)	with other students or	
content		the teacher	
• White male and female	(49 = 81.8%)	• Smiling	(40 = 70.2%)
		• Playing	(21 = 38.8%)
		• Diverse ethnicities	(5 = 9.2%)

Table 4.12. TEP Students' Real and Ideal Images about Classrooms
Features Indicating Representational Commitments (N and %)

"Real" Classrooms (N = 75)	"Ideal" Classrooms (N = 54)

• Desks organized in rows (63 = 84.0%)
• Tumultuous or violent (23 = 30.6%)
  spaces
• Inundated by external (16 = 21.3%)
  pressures and demands
• In need of repairs and (42 = 56.6%)
  lacking materials
• Overcrowded (28 = 37.3%)
	• Desks organized in circles (46 = 85.1%)
	• Neat, orderly spaces (46 = 85%)
	• Not being affected by (30 = 55.5%)
	  external elements,
	  persons, or pressures
	• Technologically equipped (18 = 33.3%)
	• Playful (11 = 20.4%)
	• Classroom outside schools (8 = 14.8%)

Table 4.13. General Trends in the Drawings about Real Schools

In a general analysis the drawings describing real situations include many of the following elements, which are considered representational commitments. (Students' phrases or words explaining the meaning of a particular element appear between quotation marks.)

In 85 percent of the situations, there are references to the social and economic crisis and/or the schools' budgetary problems in the form of:
1. Decaying materials: cracking walls, graffiti, lack of textbooks and other instructional materials, and worn-out clothing (for both teachers and students)
2. Fewer desks than the number of students
3. Empty desks, "as a symbol of the increase in the dropout rates"
4. Low salaries (in the form of small amounts of money)
5. Violence (guns in classrooms and fights)
6. Food (students being served food)

54% of the real images depict situations of "tension and control" within the classrooms as evidenced by:
1. "Authoritarian" teachers (disciplining students, giving orders regarding behaviors and/or content of learning styles)
2. Violence among students
3. Violence between teachers and students
4. Outside elements "invading" classroom environments. Students identified the following "outside" elements as problematic: bad news, "red tape," curriculum guidelines, parents, administrators, social and economic problems, and schedules

70% of the images include students, and they appear as:
1. Passive and bored (15%)
2. Hungry/receiving food (8%)
3. Violent subjects, i.e., attacking teachers and/or fighting between students (10%)
4. Being poor (50%)
5. Being "ignorant," "donkeys" (17%)

Table 4.14. General Trends in the Drawings about Ideal Schools

In a general analysis the drawings describing ideal situations include many of the following elements, which are considered representational commitments. (Students' phrases or words explaining the meaning of a particular element appear between quotation marks.)[24]

The ideal teacher:
1. The "ideal teacher" is a young and caring figure.
2. The "ideal female" teacher is helping or being attentive to the learning or affective "needs" of one or more students.
3. The "ideal male" teacher is teaching.
4. The most frequent image was of a female teacher that resembled a stereotype of a nice girl wearing "proper" clothing (feminine). Yet in some cases sport outfits were used as a way to show teachers' closeness or playfulness with students. These images of ideal female teachers closely resemble what could be considered traditional models of femininity and beauty (ideal female teachers tend to be slim and blond).
5. The ideal teacher (male and female) smiles.
6. The ideal teacher (male and female) receives a better salary.

The ideal classroom:
1. The ideal classroom is an isolated place. In most cases with the presence of a single teacher and her/his students. In those cases, the exclusion of what is "outside" the classroom is seen as a positive feature (this is particularly clear in the explanations of the drawings).
2. Tables configured in a circular manner, that allow groups to work together and not facing the blackboard, as the favorite spatial arrangement.
3. Smaller groups of students
4. Classroom libraries, and less frequently, television sets and computers
5. Out-of-the-classroom activities (field trips to a nonurban setting).
6. In some cases, more than one adult is sharing activities with the teacher.

What Can Drawings Tell Us About Schools?

Two distinctive and complementary trends emerged in the analysis of the drawings and their written rationales. First, the majority of the students chose to depict real classrooms over ideal ones. Second, these students imagined the classrooms that awaited them as troubled locations, places where indigence, distress, and hopelessness overpower discoveries, optimism, and learning. In short, poverty, violence, defiance of teachers' authority, and lack of interest about learning are among the most prominent "real" problems identified by these future teachers. Given these conditions, one cannot help but wonder about the motivations behind these students' choice of a profession with such a bleak future.

According to these images, a teacher is *a real teacher* if she stands in front of the classroom, writes on the blackboard, or less frequently sits at the teacher's desk facing several rows of students. Usually, the teacher occupies the center of the image, and does most of the talking, demanding students to do things (a favorite command is "be quiet") and writing exercises on the blackboard (a classic subject is math). However, as noted before, threats of violence and lack of discipline (usually depicted as boys not paying attention or fighting) indicate a clear concern with classroom management issues.

Based on the abundance of images about tense control in these students' representations, it is evident that what marks the reality of classrooms is chaos. These drawings show us a profusion of elements indicating teachers' strong desire to maintain their authority and establish discipline in the classroom. Among those central elements are the teachers' rigid or desperate postures, stern facial expressions and rude utterances (included in the pictures as balloon dialogue), general stiffness, and seemingly uninteresting and meaningless exercises on the blackboard. At the same time, however, there are as many markers showing the futility of the teachers' attempts at achieving complete authority and order. It seems quite obvious that when students do not pay attention, either because they are playing, fighting, or daydreaming, they are openly challenging the teacher's authority.

Evidently, images of power and authority are important for these prospective instructors. Sometimes, they appear embodied in "authoritarian" figures. In other opportunities, particularly in the "ideal" representations, power and authority are simply attributes of a teacher performing her or his job. In the real images, *power* as the imposition of the teacher's will or (its opposite) power as students' resistance is clearly depicted. In contrast, as it was expected in images depicting "ideal spaces," *power* in its dialectic relationship between imposition/resistance has vanished. It is possible to speculate that for these students the *ideal classroom* is one where power and authority are not represented because they have no longer any function.

Nevertheless, the absence of conflict (including power conflicts) in the ideal images produced by the future teachers reinforces the presence of a dilemma clearly depicted in the real drawings, a dilemma that is more easily denied than brought to consciousness for its lack of a clear answer. Can a teacher be successful without being the authority or the disciplinarian? How can teachers embrace the ideals of democracy and meaningful teaching and learning in a context that is viewed as saturated with poverty, violence, and authoritarianism?

Given this diagnosis, the implicit portrait that emerges is that successful teaching cannot be concerned with fostering intelligence, creativity, or even good scores in the assessment instruments but should rather focus on asserting discipline and order. Issues of control dominate the imagery of these future teachers, but not in a direct and unidirectional manner. The fluctuating stereotypical representations of rigid and/or older teachers, in which they are by turns hypereffective drill sergeants or impotent would-be disciplinarians, show the tension between control and lack of control as a central preoccupation. The oscillation between control and chaos seems to be augmented by other intervening elements. Not only do teachers attempt to discipline students unsuccessfully in many cases, but also they cannot control other external and internal conditions that make teaching a quite unpleasant experience. Insufficient salaries, crumbling buildings, physical and emotional violence, and indifference are real threats to teachers' ability to teach and manage classroom time, space, and power-knowledge.

Only after chaos recedes and order is reestablished can these future teachers entertain the possibility of pursuing more creative tasks. Unfortunately, there is skepticism about ever attaining the latter. As Deborah Britzman (1996) points out there is an implicit myth surrounding the incapability of students to lead the process of learning.

> Both teachers and students implicitly understand two rules governing the hidden tensions of classroom life: unless the teacher establishes control there will be no learning, and, if the teacher does not control the students, the students will control the teacher. A teacher-centered approach to learning is implicitly sustained since this myth assumes that students are incapable of leadership, insight, or learning without a teacher's intervention (Britzman, 1996: 449).

Britzman's contention about students' activism in classrooms is also reflected in the drawings about the reality of schools. In them we can see that students are able to initiate activities (though not academic ones) to resist the intervention of teachers.

It is possible to conclude then that in the imaginations of these students, discipline in classrooms is the primary concern. And yet, an important question begs to be asked. What combination of magical tools will solve the discipline problems? The analysis of the drawings indicates that for the majority of the TEP students there are three changes that if implemented may lead to the improvement of schooling. First, increase the number of male teachers. Second, have super-caring-smiling-teachers, and last, change the physical arrangements of classrooms.

In the next pages, the reader will encounter an array of images (figures 4.4 to 4.8) introducing several situations ranging from the traditional stereotypes used by the media (the wicked old teacher, the dreamer, the understanding young (fe)male teacher, and obviously, the penniless teacher) to depictions of common teachers, lacking the glamour and romantic features of the Hollywood counterpart. This selection of images is not "representative" in statistical terms, yet, it provides a good sampling of the main tendencies found and explained in table 4.14. I invite the reader to first look at the images in their totality and then read their rationales.

Figure 4.4. "Craving for Food" (original title)

"In most of the poor areas students go to schools to eat."

Figure 4.5a. Poor Classroom and Male Teacher

The author of this image (male student, 24-years-old) says in his rationale: "The worst part of being a teacher is not being able to teach. The buildings are a complete disaster and the classrooms are so overcrowded, we even have mouse-holes in this classroom. Looking at my drawing I feel pity for the students."

Figure 4.5b. Poor Classroom and Male Teacher

This drawing was produced by a male student (24-years-old). His rationale: The ideal situation has enough school supplies, classrooms and students.

Figure 4.6. The Old Witch (original title)

This drawing was produced by a female student (19-years-old). The original is in color. It is complemented by an ideal image (see figure 4.7). The blackboard says: "Mrs. Olga does not want to hear any student talking. The student that is sitting most properly gets an A+."

The author of this image notes in her rationale that: "Mrs. Olga [name of the teacher in the image] is like many of my own teachers and like many others I see daily in schools. They need silence, and they praise silence, the only thing that matters is silence."

Figure 4.7. Teaching Multiculturalism?

This drawing was made as a companion to the "The Old Witch" drawing. The rationale reads: "I became a teacher because I want to teach the indigenous people. I want to help them for all the damage caused by the so-called civilization. In the meantime, I will teach the city kids about the amazing indigenous cultures."

On the blackboard is written: "OUR BROTHERS! Latin American Aborigines."

The student on the left says, "I have an arrow."

The student on the right says, "I have a hair band and I will put a feather in it."

Figure 4.8. Violence

The original image is in color. The teacher and the student on the right side are blond. The student who has the gun as well as the second one on the right side have dark hair. The other two students have brownish hair. The only word written in this image is arma (gun). The walls of this classroom show signs of graffiti (*viva yo*, "long life for me"). On the back of the page the student provided the following rationale: "I wanted to depict the violence there is in public and private schools in our country. Also, there is poverty in municipal schools. The country 'doesn't have' money in order to buy the appropriate materials for the public schools (i.e., chairs, chalk, etc.)."

Male Teachers and the Problem of Discipline

If real classrooms are seemingly unruly spaces, real teachers are undoubtedly women. Even though ideal teachers are also mostly females, in the "ideal" situations, the number of male teachers increases quite substantially. More precisely, 5.8 percent of the images about real teachers use men as models, but 30 percent of the ideal images portray men. Only two female students drew men as "real" teachers, but eight of them drew male ideal teachers. Similarly, whereas male students drew only three masculine figures as real teachers, they produced ten male teachers in their ideal drawings.[25]

It is clear that expanding the number of male teachers is imagined as a desired change in the landscape of schools. As in the case of the interview with the principal of a TEP,[26] many students and faculty concurred with the idea that having more males as elementary education teachers could be a positive change in schools, especially by improving discipline and, as in the case of image 4.9b, salaries.

Nevertheless, both students and their teachers noted that the possibility of having more men in elementary classrooms was also a cause for anxiety. Particularly because of fears that some men might later reveal themselves as homosexuals, fail to demonstrate the right vocation, or even worse, turn out to be sexual predators.[27]

Without contending the validity of the explicit reasons offered to explain the anxiety, the previous reasons are all focused on teachers' interactions with students. Instead, if we look at teachers as adults with adult interactions, an additional hypothesis appears very plausible. By increasing the number of men in schools, sexuality as an undercurrent may spread out and upset the supposedly tamed pastoral sexual homogeneity of teaching. In other words, more men may bring not only the desired promises of discipline and money, but also the risk of a sexually charged environment which may threaten some valued "feminine" aspects of the institution.[28]

A clear example of this introduction to a sexual undercurrent is shown in case 1. In this case, Pepe, a young male student, jokingly presents his ideal of a teacher as a sex symbol justified with a rationale criticizing mass media. In the discussion that followed, the combination of words and drawings not only gets all the women's attention but also manages to provoke first acceptance followed by an outburst of indignation and condemnation. This type of interaction (which I discuss in more detail in case 1) would probably be constant, as the school might provide another space for males and females to air their differences, desires, identities, and fears. Would this be so bad? Not necessarily. But what seems essential at this point is not so much to support one position over another, but to look closely at the many levels of complexity that this issue presents.

Pepe's case gains relevancy when seen against the main model of an ideal teacher represented in the next four images (4.9a–b, 4.10, and 4.11) that illustrate the tendency of teachers as pastoral-caring figures.

Figure 4.9a. Ideal Male Teacher

Figures 4.9a and 4.9b were produced by a 28-year-old female student. Her example of a real teacher is a woman who works the morning, afternoon, and night school shifts. The student did not write an explanation for this image.

Figure 4.9b. Ideal Male Teacher

In this case, the ideal teacher is represented as a male and the student wrote an explanation for the image. The rational for the ideal image was very synthetic, with only two words: "decent salaries."

Figure 4.10. Caring and Affection

Rationale: "A happy teacher, open to dialogue and new proposals. CARING AND AFFECTIONATE. Respectful of the children's needs and makes others respect her" (capitalized in the original).

Figure 4.11. Caring

This was drawn by a 29-year-old female student. Her rationale states that "teaching is above all, caring for our students. Being patient and loving is the key to a great classroom."

Fears aside, then, why would it be significant to have more men in elementary education? Are these students concerned with gender inequalities at all? Or are they convinced that the idealized presence of males in elementary schools promises to provide conditions that the current majority of women in elementary schools are unable to obtain? Perhaps the most likely explanation is that for these students the association between discipline and masculinity is very strong and dominating the gender regimes of TEPs.

Within the confines of the operating gender regime, it is imagined that the mere presence of more men in schools will improve material conditions and discipline. Whether this change delivers the results expected or not, it is also likely that those men would continue to be "encouraged" to compete and advance to positions of leadership outside the classrooms. Why? Because this unchallenged gender regime reinforces the patriarchal dividend by privileging the masculine supervisory gaze over the caring women while, at the same time, keeping sexuality at bay.[29]

This hypothesis is also sustained by the fact that several of the images of ideal male teachers are also connected with improved material conditions (better salaries, better classrooms). This association is also a stereotypical recognition of essentialist values of masculinity. Moreover, whereas males are portrayed as the standard carriers of discipline and material conditions, women are depicted along traditional places in the gender regime of TEPs. Female teachers have to care and smile.

Smile! You Are a Teacher

Perhaps no other trend is more evident in the ideal drawings than the constant representation of teachers (especially females) and students' smiling. The great majority of the ideal drawings show the instructors (58.3 percent) and participants (70.2 percent) grinning happily, reminding us of the classic rendering of a Kodak moment of fulfillment and joy. Given the gloomy scenario portrayed in the depictions of the real classrooms, this unexpected extreme show of optimism and renewed confidence breaking through the troubles and tribulations of reality seems at best forceful and fake, as if there were a need to balance the harshness of teachers' everyday lives. But, what exactly does a teacher's smile communicate?

John Hartley in his study about the *Politics of Representation* analyzes what he terms the *smiling professions* in the following way:

> Jobs where work, preparation, skill, and talent are all necessary but hidden, where performance is measured by consumer satisfaction, where self is dedicated to other, success to service, where knowledge is niceness and education is entertainment. Such professions are often

associated with women, and often enjoy less than perfect social prestige, with marginal rather than centralized power. (Hartley, 1992: 136)

He further comments:

> Teaching as such has never been fully accepted as a branch of learning in itself, and the teaching profession is one of the clearest examples of an institution whose hierarchy is both feminized and lip-synched; the "lower" you go towards primary teaching, the more women you encounter and the more they must smile as part of their professional skill. Conversely, the higher up the professional ladder you go the more you encounter men whose smiles are of the Dylan Thomas variety, like razor blades. (Hartley, 1992: 136)

By looking again at the images of ideal teachers, it is easy to see Hartley's point. Female ideal teachers openly smile, whereas in the portraits of male teachers this trend is less evident. Is it possible that the smiles of these ideal teachers are a reflection of conformity? Or on the contrary, are these smiles a demonstration of the optimism of the will, manifestations of satisfaction in finding a profession that is meaningful for its practitioners and beneficial for its users?

A closer look at the images that were selected by two groups of TEP students and their rationales may help us shed some light on these complex matters. Case 1 presents and discusses how Pepe's drawing of an ideal smiling female teacher was first accepted and then challenged by his female classmates. The second case presents two contrasting images selected by a group during a workshop in which the image of teachers as transformative intellectuals challenges and is challenged by the limits posed by the social and economic poverty of the Argentinean situation.

Case 1: What Happens When Bad Girls Become Teachers

The twelve students are informally sitting in a semicircle: some of them are smoking. A couple of students are working alone, others in pairs. It is a chilly day. After twenty-five minutes, most of the students have finished their drawings. The researcher gathers the images and begins to show and read the explanation of each picture to the whole group.

A range of comments and questions spontaneously stirs the general discussion. The students seem to enjoy this activity and are enthusiastic: sometimes they even applaud when an image is well crafted or its humor is noted. In this particular group, most of the students have presented images of real teachers, except for one image produced by the only male in the group. At first it provokes laughter and the comments are voiced loudly, but soon they are replaced by a very controversial discussion.

This drawing was made by Pepe, a nineteen-year-old student who is also working as an office supply salesperson. Pepe works approximately eight to ten hours a day and attends the TEP four to five hours daily. He states that he wants to be a teacher because he "likes the spontaneity and freshness of small kids."

His image represents an "ideal" situation. His drawing is shown in figure 4.12, along with his rationale.

What follows are substantial parts of the exchange between Pepe, his classmates, and the researcher.

Claudia: I think Pepe [author of the drawing] is right. TV and commercialism are destroying everything. I remember how people laughed at me when I told them I wanted to be a teacher [students laugh].

Researcher: Why?

Claudia: Well, I'm skinny, don't you see? [more laughs]. The joke was that I could only teach in kindergarten because the second graders are stronger than me.

Luisa: She is right. Until not long ago, it was legal to discriminate against short, fat and the like. If I had wanted to be a teacher before, I couldn't have passed the physical test! This country. . . ! [Luisa seems to refer to her weight, other students are nodding as in implicit agreement].

Mara: But, why is she [the woman in the image] smiling and standing like that? She seems drunk or something. . . .

Pepe: I don't know, I wanted to have something different and ended up with this "chick." I guess I could choose something different . . . I'm concerned with the media stuff.

[Many students at unison, interrupting and imitating Pepe's voice.]

Some student: Yeah, we know we should ban TV! It is rotting our kid's minds [laughs].

Vero: Why did you write "mamá" in the blackboard? It sounds like: *mi mamá me mima* [my mother cuddles me, a stereotypical phrase used to teach first graders how to read, using the phonetic system]. You should have written something else.

Claudia: Yes, in fact she looks like a . . . like a stupid . . . like a stupid whore. It is a miracle that "mamá" is spell correctly [many students are laughing; two or three students are commenting on Claudia's statement].

Vero: I think . . . no, I disagree with you! [talking to Pepe]

Iris: Shut up! [trying to silence the rest of the students who are all talking at the same time]. She is right [referring to Vero], Pepe wanted to criticize TV and commercialism, but he is doing exactly the same thing he criticized. . . .

Figure 4.12. Pepe's Ideal Teacher

"From my point of view this should be the 'ideal' teacher. Because if they keep selling us a culture of appearances and discriminate against those who are not that well 'physically equipped,' this is the only type of teacher that will attract the children's attention."

Pepe: [Interrupts Iris and sounds very disappointed] What do you mean? What is wrong? . . . She looks like that but is not dumb . . . the way she smiles . . . and standing up . . . well, I don't know . . . this is a stupid drawing. I wasn't thinking about the details.

Iris: I don't mean that, and let me talk [Pepe has blushed and he looks quite angry, as if he were embarrassed or didn't expect to be criticized by a classmate]. The problem, as I see it, is that you are only thinking about the boys. I can't imagine a girl that would be attracted by that "Lolita."[30] Moreover, I don't think many boys would be attracted by her either.

[At this point the constant background chattering is now replaced by an exchange of embarrassed looks, and stares directed at Pepe, who is on one side of the classroom, and Veronica and Iris, who are on the other. Pepe seems to be listening, still blushing but not angry any longer.]

Vero: This is not against you [looking at Pepe] but I think that we all are part of the same situation. . . . You need to think about how I feel when I look at your picture of the "ideal" teacher. Yours is the only one that . . .

Pepe: [interrupting Vero] You are right! Completely, I'm . . . well, yes I think I'm kind of machista too. It is hard, I wasn't thinking right and it's true, who will pay attention to her . . . I guess, no, I'm sure that type of teacher can only be found on TV. . . .

Claudia: [interrupting Pepe] Yes, but on the porno channel!

[Everybody laughs and the chattering resumes.]

Pepe: [talking to the researcher] Can I do it again? I don't want you to have that, I mean, I'm changing and you should have the real me.

Researcher: Yes, I. . . .

[Several students interrupt and say "no."]

Researcher: What's happening?

Claudia: No, you should have the original, you are recording and you can explain what has happened here. If you [addressing Pepe] want to have a second version, do it, but give him [the researcher] the original one. In that way you will learn. Think before you act.[31]

The discussion is over and everybody seems eager to leave the room. Pepe and a couple of other students approach me to talk. It is a total surprise. They thank me for "the lesson." I feel puzzled and tell them that I did not intend to teach anything but had hoped to open a space for sharing and talking. I thank them for helping with my research. I have the feeling that something meaningful has taken place, perhaps a small moment of learning. I feel emotionally exhausted but happy. However, I am not sure what it all means.

Rethinking the Masculine Gaze

The development of teachers' self-images is part of a long and complicated process of identification. The sense of professional identity is not formed in a single instance, nor is it merely modeled by professional training and previous experiences (though all of them do play a role). Teachers' identities are developed through multiple levels of reconstruction and conflicts in which metaphors, images, and memories interact, creating contradictions, desires, anxieties, and fears.

In the case of these TEP students, there is no doubt that they produced metaphors and images charged with extreme dualism. Teachers are nice and good or absolutely horrifying. In many cases, the student teachers' drawings resembled the aesthetics and characters of a soap opera, which in Argentina is a popular outlet for viewers' imaginations. In fact, the influence of popular culture and mass media cannot be ignored when we look for models of identification, metaphors, and images. Nor can the powerful and pervasive sources of popular culture such as tango be minimized. Images and elements of popular culture circulate through books, cartoons, and television series, producing stereotypes of women and men that are in turn reincarnated into models of the good, caring, loving, self-sacrificing teachers (and their counterpart, the old, spinster, bitter witch). In the particular context of Argentina, the popular mythology about mothers in tango seems to reappear embodied in the images of the caring motherly teachers. Some of those ideals take a hold of society's imagination across generations. They should not be underestimated because in truth, they become part of the thread of culture and mores by being adored and hated as the everyday recycled characters in the media.

In addition to the cultural elements that may play an important role in molding the identity of the teacher, equally important are those factors that are particular to each potential teacher. For example, we may find that some of the features represented in the ideal drawings may indeed be triggered by the students' loving memories of great teachers who cared and stimulated them, who helped them to develop a passion for learning and teaching. The opposite may be true as well. The hated teachers of their childhood may provide the necessary fuel to imagine a desired teacher they may have never known.

In any case, as noted before, most of the ideal portraits reflect romantic figures, who sometimes resemble heroic defenders of enlightenment or idealized, powerful mothers able to guide their students through the mysterious world of school. Clearly, the romantic figure of the all-loving teacher has great appeal for these students, perhaps because it also sets a pacifying limit, a boundary between normal and abject. It is also a silent boundary that no real teacher should dare to speak about or attempt to cross. In simple words, teachers (just like mothers in tango) may have gender, yet they are not sexually charged. Even though leading female actresses playing teachers are rare, most recently in some movies female educators are portrayed as able to "caringly" seduce students (e.g., Michele Pfeifer in *Dangerous Minds*); in many more (e.g., *Matilda*) female school teachers are vivid embodiments of authoritarian demeanors or inquisitorial inclinations. Seductress, or authoritarian, they are some sort of modern-day witches; however, a common trend is shared in both the positive and negative images. These teachers appear to be powerful; that is, they look like they are in command, exercising their "control," and are recognized by others as powerful figures that are threatening the "normal" school situation. Even in the case of Pepe's depiction of an ideal teacher, we find a very self-confident voluptuous figure, her back straight, openly smiling, staring straight at us and able to spell.

The threatening aspect of this clearly sexualized teacher was noted by the female students, one of whom quickly interpreted Pepe's drawing as the image of a "whore." Many questions arise. First, what was it about this drawing that made the students perceive this teacher as a whore, a *bad girl*? Why did this perception become so unanimous? Why did it spark such intense discussion and debate? What is censurable in the image's posture and smile? Similarly, why did the female students object so strongly to the presence of this "bad girl" in a school? Why was this image so different from the majority of the images produced by the rest of the group, which portrayed caring, nonsexual, and benign models of womanhood (see especially figures 4.4, 4.10, and 4.11).

If the dominant metaphor for this group of students was the school teacher as the good smiling mother of tango, Pepe's drawing was a challenge, an invitation to cross boundaries in the tradition of Martin Heidegger: "A boundary is not that at which something stops, but, as the Greeks recognized, the boundary is that from which something begins its presencing" (in Hebdige, 1988: 228).

Granted, Pepe's ideal teacher may have several shortcomings, and yet it provided an image of a different future, pointing to other possible models of teaching. What is dominant in this particular image is a certain "badness" akin to sexuality and eroticism, characteristics completely absent in the majority of the ideal drawings. In this image even the smile, one of the few general symbols of "good teaching" found in most of the ideal images, was perceived as a not-so-good (or challenging) smile. Conceivably, this smiling teacher was disapproved of because of her explicit sexuality. If that is the case, Pepe's drawing and the discussion and reflections developed around it could be better understood by using Foucault's notion of sexuality:

Sexuality must not be thought of as a kind of natural given which power tries to hold in check, or as an obscure domain which knowledge tries gradually to uncover. It is the name that can be given to a historical construct: not a furtive reality that is difficult to grasp, but a great surface network in which stimulations of bodies, the intensification of pleasures, the incitement to discourse, the formation of special knowledge, the strengthening of controls and resistances, are linked to one another, in accordance with a few major strategies of knowledge and power. (Foucault in Britzman, 1996: 5)

Pepe, by making explicit his masculine gaze, was also showing (as Foucault pointed out) correspondence with a few major strategies of knowledge and power. This image was in a way reproducing the hegemonic gaze of mass media (as some of his classmates readily pointed out), unveiling "sex" by giving primacy to exuberant and voluptuous bodies while at the same time reinforcing the idea that "bad girls" have no place in schools. This should not come as a surprise, because as Carmen Luke comments the absence of "bad girls" is also a significant feature of even feminist positions:

First, feminism's moral discomfort with publicly claiming individual power and authority has produced a concept of the feminist teacher characterized by a series of lacks, including the lack of [bad girl] authority and sexual identity. . . . Second, because her role as a teacher is conceived in "good girl" feminism—selfless dedication and nurturance of her students—her identity is desexualized and repackaged as the nurturing maternal subject. (1996a: 299)

Pepe's ironic view of the future triggered much needed reflections for the whole group. Portrayals of female teachers as seductresses, witches, vampires, or even as good mothers appear to be loosely connected with women's "nature," dispositions, and performances. These images seem to be more strongly related to the myths that (mostly men) have created through literary, pictorial, and scientific productions that in Chodorow's words happened because "men create folk legends, beliefs and poems that ward off the dread by externalizing and objectifying women" (1989: 189).

Notwithstanding the factual or mythological origins of the "seductive woman," such images are used by many men like Pepe as one of the key devices that allow them to acquire, maintain, and express their desire for a normalized masculine heterosexual behavior (Lord, 1994). The desire of reasserting an "essentially" masculine perspective in this case should be understood in a context in which fears about male teachers as homosexuals are openly voiced.[32] Therefore, it is possible to speculate that Pepe's erotic-ironic gaze about women is also part of a defensive device to express his masculinity. In a similar way, the discomfort and protests expressed by Pepe's classmates could be related to the desire of these female students to defend their own bodies and identity against the normalized standards of beauty so pervasive in contemporary culture.

Pepe's sexualized drawing and the reactions it has created (not only with these TEP students but also at conferences and academic meetings where the drawing was presented), are strong reminders of the moral discomfort provoked by references to sexuality in education. This discomfort is in Luke's (1996a) terms a symbol of "our passion for ignorance," because sexuality and eroticism are powerful weapons able to injury an imagined state of familiar innocence, purity, and a sense of normality which should prevail in classrooms.

This drawing activity was created with the intention of imagining teaching within a context of openness, to produce fractures in our passion for ignorance. The transcript of the dialogue established between Claudia, Luisa, Mara, Vero, Pepe, Iris, and others shows that such discussions are possible, and perhaps more important, necessary in order to transform our ignorance into active imagining teacher education.

Case 2: The Contradictions of Teaching: Between Donkeys and Superteachers

While doing fieldwork I was invited to conduct a nonformal education workshop with students of TEPs, school teachers, adult educators, and community organizers (most of them women in their mid-twenties and thirties) in a very poor district of the city of San Miguel, Argentina. Even though not all the participants of this workshop were students of a TEP, many were studying to become teachers, and the other participants were either working as school teachers or in literacy programs. In that sense, they added depth to my study and their inclusion in this research is justified.

In this workshop, the researcher used the same technique of asking the students to draw two situations related to education, either representing a "real situation" or an "ideal" one or both. In general terms the same representational commitments about the reality of schools that were discussed previously were also present in this group, namely poverty, lack of discipline, and caring. However, when this particular group selected two drawings for the follow-up discussion, the defining topics were the politics of education, the possibilities of transformative actions, and the role of teachers and communities in changing or maintaining the status quo.

Figure 4.13 was made by two women, an elementary school teacher and a TEP student who is teaching literacy to women in a nearby shantytown. It represents a "real" situation.

This drawing shows a very poor public school; the building displays signs of decay and even the flag is torn. The flag as well as the white uniforms that the teacher and students are wearing symbolize a public school. In front of the

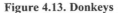

Figure 4.13. Donkeys

"This school is forgotten (because of the lack of economic resources)."
"So what? Only children and those who don't know anything go to this school."

building, there is a female teacher and near her, one faceless figure with donkey ears. The two dominant figures to the left are well-groomed donkeys.[33] One of them is carrying a bag or briefcase, missing one hand, has longish hair, and, according to the "artists," is a female. The second one is standing next to her in exactly the same position, with a smile on his face.

In selecting this drawing the participants indicated that this was a clear example of the reality of education in Argentina. One participant mentioned:

> Participant 5: It was a good description of the effects of the social and economic policies towards public schools.

> Participant 4: [Because] it was unclear whether the two big donkeys to the left were students or teachers [it] make[s] the whole picture more interesting.

The importance of the last point is related to the traditional criticisms of many nonformal educators toward public school teachers. In other words, the ambiguity of the picture produces a remarkable result. It suggests that the teachers, and in truth anybody who attends a public school, must be dumb (donkeys) to be supporting the system. This categorization does not include only teachers and children, but also adults who attend classes.

In the participants' view, the images both complemented the written explanation, "This school is forgotten (because of the lack of economic resources)," as well as stressed the message that "those who go to public schools—teachers and students, children or adults—don't know the reality. They are like donkeys." What is not clear is what alternative those teachers and students would have in terms of schooling. The criticism is incisive and reveals an overall feeling of powerlessness and hopelessness, as well as an evident bitterness expressed in the following comments:

> Participant 1: These people [popular sectors and teachers] do not know they are helping the reproduction of the system. See, they are donkeys [laughs] they support the government.

> Participant 2: The teacher looks powerless . . . the student-donkeys are adults that are unconscious of their situation, that is why they are smiling.

This drawing of a "real" school is a sad reminder of the perceived or real sense of unequal relationships in Argentina's education and indicates a specific sense of dislike or frustration. In this case teachers and students/parents are blamed for its docility because they seem unable to control or alter their poor working conditions and are unable to modify external elements like salaries, students' poverty, and decaying schools.[34]

The sense of dislike expressed by the participants in this workshop gives us a glimpse of some of the elements used to support the group's selection of the second drawing, figure 4.14, which represents an "ideal" situation.

In this ideal situation, we see a single figure that is neither male nor female who is supporting the world over his or her head and is of course bearing a big smile. The right hand of the subject is not touching the world and the left hand barely touches it.

One of the key reasons some members of the workshop give to justify the selection of this picture is the fact that the gender of the subject is not defined. It is interesting to note that the author admits that she had a man in mind, even though she consciously tried to avoid sexual stereotypes. For other members, the representation of a popular educator as being gender-neutral is "a recognition of the importance of gender equity for popular education" (participant 5).

Another engaging element is the message of hope. The eyes in the drawing look up with an expression of innocence or naiveté that reveals, according to some members of the group, "the hope of transformation, and the required foolishness needed to dream of that" (participant 12). Both of these feelings are ones that "all the members of the workshop share" (participant 4).

Ambiguity is also part of the rationale for selecting this picture. On the one hand, he or she does not look strong enough to sustain the world in that position. On the other, all the members of the group like the written message because it is "clear and strong." Participant 3 states, "It is exactly what teachers should do" and participant 4 adds, "It has hope, I also believe in utopias, otherwise I wouldn't be here."

Finally, others associate the position of the educator and his or her supporting the world over his or her head with Freire's ideas about "reading the word and reading the world."

Issues of *conscientization* and self-awareness as means of empowerment and effecting change in education figure prominently in these images. In addition, it appears that these group members are willing to extend themselves in images of leaders, promoting students' learning as teachers who are "proud of their chosen work and life choices. Perhaps not in the school or in the community, but certainly in the classroom, there are images of teachers as leaders" (Bolotin Joseph and Burnaford, 1994: 17).

Clearly, this leading "superteacher" is the closest example of a Gramscian-inspired transformative educator.[35] This supereducator (she/he) goes beyond narrow definitions of schooling and basic literacy concerns in order to promote experiences that will empower the students as members of an oppressed social group. In this case the teacher is a promoter, and to a large extent a leading figure in the organization of counterhegemonic pedagogical practices.

However, what seems to be clear is that the participants of this workshop are entrapped in a dilemma that is very hard to resolve. On the one hand, they point to the difficult economic situation and to the role teachers (like themselves),

Figure 4.14. Superteacher

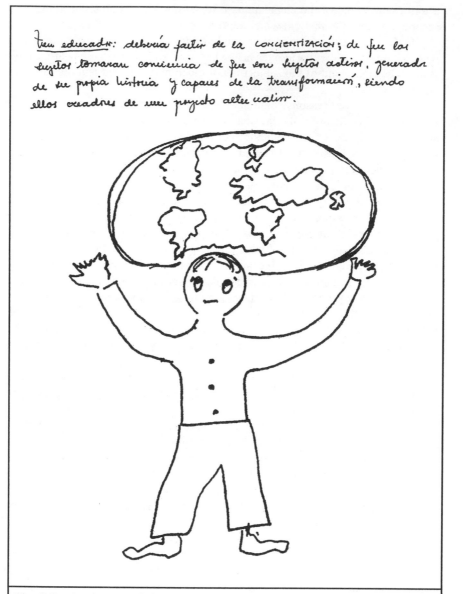

The following is a translation of the written explanation given by the 29-year-old female social worker who produced the drawing: "An educator should start from *conscientization*; people (subjects) realizing that they are active subjects, makers of their own history and capable of transformation, being the creators of an alternative project." On the side of the picture, it reads: "I believe in utopias (they exist)."

students, and communities play in enabling the system (perhaps the state?) to continue its path of destruction and poverty in terms of programs, resources, and buildings. On the other hand, Gramsci's idealized version of the superconscious, all-resourceful teacher as an organic intellectual of the popular sectors remains very vivid for them. This polarization, the donkey versus the superteacher as it were, seems to strongly affect these teachers as they explore contradictory personal and collective situations.[36]

As the examples from case 2 show, in at least a small group of students there is an explicit attempt to make visible the political nature of schooling and the relations of power that characterize schools in any society. These students are willing to challenge the largely ahistorical, apolitical guiding fiction of dominant pedagogical theories and practices (McLaren and Lankshear, 1994) and rebuke the myth of educational "meritocracy" held by so many within, and outside of, the educational establishment.

This understanding of schools as politically charged places has undoubtedly influenced envisioning the ideal teacher-based solutions imagined by the participants in case 2 and to a lesser extent in case 1. In the other workshops the majority of students opted for ideal solutions that were less dependent on the personality or appearance of the teacher and more related to their practices. The next section discusses one of them, arranging the classrooms' desks in circles from the perspective of rituals.

Rows, Circles, and Ritual Performances

The emphasis on changing spatial arrangements, such as circle seating formations instead of rows, seems to be the privileged marker and at the same time a limiting factor in the pedagogical imagination of these students. Student circles represent, in most of the ideal drawings, nonauthoritarian pedagogical practice. This is supposedly a more democratic practice because it counteracts rigidity in classrooms:

> Stillness is the achievement of the science of supervision, an arrangement of persons in collective units accessible to constant surveillance. By arranging students in rows, all eyes facing front, directly confronting the back of a fellow's head, meeting the gaze only of the teacher, the discipline of the contemporary classroom deploys the look as a strategy of domination. (Grumet, 1988: 111)

However, there is nothing inherently democratic or oppressive in arranging the desks in rows over the circular seating. Men and women have always envisioned and searched to create "liberating machines" (Foucault, 1993) through religion, ideologies, and science. However, regarding the use of different spatial arrangement as markers of nonauthoritarian pedagogies, it is important to remember what Foucault pointed out regarding other innovative technologies:

Figure 4.15. Students as Actors and Teacher as Spectator

The rationale for this drawing is the following: "I wanted to make something symbolic. I believe that an ideal situation for me would be to give the kids more chances to participate, that is, to motivate them to do creative things, research and meaningful experience. I think that these days, this does not happen everywhere. On the contrary, there are many traditional schools where kids feel trapped and forced to listen to the teacher without a fly passing by and when the bell rings for recess they get desperate to go out and play, run, shout. With this we realize that in many cases the classes taught do not appeal to them."

Figure 4.16. Good Classrooms/Poor Classrooms

This drawing was done by a 20-year-old female student. The ideal situation is a well-equipped classroom, with good distribution, maps, library, videos, information and with the right number of studnets to be able to attend them. The real situation is a lack of materials, a run-down building, too many cluttered students—without space.

> It is impossible to think that it [technologies] would have been developed and adapted had there not been in the play and strategy of human relations something which tended in that direction. What is interesting is always interconnection, not the primacy of this over that, which never has any meaning. (1993: 169)

In other words, the circles students represented in their drawings are not necessarily a liberating device. Referring back to the "real images," it appears that most of the students who sit in rows are able to avoid and resist the teacher's control in direct contradiction to what is often described as "authoritarian classrooms." Ironically, in many of the ideal representations showing circular arrangements, it is the teacher who occupies the center and seems to control more, not less, of what circulates within the classroom. In other words, circle seating appears as a particular technology, a reified ritual that classifies and distinguishes good teaching from bad teaching. In the images analyzed here, circular seating is not only a methodological tool, it has acquired ritualistic features, invested with power and meanings.

Yet, as McLaren points out, "rituals never convey meaning in a vacuum or outside of history. . . . As carriers of culturally and politically coded meanings, rituals are never self-evident or unproblematic" (McLaren, 1993: 255). He argues that ritual performances, in effect, inscribe power on the body of the subject and that those subjects (or subjected bodies) subsequently utilize different rituals as instances of social constructions of shared meanings. The micro- and macro-rituals (from smiling to changing the spatial arrangements in classrooms) represented in many of the images analyzed here should be understood not only as critical observations of Argentina's classrooms, but also as expressions of imaginary performances that delimit good teaching from bad teaching.

The emphasis on circular seating could be seen as an expression of certain methodological limitations, but that is a partial explanation. These images are also a clear attempt to communicate to an audience that these future teachers are different from the *current real teachers* because they *will* encourage group participation and *will* care about the students. I suggest here that some TEP students have taken advantage of the drawings as tools that allow public display of marks of "good and bad teaching." These teacher education students endowed circular seating with a positive value and needed to communicate this value to an audience, in this case other students and the researcher. This communicative action is crucial because the interactions between participants and audiences are critical in order to confer meaning and increase the efficiency of a ritual

Looking at the ideal and real representations of classrooms produced by these students as graphic representations of rituals also points to the fact that not all the participants of a ritual experience the same significance or efficacy of that ritual. "Indeed, it seems that unless there is some supervision of both performance and interpretation by guardians of orthodoxy, the performance is bound to mean different things for different people" (Schieffelin, 1990: 722).

Figure 4.17. "Ear"

The "Ear" was drawn by a 33-year-old female student. Her rationale for this picture is: "Ideal situation, in my opinion, is that in which education finds support and there are opportunities for the wonderful minds to grow and blossom wider day by day. Even though financial support is important, more would be achieved with effort and much passion to see the fantastic working minds."

Figure 4.18. Curriculum and Discipline

The rationale of this picture says: "Nowadays teachers are more concerned about covering everything in the syllabus, forgetting something that is important to the students. They do not worry about the circumstances each of them [the students] is going through nor about having a good relationship. Students fear the teacher in the drawing and their parents" (female student, 22-years-old).

The teacher (words on the right side): "I give you only one hour to do it, because you come to school only in order to study."

The teacher (words on the left side): "Today we will look at the digestive system. Take out a sheet of paper and write everything you know about this organ and this will be graded."

Student (words on the left): "They are going to beat me up at home if I get a 1 [low grade]."

Student (words on the right): "I don't know anything. I am going to get a 0."

Figure 4.19. Discipline and Control

This was produced by two students (male and female). The rationale for this image is the following:

"The teacher feels hopeless as she faces the students' aggression and the lack of interest. In terms of the aggression, there is verbal aggression that consists of answering the teacher very badly, sarcastically, a situation that didn't used to happen in the past. She does not feel stimulated or supported since the principals and parents represent another hindrance to get respect from the students. In private schools, students are clients and teachers feel limited. The salary does not serve as a motivation since to make a sufficient salary teachers have to teach two shifts. A very tiring task!"

Figure 4.20. School's Mission

This image was created by a 22-year-old male student whose rationale is as follows: "Schools must help students become capable people who can manage them-selves in the world so that they can live together with others despite the differences."

Figure 4.21. "The Scale"

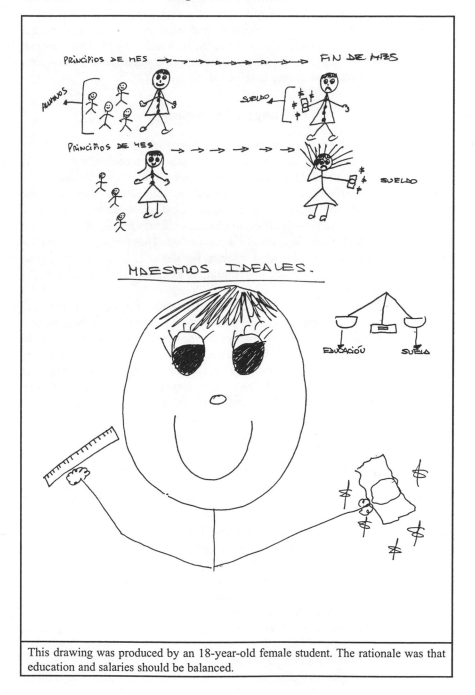

This drawing was produced by an 18-year-old female student. The rationale was that education and salaries should be balanced.

It appears, however, that for most of these students and their instructors in the TEPs, rows in classrooms are reified, condensing many of the elements of bad teaching. In this process of reification, both students and teachers are not able to accept that the efficacy of school rituals, such as sitting in circles instead of rows, should be located in the emerging relation between school authorities, teachers and students (and among each of these groups).

The Tango of Schooling

The situations depicted in these drawings are neither very "optimistic" nor "pessimistic." It seems that the representation of schools, teachers, and students in these drawings is mainly critical. At the same time these drawings have provided an opportunity for the participants in this study (including the researcher) to deal with those shadowed, nonrationalized sides of the insecure human identity, especially with all those elements that do not fit, which cannot be clearly identified, classified, and, thus, surveilled. That permanent interplay produces unfinished identities that cannot be derived from homogeneous collective identities (i.e., race, class, religion, or gender), nor be mechanically imposed (Donald, 1992).

Looking at many of the images produced by students in this research, it is clear that they have developed a critical perception of Argentina's school system and current educational problems. However, these critical understandings do provide an opportunity to search for alternatives, even in the middle of a very pessimistic and uncertain scenario. These students are challenging our imagination as teachers and professors. Any attempt to give quick or easy answers to their challenges will be met with definite failure. Some of the elements presented in these images and testimonies are pressing problems: overcrowding of classrooms; budgetary problems; lack of stimulus to learn and to teach; decline of working conditions for teachers and of learning conditions for students; irrelevancy of curriculum; violence, hunger, boredom, and indifference; discriminatory practices.

Given these pessimistic perceptions of real classrooms it is not surprising that in the ideal representations, anything and everything that goes beyond a strictly defined relationship between teachers and students is obliterated. A good ideal classroom is often portrayed as a peaceful and orderly space. This expression of order seems to be the main goal and/or desire of these future teachers. However, the need for order and discipline in the ideal classrooms seems to carry the price of working in isolation because curricula, textbooks, parents, and administrators are not part of the ideal space.

And yet, in spite of their shortcomings and contradictions, ultimately, these students are able to formulate and express their reasons and hopes about the social importance of a different kind of schooling. The school these students imagined is almost like a tango in reverse. Many of the best-known tango lyrics have contributed to the development of discourses about an idealized past that cannot be recovered. In contrast, TEP students look at the past and the present with aversion. Eagerly, they escape into an idealized future, which echoes the same nostalgic tones of the romantic pure love of mothers in tango, censuring the "Other" woman—*la otra*[37]—who dares express her sexuality, and who is always the cause of pain and suffering. This is a first step to obliterate any alternative model of teacher who may present herself as a whole woman or man, without hiding her sexuality.

Furthermore, these images also share other qualities with tango. As noted in chapter 1, tango and its women and men resist any reductive logic. The drawings and discussion these students have shared with the researcher and among themselves stress many conflictive areas and new lines for research. Among them it is important to emphasize that past schooling experiences, popular culture, and deeply gendered structures of thought and action must be taken into account in imagining teacher education.

Thus, these images of the nice girl, the mother-teacher, the authoritarian women, and the bad girl have condensed societal models, lived experiences, memories, ideologies, and future expectations. At the same time, these images offer an opportunity to uncover fears and fantasies, to reveal contradictions between different ways of seeing and expressing, in order to exercise criticism and challenge existing ideologies. By the same token, this technique has been invaluable in bridging the traditional gap between researcher and the "subjects of research," an unplanned but absolutely welcomed by-product. The exchange of ideas, images, and metaphors allowed all the participants to experience meaningful and challenging moments of learning.

Finally, these images present another great challenge to researchers and practitioners in education. It is the simplicity of the presentation of the problems that strikes the reader's attention. The implicit challenge to any practitioner and scholar of education is the following: Can we look at these students' dreams and the power of their metaphors and images to summarize problems and challenges in schools without falling into ambivalent or naive explanations? Or as Freire posits, can we "try to be simple without being simplistic?" The next and final chapter of this book attempts to explore the connections between images, representations, identities, and the development of their geographical, historical, and cultural contexts.

Notes

1. It is interesting to note that similar somber prospectives are also perceived in the United States. Current estimates are that the United States will need to hire as many as two million new teachers during the ten year period of 1995 to 2005. Nevertheless, during the period of 1975 to 1996, fewer college graduates have shown interest in becoming teachers while student enrollments have increased. The combination of these factors has

contributed to put teacher education and recruitment at the center of the educational arena
and as an area of highly contested debates among policymakers and colleges of education
(Henke, et al., 1997).

2. At this point it is important to clarify that the references to TEPs as sick places
could be related also to the particular regime of truth about gender in Argentina. In thirty
interviews conducted with informants, "sick places" was a common portrait used to
describe environments with a majority of women (such as schools). What is perhaps most
striking is that when the informants were queried about places where the presence of men
is almost exclusive (the soccer stadium, the army, financial firms, and the typical
Argentinean "Café"), the responses were at best defensive and evasive ("Well, it is hard
to tell") and at worst, plain discriminatory ("Women are so emotional and irrational that
they will always need a man to provide some order").

3. All names are fictitious.

4. During the military dictatorship (1976–1983), admission to the university required
an entrance exam, and certain majors had limited enrollment. These and other restrictions,
coupled with censorship and repression, discouraged many, including myself, who wanted
to pursue higher education degrees. During the first years of the democratic transition
(1984–1987) the number of students in universities tripled because of a policy of open
enrollment. For a thorough discussion of these issues, see Schugurensky (1994).

5. According to preliminary data, prepared by the INDEC (Argentina's National
Statistics and Information Institute), in 1995 one out of three young adults (age 18–25)
was unemployed nationwide.

6. By 1999 TEP enrollment figures indicate that in the near future there will not be
enough certified teachers to attend to the normal expansion of the system.

7. Only a few TEP faculty have expressed hopes of positive change based on the
alleged changes of social conditions of the new students. (I return to this point later.)

8. Because of absence of accurate information there is a lack of definitive data that
would allow a definitive comparison about this particular phenomenon. In addition to the
lack of reliable statistics that this research has faced in every single aspect investigated,
there are other factors that inhibited accurate comparisons. The most important of these
factors is that many men are not studying in TEPs to become teachers; they begin their
careers as teachers using other educational credentials, such as university degrees, that
allow them to teach (particularly at the secondary level). The next section in this chapter
discusses the explicit rationales presented by male and female students relating to these
issues.

9. Men are "alien" in many TEPs in the city of Buenos Aires, but less so in other
provincial states. Also, there is a unique and not surprisingly prestigious Normal School
in the city of Buenos Aires that was for almost eighty years a men's only institution. Its
graduates were regarded as among the best teachers in the city and its students were
promoted to supervisory positions faster and in higher proportions than graduates (mainly
females) from the rest of the TEPs in the city.

10. This normative is call the "3x1." For every three female teachers listed in the ranking
to have access to principal and supervision positions, there must be one man included.

11. This understanding of vocation coincides with the historical construction of the
concept, showing its strength as a disciplining principle for many teachers. In Spanish and
English, vocation has similar meanings. According to the Oxford American Dictionary
(1980), vocation has three meanings: "1. a feeling that one is called by God to a certain

career or occupation. 2. a natural liking for a certain type of work. 3. a person's trade or profession." In this teacher's testimony only the third meaning of "vocation" is absent.

12. There are no empirical studies that confirm or discuss this extended idea that suspects the "risk of a hidden homosexual" in all male teachers. This researcher found, as one of the examples of the extension of this bias, that most of the male students reported having suffered many jokes and comments about their presumed homosexuality.

13. This apparent contradiction is discussed in greater detail in the next section of this chapter.

14. As noted repeatedly, historically in Argentina, teachers and especially TEP faculty come from middle classes that are mainly self-identified as being from European descent. Among those social sectors there is also a strong fascination and reverence for "Western cultural canons" that influence almost every aspect of everyday life in the country, and this aspect is often an element of mockery for the rest of Latin American societies. Since the origins of the construction of the Argentinean nation-state there has been a widespread perception about the backwardness of the native and Creole population. Marifran Carlson notes that "Alicia Moreau de Justo in her book, *The Civil Emancipation of Women* (1919) [perhaps the country's best known female socialist thinker of this century], attacked the Argentinean-Hispanic Creole mentality which promoted what she called 'the child-doll personality' and which, while allowing eighty-seven percent of Argentinean primary school teachers to be women, denied these same women civil and political equality. European immigrant women, she said, were more free both psychologically and socially than native Argentineans, and it was their mission to educate and liberate the native population" (1988: 135).

15. This situation is not exclusive to TEPs. A recent report about university students found similar results (Dicker and Terigi, 1994).

16. In Argentina, forty years is the age limit to begin a teaching career in public schools.

17. In several interviews, however, many female students acknowledged that they do perform domestic work in their homes but do not consider those tasks as jobs.

18. Davini and Alliaud (1995) present similar figures for this phenomenon. In their study involving more than a thousand students, more than 70 percent of TEP students chose teaching after attempting and dropping out of other university-level studies.

19. In Argentina, the presence of women in fields linked to science and technology is still less than ideal. Yet, there are signs that women are having more presence in traditionally masculine fields such as electronics, computer science, and information science. However, Stromquist also notes that those levels of participation are restricted to low-skill manufacturing tasks instead of design, planning, and management levels.

20. In Brazil, elementary school teachers are commonly called "aunts."

21. These homogeneous characteristics, coincide with the results of other studies (Birgin, 1995; Davini and Alliaud, 1995).

22. After this activity was concluded the students were provided with the complementary questionnaire discussed earlier. Anecdotally, it is very interesting to mention that at the beginning of this research the interpretative activities (drawings and focus groups) were not connected with the questionnaire. The first two times the questionnaire was distributed to TEP students (one group of eighteen students and the second of twenty-eight) only seven students responded. Besides the small number of responses, the commitment to the task was somehow poor (very short answers,

incomplete answers, and so on). The third time I conducted the drawing workshop and focus groups with twenty-one students first and gave the questionnaires afterwards, asking the students to return them the following day.

23. See case 2.

24. Students' phrases or words explaining the meaning of a particular element appear between quotation marks.

25. Those drawings that made explicit references to the nonrelevant gendered distinctions of either real or ideal images are not included in these percentages.

26. See Teresa's testimony in the previous section.

27. Responding to the question, What do you think about incorporating more male teachers in elementary schools? 50 percent of the students were very positive, 38 percent positive and 12 percent said they were indifferent.

28. Needless to say that when the situation was the opposite, and teaching was a male-dominated profession, the presence of women was seen as creating a sexually charged environment in schools.

29. As was noted before, even though males are a minority in the rank and file, their presence in the administration at large is rather important.

30. Lolita is used as a traditional erotic name based on Nabokov's novel.

31. After this group activity the researcher approached Pepe and asked him if he wanted his original drawing back. Pepe's answer was negative. He said, "You should take it. I am learning a big lesson here and this is part of the lesson."

32. Before this drawing workshop, the researcher interviewed Pepe, and he also expressed his discomfort with some friends and classmates, who had "jokingly" expressed doubts about his heterosexuality because he wanted to be a teacher.

33. It is important to note that the "donkey" is a very symbolic figure in many countries in Latin America, representing ignorance. As a matter of fact, until not long ago, a common disciplinary action was to place a donkey hat on the poor performer and send him or her to stand in a corner, a very humiliating punishment that earned the laughter and scorn of the other classmates.

34. Interestingly, these criticisms are echoed in the United States context: "The docile teacher is a pervasive stereotype. Moreover, submission enters into interviews with contemporary teachers. We find that the image of docility and submission outrages them, not because they feel it is incorrect portraiture, but because it points out the worst frustration in their work—that of perceived or real powerlessness" (Bolotin Joseph and Burnaford, 1994: 17).

35. According to Giroux, "Acting as a transformative intellectual means helping students acquire critical knowledge about basic societal structures, such as the economy, the state, the workplace, and mass culture, so that such institutions can be open to potential transformation" (1988: 138–39).

36. In different workshops, working with groups of Chilean, Uruguayan, and North American educators (mostly Chicano/a, Latino/a, and white), the same polarization was found. This polarization is explored in more detail in the last section of this book.

37. Even though it was not noted in any of the interviews or drawings, one of the hypotheses of this research is that the most threatening "other woman" in TEPs is the lesbian teacher. I base this hypothesis in the telling fact that male homosexuality was explicitly condemned but nobody ever mentioned female homosexuality. In this case the old saying that there are silences that speak volumes clearly applies.

CHAPTER 5

IMAGINING TEACHER EDUCATION

What it all comes down to is that we are the sum of our efforts to
change who we are. Identity is no museum piece sitting stock-still in
a display case, but rather the endlessly astonishing synthesis of the
contradictions of everyday life. (Galeano, 1991: 125)[1]

Gender, Teaching, and the Elusiveness of Caring

The teacher education program students' perception of themselves as caring
professionals clearly contrasts with the perception expressed by TEP faculty,
educational researchers, and the media. These conflicting perceptions and
interpretations constrain and saturate the field of teacher training, setting the
boundaries of what can be spoken and what can be heard as the "true" discourses
regarding who can be a teacher and how teachers should be trained.

In particular, most TEP faculty members are not able to see and listen to the reasons that students provide for their vocational choices. They only see what the students are not—they are not from the traditional middle classes, they are not academically well prepared, and their sexuality is somehow threatening. This threat to TEP faculty habitus is exacerbated by two factors. First, there is the "cursed-blessed" increase in the number of men in TEPs and the implicit threat of homosexuality and competition for leadership positions, which is combined with the desire to have more men to "fix-cure" schools by disciplining and bringing order into them. Second, there is the arrival of "poor" male and female students to the traditionally middle-class milieu of the TEPs. These newcomers are also cursed-blessed. Their presence gives TEPs a reason to exist while at the same time jeopardizing the habitus of these institutions because this segment of society is stereotypically defined as lacking knowledge, skills, and to a certain extent, moral values.

The ambivalence created by these factors, in addition to the social and economic pressures for adjusting teaching to the demands of the market and the TEP's internal gender regimes, influence students' discourses and how they are manifested. These discourses are not homogenous constructions and therefore allow for internal contradictions and competing messages that nevertheless provide pathways to navigate the murky waters of gender regimes in schools.

A clear example of this situation is found in the different ways that the TEP students recovered and assigned new meanings to the most influential social representations of teachers: the "mother-teacher" and the "teacher as a technician." Chapter 4 has shown that an ideal classroom was imagined within the confines of stereotypical feminine and masculine models. In addition, those spaces showed weak or nonexistent connections between classrooms and schools, and schools and society. However, despite the strong presence of stereotypes and the weak overall links, these future teachers managed to include expressions of caring practices, nonauthoritarian pedagogies, and meaningful, contextualized and playful learning in their representations.

This research has found evidence to suggest that the ideal classroom imagined by teacher education students is mainly a response to their diagnosis of current classrooms as chaotic spaces. As one might expect, the ideal spaces do not have any "visible" signs of disciplinary problems or challenges to teachers' authority. What is visible then? Smiles, young caring female teachers, more male instructors, properly heterosexual representations, circular seating, more books and supplies, and better salaries are all seen at first glance.

However, the constant prevalence of caring throughout the analysis of the data (from the historical overview, interviews, questionnaires, and images) deserves particular attention. Whether the overwhelming presence of it, or the threatening possibility of its absence, caring defines teaching. In many respects, these students appear to be embracing Nell Noddings' conceptualizations about teaching and the ethics of care.

Undoubtedly, these students' desires to be caring teachers is a worthy and compelling goal. However, it is important to reflect about the possibilities and limitations of TEP students' understanding of what it means to be a caring teacher.

As noted previously, these students see caring less as a social practice that encourages the simultaneous development of groups of individuals through multiple social relationships and more in sync with Noddings' model of caring as being an individualized and unique relationship developed by the teacher (especially female ones) with her students. Is in this sense, that in the representations analyzed in this project, caring is especially stripped of its social characteristics. It is worth quoting Schutz on this point:

> As we initiate students into the practices of caring, we must also develop with them the skills that we need to respond collectively to oppression, to what (Maxine) Greene calls the obstacles in the way of our self and collective becoming. Failing to engage in practices of the "public" with our students even though these are practices that require a shift away from the engrossment of caring, represents, paradoxically, a failure on some level to care for them and their futures in an often unforgiving world. (1998: 392–93)

For these TEP students, caring has been reified and ritualized. It seems clear that in this model of caring, the state has no influence, and classrooms are not workplaces. Indeed, caring practices and ideologies, either performed by women, or men teachers and students, do not happen in a historical vacuum. Caring has a genealogy, and as this book has repeatedly stated it is strongly associated with mothering in multiple ways. Therefore, the strength of the mother-teacher association cannot be underestimated.[2] As discussed in chapter 3, the notion of the caring teacher is also promoted by the state and it arouses in the public—and often in some teachers—a set of expectations, from abnegation to altruism or lack of economic expectations. Madeleine Grumet (1988) describes the effects of these expectations quite well.

> For those who sustain the emotional and physical lives of others, there is no time out, no short week, no sabbatical, no layoff . . . even though we secretly respect this maternal pedagogy of ours, it seems personal to us, not quite defensible in this public place, and we provide this nurturant labor without demanding the recompense it deserves. (1988: 86–87)

This book has shown how different conditions that range from historical low salaries to the social status of women have contributed to the image of teachers as surrogate parents (particularly as second mothers) who are caring, have a strong vocation, and provide emotional and intellectual guidance to the children.

All those elements have conjured up an image of a "teacher who selflessly does what s/he does for the sake of the children rather than from any desire for personal monetary gain or worldly satisfaction" (Duncan, 1996: 163).

Thus, it is important to rethink caring and not to throw out the baby with the bathwater. How do we do that? Perhaps we can begin by understanding that the way in which teachers' work is imagined and defined both *questions and reinforces* gender dynamics.

In particular, during this research, the prevalence of two semantic equivalences between women-teacher-caring and men-teacher-discipline, reinforces the gender regime of TEPs. As such, these equivalencies strengthen the relationship between the pastoral and productive character of teaching by including a set of discourses and mechanisms that attempt to hide the political, economical, and cultural rationales intervening in the process of teacher education behind the curtains of a neutral socialization process.

However, there is no doubt that not all the students (regardless of social conditions, gender, or ethnic backgrounds) share the same ideals of discipline caring, and motherhood, nor are they in a position to develop coherent alternative models of schooling. What they do share are positions of resistance to some of the more oppressive elements of TEPs and by extension to education in general, whether openly contesting the second-mother ideology, or by incorporating only certain elements of it into their own narratives and alternatives. Notwithstanding, without significant efforts to redefine the gender regimes in schools, these future teachers will have few opportunities of transforming resistance into agency and breaking with the essentialist view of "caring" as a feminine activity and "discipline" as the exclusive realm of men.

It is quite relevant to remember that even when the TEP students attempted to resist the limits of a pastoral pedagogy and gender dynamics they searched for help in different forms of "normal" class, gender, and professional identities. Their persistent verbalization and representations of the importance of caring and always placing children first are cases in point. This "children-first" model of teaching not only reinforces and reinvigorates the second-mother ideology, but also undermines possible alternatives developed and expressed by the TEP students themselves in their interviews, questionnaires, and drawings. In order to sustain the children-first discourse or model, these students, especially female ones, are placed in a double bind. First, they have to be selfless, and second, they have to be asexual. Even though these two conditions are never fully achieved in any individual, the gender regime of teaching dictates that sexuality and self-interest must be repressed. Men and women in TEPs (whether heterosexual or homosexual) appear to be confined to the traditional stereotypes of tango. They should perform a patriarchal choreography within the gender regimes of TEPs, without losing the smile in order to simulate the perfect teacher.

In the case of the female students, the hegemonic gender regime operating in TEPs presents important challenges in the form of an ideologically charged model that does not question the "feminine condition of teaching" and the connections of teaching with mothering (Morgade, 1992a, 1992b). These future teachers have to find strong justifications to affirm their professional choices when they know that at the end of their studies await low salaries, relative autonomy within classrooms and high levels of dependency outside of them, simplistic assumptions about teachers' work, and even hostile discourses when they cannot embody the ideal of the all-caring, all-knowledgeable teacher of people's imaginations.

Historically, the ideology of teachers as second mothers embodied the romantic model of the all-caring puritan mother. However, the concept of motherhood is historically mutable. As such, it is not a single, non-contradictory identity, even though in its current regime of truth, mothering appears to be "naturalized" and its most romantic versions have an almost universal appealing. When faculty in TEPs proclaim the disappearance of the second mother ideology, they do so without considering the fact that the structures which contribute to the reproduction of this ideology remain intact and that there are alternative meanings embedded in the figure of the mother.

In contrast, the TEP students, by asking for improved working conditions, more professionalism, and the transformation of the domestic and external causes of poverty and violence in classrooms, recover, resignify, and sometimes carnivalize the figure of mothering teacher.

Carnivals, Laughing, and Teaching

The most pervasive discourses on education in the modern period have been framed with the same dual and unpleasant logic—that of liberation versus control. The more general goal of schooling has been seen as either to prepare individuals for citizenship and productive work or to develop their full creative and cognitive potential (or some combination of the two). However, following the arguments about power developed in the theoretical section of this work, these positions do not take into consideration the following:

> In modern democracies, power works *through* "freedom;" any particular account of the human individual and how he or she might achieve self-realization . . . can equally be read as "a normative grid for the observation and classification" of children or adults/citizens. In other words the "liberation of the individual" is always about constructing a particular notion of the individual and providing mechanisms of surveillance and regulation. (O'Shea, 1993: 503)

One of the noticeable characteristics of the data is that students of TEPs are permanently borrowing from and dialogically relating to other voices. In other words, the well-known Bakhtinian statement that "the word in language is half someone else's" seems to perfectly apply to the production of their discourses (verbal and pictorial). Again, perhaps the clearest example is expressed in the TEP students, complex maneuvers with the historical models of teachers they may have both witnessed and learned (particularly the second mother, the technician, and the adjusted teacher).

The images created by the TEP students have shown that in schools the voices of students and the voices of teachers collided with and assessed each other. And yet, the juxtaposition of the two results in the implicit ridiculization of teachers' desire of achieving total control of students and classroom situations and of the ideology this desire implies. That effect is part of the process of carnivalization in Bakhtinian terms.

> In order to carnivalize the voice of authority and power the rebel comic voice must use that authoritative voice, must parody or mimic it. As Derrida describes the process, a deconstructive discourse borrows from heritage the resources necessary for the deconstruction of that heritage itself. (Holquist, 1990: 241)

Yet, there is more than carnivalization in these discourses about classrooms and students. As was previously discussed, contexts such as socialization, culture, schools, and domestic units constitute orders of discourse and regimes of truth, constraining who can speak and what can be stated. However, there are always contradictions, subjugated knowledge, and alternatives to the particular regime that is operating in a given context. As the examples reveal, space is almost always available for people to cross firmly established borders in rigidly defined situations. Students and teachers navigate various contextual geographies, and in this navigation they are compelled to develop and construct *alternative* voices. By doing so they have to confront the already established "true" discourses of modern pedagogies. Nevertheless, the data show with clarity that people elaborate discourses, including alternative or oppositional ones, in contexts saturated with factors, which limit or control what can be said and heard.

What is the importance of listening to the students' and teachers' voices and looking at their metaphors and pictorial creations? What are their stories? What do they reveal about education? I propose that these acts of listening and seeing allow us to go beyond the overrationalistic discourses in education, without having to accept either/or explanations that only see schooling and culture as mere technologies of socialization or liberation of the students' souls.

One of the most important elements uncovered by this research is that the (re)production of certain discourses is not *imposed* on the minds of unthinking and entirely manipulable subjects. Meanings, interpretations, and discourses are played out in discursive fields in which unequal relations of power are pervasive. And yet, these relationships do not happen through simple imposition; they require creative work on existing problems, themes, contradictions, and feelings.

The data analyzed in this research also direct our attention to different modes in which social groups and individuals engage in the creative work that is needed to achieve and then maintain the leading hegemonic position, or do the opposite: resist and then develop counterhegemonic practices.

The drawing of the superteacher and some of the testimonies and metaphors used to describe teachers are just a few examples of romantic visions of agents of change (intellectuals, heroes, or superteachers). These figures always have to face the same problem: How is it possible to turn mere resistance into agency? Particularly if we understand agency as more than the power to act, but also as "access to particular places—places at which particular kinds of actions, producing particular kinds of effects, are possible—places at which one can intercede and influence the various 'forces' and vectors that are shaping the world" (Grossberg, 1999: 32).

I would like to argue that one of the main challenges for the improvement of teacher education, in particular with regards to the issue of educating teachers within a framework of professionalism and agency, is to overcome the categorical assumption that only considers power in a negative sense (as imposition or a possession of a person or institution) and not as relational or productive. Given this assumption, the only way these future teachers can conceive of becoming good teachers or agents of change is by developing supernatural powers. These superpowers appear to translate in the infinite capacity for caring, hyper-repressed sexuality, constant smiling, and superior levels of consciousness.

In this book, I would like to propose that the alternative to and companion of the resisting, hegemonized, and fragmented teacher is not the critically smiling-super-conscious-all-caring-asexualized teacher, but the committed and laughing teacher. To be committed is a characteristic that everybody expects in a teacher, and in fact perhaps most teachers are, but a laughing teacher? In the midst of all the calls for higher standards, zero tolerance, imposing more discipline, raising the stakes, who can seriously propose that we need to incorporate laughter when rethinking such a serious matter as teacher education? Jorge Larrosa gives some interesting clues about the importance of laughing in pedagogy.

> Perhaps my main goal in talking about laughter is a conviction that laughing is forbidden or at least amply ignored in the field of pedagogy. And it is always interesting to know why a field forbids or ignores something. In fact, omissions and prohibitions are the best

> ways to know the structure of a discipline, the rules that structure it
> and its deep grammar. (1998: 213)

Larrosa, Mikhail Bakhtin, and others have argued that laughter is an indispensable recourse in processes of social renovation. By carnivalizing societal structures, laughter produces, reproduces, and transforms cultural elements from both the popular sectors and high-academic circles. It is in those laughing moments when regimes of truth can momentarily be turned upside down, and thus the social hierarchical regimes that appear natural and necessary can begin their transformation.

> Mikhail Bakhtin once suggested that laughter has an all too often
> unacknowledged role to play in history. It is the joker in the pack: the
> "wild card." It stands on the other side of order "without rhyme or
> reason": the exception to the rule. Its appearance is always an
> interruption. It disrupts the players' concentration. It stops us taking it
> all too seriously. It makes the game a game again. Laughter is the
> joker in the pack of time. (Hebdige, 1988: 242)

The laughter I am proposing is not the ludic chuckle limited to entertainment and dissipation, placed on the opposite side of the "real world." Nor is it the humorous irony or pun about the "problems of the real world" that by merely giggling at the reality confirms the normality of racism, sexism, and multiple form of oppression. It is not the laughter sometimes used in order to deny the pain, in attempts to pretend that danger and humiliation have disappeared. Nor is it the laughter that proclaims itself not to be serious, that is just making fun, and by the same token creates a barricade around itself. Larrosa describes the latter as "that laughter which used to be as moralizing and rationalizing as the solemn system it is opposed to, in the name of another solemnity. That non-reflecting laughter which is not able to laugh at itself" (1998: 212).[3]

Larrosa (1998) points out to two functions of laughter in the development of thought that I would like to suggest are rather important in rethinking teacher education. First, laughter isolates, makes relative, and puts distance with the rhetorical masks that structure language. Second, it allows for a reflective moment, a self-analysis of our own rigidities, those that appear to provide inflexible characteristics to our imagined-structured identities.

Accordingly, it is possible to speculate that laughter's contributions to pedagogy reside in the combined functions of relativizing and self-analysis. Not in destroying masks, but in the acknowledgment of the masking characteristics of any pedagogical project and in impeding its solidification. Laughter gives us new wings in rethinking teacher education, allowing consciousness to play, and thus imagining without moralizing the acts of teaching and learning.

For these reasons, the laughing and committed teacher (he or she) is sometimes conscious, active and critical, but at other times is confused, or even unaware of his/her limitations or capacities to be an active promoter of social change. Or as Paulo Freire has noted: "*Conscientizacion* is not exactly the starting point of commitment. Conscientization is more of a product of commitment. I do not have to be already conscious in order to struggle. By struggling I become conscious/aware" (Freire, et.al., 1988: 114).

It is important to acknowledge that consciousness always implies that the subject has some awareness of the immediate world that concerns him or her. Indeed, critical consciousness is the capacity to recognize the historicity of human beings as social actors. However, as Freire (1989) recognized, having a deep understanding of the complex processes of oppression and domination is not enough to guarantee a personal or collective transformative praxis.

The examples provided by the students and teachers during this research demonstrate, with different degrees of clarity, that the field of teacher education is populated by women and men who are willing and could challenge and transform if not the whole system, at least some parts of the existing and historically permeable structures of domination. The former may not sound very ambitious, and yet, as Walter Benjamin put it, "the fragment is the gateway to the whole" (in Hebdige, 1988: 230)

Rethinking the issues around gender, teaching, caring, resistance, and agency is a pressing challenge for those who are committed to developing not only better education programs, but also more egalitarian systems of social life. In this project, rethinking teacher education has required an engagement in analyses that goes beyond reducing the institutional life of educating teachers into two subject positions, i.e., oppressive educators and oppressed students, male vs. female, and instead attended to the multifaceted everyday struggles developed in the intersection of class, gender, race, age, and sexual preferences.

In this book the deliberate attempt to abandon either/or type of analyses allowed the advantage of "seeing" those everyday struggles from different perspectives and thus, imagine alternatives for the dilemmas of the "real world." Rethinking teacher education, therefore, implies the recognition that in many programs there are oppressive educators and oppressed students and discriminatory gender regimes, but there are also other actors who are committed learners and teachers, down-to-earth thinkers, and sophisticated practitioners, mindful and hardworking people who have difficult times questioning teacher education programs while trying to keep them alive during this restructuring era—all of them individuals who are also in the process of finding meaning in the not often recognized, everyday political act of being present in schools, despite the low salaries, lack of social recognition, and boredom that plagues some programs.

This book was created with the purpose of contributing to the understanding that the institutional patterns and systems of production of knowledge about teacher education programs have histories, particularly gendered ones. These gendered histories have operated as contextual parameters of what can be imagined in the present. It is not simply a matter of looking for the origins of discourses of power in a profession, or determining that Pepe was the perfect example of hegemonic masculinity while Claudia embodies the mother-teacher ideal. It is rather a manifold question of recognizing that alternative conceptualizations of a given discourse always support or undermine distinctive discursive traditions (Sawicki, 1991).

In other words, if we want to imagine, understand, and construct teacher education as a dialogic instance involved in the production of socially relevant knowledge and participating in the deepening of democratic processes, we need to be committed to deconstruct all discourses of truth. When facing those discourses, we need to engage in the very real and complex processes of deconstruction of the concepts and structures supported by those regimes of truth.

> To deconstruct the concept of matter or that of bodies [teaching and caring I may add] is not to negate or refuse either term. To deconstruct these terms means, rather, to continue to use them, to repeat them, to repeat them subversively, and to displace them from the contexts in which they have been deployed as instruments of oppressive power. (Butler, 1993: 16)

Where to begin? Perhaps by laughing at those discourses that naturalize associations between women, teaching and suffering; equate homosexuals with sexual predators; erase the sexualized bodies of teachers and students; associate discipline and leadership exclusively with masculinity, and caring with femininity; ignore that classrooms are workplaces; and, lastly, claim that the best rewards for teachers are love and understanding and not professional recognition, intellectual independence, and adequate monetary compensation.

Granted, if anything, committed laughing is only one possible beginning in the hard and long-term process of transforming some of the most discriminatory and oppressive practices in teacher education. It may also be seen as a naive proposal, one that offers no guaranty, no assurance of results, slight benchmarks, unclear directions, and very little moralizing—this at a time when teachers are facing increasing demands and hostile criticism by a seemingly angry and disenchanted coalition of people obsessed by test scores, discipline, obedience and financial savings. There are no guaranties. There are no assurances. And moralizing will not help us. We are left with our knowledge, our hopes, our commitment, and the power of imagining the challenging, exciting, and at times daunting task of reinventing teaching and learning every moment, every day, making choices as we go, dreaming possibilities and having the courage to persist in our intent.

Notes

1. I want to thank my friend and colleague Julie Thompson for directing my attention to this quotation by Eduardo Galeano.

2. Noddings would argue that the quality of the caring relationship depends on the type of care that the mother received when she was a child. My objection to this is directed to the fixed reproductive qualities of early caring. It assumes that whatever early influences teacher and students were exposed to are necessarily going to be reproduced later. I am not claiming that early socialization is not a powerful influence, but as in the example of the *Madres de la Plaza de Mayo*, there is no one *essential* way of being a caring mother, and the same can be argued about teachers.

3. I am not arguing for the exclusion of those perhaps more commonly humorous forms of laughter from schools but only that we should not misunderstand entertainment with the potentially disruptive and regenerating power of laughter and humor. Already in the 1960s Rose Laub Coser (1960) described five functions of humor in her study of laughter in the workplace: (1) entertainment; (2) a means of escape or release from uncomfortable situations; (3) self-validation (mainly for the joker), which is an inclusive device when it provides or promotes cohesiveness within a group and by the same token, can be an exclusive device; (4) an expulsory function may take at least two forms: being the subject/object of the joke and/or not understanding the joke; (5) and a subversive device against well-established norms or power. While schools tend to accept the milder forms of the first four functions it is a rare case where the schools admit the last.

BIBLIOGRAPHY

Acker, Sandra, ed. 1989. *Teachers, Gender, and Careers*. New York: Falmer Press.

———. 1992. "Creating Careers: Women Teachers at Work." *Curriculum Inquiry* 22:141–63.

———. 1994. *Gendered Education: Sociological Reflections on Women, Teaching, and Feminism*. Buckingham: Open University Press.

———. 1996. "Gender and Teacher's Work." *Review of Research in Education* 21:99–162.

Alcoff, Linda, and Elizabeth Potter, eds. 1993. *Feminist Epistemologies*. New York: Routledge.

Alexander, Jeffrey C. 1989. *Structure and Meaning: Rethinking Classical Sociology*. New York: Columbia University Press.

Alliaud, Andrea. 1993. *Los Maestros y Su Historia: Los Orígenes Del Magisterio Argentino*. Buenos Aires: Centro Editor de América Latina.

Alliaud, Andrea, and Laura Duschatzky, eds. 1992. *Maestros Formación Práctica y Transformación Escolar*. Buenos Aires: Miño y Dávila Editores.

Almandoz de Claus, Maria R., and Sonia Hirschberg de Cigliutti. 1992. *La Docencia Trabajo De Riesgo*. Colombia: Tesis Grupo Editorial.

Anderson, Benedict. 1993. *Imagined Communities*. 2d ed. London: Verso.

Anderson, Gary L. 1998. "Toward Authentic Participation: Deconstructing the Discourses of Participatory Reforms in Education." *American Educational Research Journal* 35(4):571–603.

Anderson, Gary L., and Maria Santillan. 1997. "Challenging Non-Democratic Approaches to Staff Development in Latin America." *Democracy and Education* 11(2):26–30.

Anderson, Perry. 1978. *Las Antinomias De Antonio Gramsci*. Barcelona, Spain: Fontanara.

Apple, Michael W. 1979. *Ideology and Curriculum*. Boston: Routledge.

———. 1986. *Teachers and Texts*. New York: Routledge.

———. 1993. *Official Knowledge: Democratic Education in a Conservative Age*. New York: Routledge.

———. 1995. *Education and Power*. 2d ed. New York: Routledge.

———. 1996. *Cultural Politics and Education*. New York: Teachers College Press.

Applebaum, Barbara. 1998. "Is Caring Inherently Good?" *Philosophy of Education Society*. <http://x.ed.uiuc.edu/PES/1998/applebaum.html>.

Archetti, Eduardo P. 1992. "Argentinean Football: A Ritual of Violence?" *The International Journal of the History of Sport* 9(2):27–40.

———. 1996. "Playing Styles and Masculine Values in Argentine Football." In *Machos, Mistresses, Madonnas: Contesting the Power of Latin American Gender Imaginery*, ed. Marit Melhuus and Kristi A. Stølen, 34–55. London: Verso.

———. 1997. "Multiple Masculinities: The Worlds of Tango and Football in Argentina." In *Sex and Sexuality in Latin America*, ed. Daniel Balderston and Donna J. Guy, 200–18. New York: New York University Press.

Arnove, Robert F. 1999. "Introduction: Reframing Comparative Education: The Dialectic of the Global and the Local." In *Comparative Education: The Dialectic of the Global and the Local*, ed. Robert F. Arnove and Carlos A. Torres, 1–25. Lanham, MA: Rowman & Littlefield.

Aronowitz, Stanley. 1992. *The Politics of Identity: Class, Culture, Social Movements*. New York: Routledge.

Aronowitz, Stanley, and Henry Giroux. 1991. *Postmodern Education: Politics, Culture and Social Criticism*. Minneapolis: University of Minnesota Press.

Astor, Ron A., Ann H. Meyer, and William J. Behre. 1999. "Unowned Places and Times: Maps and Interviews about Violence in High Schools." *American Educational Research Journal* 36(1):3–42.

Avalos, Beatrice. 1987. "Moving Where? Educational Issues in Latin American Contexts." *Educational Development* 7(3):151–72.

Ayers, William. 1989. *The Good Preschool Teacher*. New York: Teachers College Press.

Balibar, Etienne, and Immanuel Wallerstein. 1991. *Race, Nation, Class: Ambiguous Identities*. London: Verso.

Ball, Stephen J., ed. 1990a. *Foucault and Education: Disciplines and Knowledge*. London: Routledge.

———. 1990b. *Politics and Policymaking in Education: Exploration in Policy Sociology*. London: Routledge.

———. 1994. *Education Reform: A Critical and Poststructural Approach*. Buckinghan: Open University Press.

Ball, Stephen J., and Ivor F. Goodson, eds. 1985. *Teachers' Lives and Careers*. London: Falmer Press.

Balley, Susan. 1992. *How Schools Shortchange Girls*. Wellesley, MA: Wellesley College Press.

Barbeito, Alberto C., and Ruben M. Lo Vuolo. 1992. *La Modernización Excluyente: Transformación Economica y Estado De Bienestar En Argentina*. Buenos Aires: UNICEF/CIEPP/Losada.

Barman, Chris. 1997. "Students' Views of Scientists and Science: Results From a National Study." *Science and Children* 35(1):18–23.

Batallán, Graciela, and Fernando García. 1992. "La Especificidad Del Trabajo Docente y La Transformación Escolar." In *Maestros: Formación, Práctica y Transformación Escolar*, ed. Andrea Alliaud and Laura Duschatzky, 217–34. Buenos Aires: Miño y Dávila Editores.

Beare, H. 1993. "Different Ways of Viewing School-Site Councils: Whose Paradigm Is in Use Here?" In *Restructuring Schools: An International Perspective on the Movement to Transform Schools and Performance of Schools*, ed. H. Beare and W. L. Boyd, 200–17. London: Falmer Press.

Berger, John. 1972. *Ways of Seeing*. London: Penguin Books.

———. 1980. *About Looking*. New York: Vintage Books.

Berliner, David C., and Bruce J. Biddle. 1995. *The Manufactured Crisis: Myths, Fraud and the Attack on America's Public Schools*. New York: Longman.

Best, Steven, and Douglas Kellner. 1991. *Postmodern Theory: Critical Interrogations*. New York: The Guilford Press.

Bhabha, Homi K. 1994. *The Location of Culture*. London: Routledge.

Biklen, Sara Knopp. 1995. *School Work: Gender and the Cultural Construction of Teaching*. New York: Teachers College Press.

Birgin, Alejandra. 1993. *Panorama De La Educación Básica En La Argentina*. Buenos Aires: FLACSO.

———. 1995. *Viejas y Nuevas Tensiónes En El Trabajo Docente*. Buenos Aires: FLACSO.

———. 1996. "La Crisis Docente." *Clarín* (March 25): 5.

———. 1999. *El Trabajo De Enseñar: Entre La Vocación y El Mercado*. Buenos Aires: Troquel.

Blackmore, Jill. 1994. *Gender and Administration*. Sydney: Sydney University Press.

———. 1995. "Policy as Dialogue: Feminist Adminstrators Working for Educational Change." *Gender and Education* 7(3): 293–314.

———. 1999. "Localization/Globalization and the Midwife State: Strategic Dilemmas for State Feminism in Education?" *Journal of Education Policy* 14(1):33–54.

Bolin, Frances S., and Judith McConnell Falk. 1987. *Teacher Renewal: Professional Issues, Personal Choices*. New York: Teachers College Press.

Bolotin Joseph, Pamela, and Gail Burnaford, eds. 1994. *Images of Schoolteachers in Twentieth-Century America*. New York: St Martin's Press.

Bonder, Gloria. 1992. "Altering Sexual Stereotypes through Teacher Training." In *Women and Education in Latin America*, ed. Nelly Stromquist. Boulder: Lynne Rienner.

Boron, Atilio. 1995. *State, Capitalism, and Democracy in Latin America*. Boulder: Lynne Rienner.

Boron, Atilio, and Carlos A. Torres. 1996. "The Impact of Neoliberal Restructuring on Education and Poverty in Latin America." *The Alberta Journal of Educational Research* 17(2):102–14.

Bourdieu, Pierre. 1984. *Distinction: A Social Critique of the Judgment of Taste*. Trans. Richard Nice. Cambridge, MA: Harvard University Press.

Braslavsky, Cecilia. 1985. *La Discriminación Educativa En Argentina*. Buenos Aires: FLACSO/GEL.

———. 1992. "Educational Legitimation of Women's Economic Subordination in Argentina." In *Women and Education in Latin America*, ed. Nelly Stromquist. Boulder: Lynne Rienner.

———. 1993a. *Autonomia y Anomia En La Educación Pública Argentina*. Buenos Aires: FLACSO.

———. 1993b. *Transformaciones En Curso En El Sistema Educativo En La Argentina*. Buenos Aires: FLACSO.

Braslavsky, Cecilia, and Alejandra Birgin. 1995. "Quienes Enseñan Hoy En La Argentina." In *Las Transformaciones De La Educación En 10 Años De Democracia*, ed. Guillermina Tiramonti, Cecilia Braslavsky, and Daniel Filmus, 65–106. Buenos Aires: Tesis-Norma Grupo Editorial.

Braslavsky, Cecilia, and Daniel Filmus, eds. 1988. *Respuestas a La Crisis Educativa*. Buenos Aires: Cántaro/FLACSO/CLACSO.

Braslavsky, Cecilia, and Nora Krawczyc. 1988. *La Escuela Pública*. Buenos Aires: Cuadernos de FLACSO.

Brennan, Teresa. 1996. "The Contexts of Vision from a Specific Standpoint." In *Vision in Context*, ed. Teresa Brennan and Martin Jay, 217–30. New York: Routledge.

Brennan, Teresa, and Martin Jay, ed. 1996. *Vision in Context*. New York: Routledge.

Britzman, Deborah P. 1996. "Towards a Polymorphous Perverse Curriculum." *The Review of Education/Pedagogy/Cultural Studies* 18(1):1–13.

———. 1998. *Lost Subjects, Contested Objects: Toward a Psychoanalytic Inquiry of Learning*. Albany: SUNY Press.

Brook, Colin, ed. 1996. *Global Perspectives on Teacher Education*. Oxfordshire: Triangle.

Brown, Lalage. 1999. "Beyond the Degree: Men and Women at the Decision-Making Levels in British Higher Education." *Gender and Education* 11(1):5–26.

Brunner, Joaquin, and Jeff Puryear, eds. 1995. *Educación, Equidad y Competitividad Económica En Las Américas*. Vol. 1, Key Issues. Washington, D.C.: Organization of American States.

Bunster-Bunalto, Ximena. 1993. "Surviving Beyond Fear: Women and Torture in Latin America." In *Feminist Frameworks*. 3d ed., ed. Alison Jaggar and Paula Rothemberg, 252–61. New York: McGraw-Hill.

Butler, Judith. 1990. *Gender Trouble: Feminism and the Subversion of Identity*. New York: Routledge.

———. 1993. *Bodies That Matter: On the Discursive Limits of "Sex."* New York: Routledge.

Butler, Judith, and Joan W. Scott, ed. 1992. *Feminists Theorize the Political*. New York: Routledge.

Cancian, Francesca M. and Stacey J. Oliker. 2000. *Caring and Gender*. Thousand Oaks, CA: Sage.

Carlson, Marifran. 1988. *¡Feminismo!: The Women's Movement in Argentina from Its Beginnings to Eva Perón*. Chicago: Academy Chicago Publishers.

Carnoy, Martin. 1994. *The State and Political Theory*. Princeton: Princeton University Press.

———. 1997. Foreword to *Pedagogy of the Heart* by P. Freire. New York: Continuum.

———. 1998. "National Voucher Plans in Chile and Sweden: Did Privatization Reforms Make for Better Education?" *Comparative Education Review* 42(3):309–37.

Carnoy, Martin, and Claudio de Moura Castro. 1996. *Improving Education in Latin America Today: Where to Now?* Seminar in Educational Reform. Buenos Aires: Inter-American Development Bank.

Carnoy, Martin, and Carlos A. Torres. 1995. "Educational Change and Structural Adjustment." In *Coping With Crisis*, ed. Joel Samoff, 64–94. London: Cassell.

Carvalho, Marilia. 1996. "Between Home and the School: Tensions in the Professional Identity of Teachers." In *Gender Dimensions in Education in Latin America*, ed. Nelly Stromquist. Washington, D.C.: Organization of American States.

Casanova, Ursula. 1996. "Parent Involvement: A Call for Prudence." *Educational Researcher* 25(8):30–32.

Casey, Kathleen. 1995. "The New Narrative Research in Education." *Review of Research in Education* 21:211–53.

Caulfield, Sueann. 1993. "Women of Vice, Virtue, and Rebellion: New Studies of Representation of the Female in Latin America." *Latin American Research Review* 28(2):163–74.

Cavallo, Domingo. 1995. "Reportje." *Ambito Financiero* (August 15): 12.

CCCE (California Consortium for Critical Education). 1999. Position paper. *CCCE Solidarity News* 1(2): 1–6.

CEPAL. 1995. *Panorama Social De América Latina*. Santiago, Chile: CEPAL.

CFCyE (Consejo Federal de Cultura y Educación). 1992. *Documentos para la Formación Docente*. Buenos Aires: CFCyE.

Chaplin, Elizabeth. 1994. *Sociology and Visual Representation*. London: Routledge.

Cherryholmes, Cleo. 1988. *Power and Criticism: Poststructural Investigations in Education*. New York: Teachers College Press.

Chodorow, Nancy. 1978. *The Reproduction of Mothering*. Berkeley: University of California Press.

———. 1989. *Feminism and Psychoanalytic Theory*. New Haven: Yale University Press.

Chubb, Jon, and Terry Moe. 1990. *Politics, Markets, and America's Schools*. Washington, D.C.: Brookings Institute.

Coles, Roman. 1997. *Rethinking Generosity: Critical Theory and the Politics of Caritas*. Ithaca: Cornell University Press.

CONADEP (Comisión Nacional sobre la Desparición de Personas). 1984. *Nunca Más*. Buenos Aires: EUDEBA.

Connell, Robert W. 1987. *Gender and Power*. Cambridge, U.K.: Polity Press.

———. 1990. "The State, Gender and Sexual Politics." *Theory and Society* (19):507–44.

———. 1992. "Citizenship Social Justice and Curriculum." *International Studies in Sociology of Education* 2(2):133–63.

———. 1995. *Masculinities*. Berkeley: University of California Press.

———. 1996. "Teaching the Boys: New Research on Masculinity, and Gender Strategies for Schools." *Teachers College Record* 98(2):206–35.

Cook, Rebecca J., ed. 1994. *Human Rights of Women*. Philadelphia: University of Pennsylvania Press.

Coomaraswamy, Radhika. 1994. "To Bellow Like Cow: Women, Ethnicity, and the Discourse of Rights." In *Human Rights of Women* , ed. Rebecca J. Cook, 39–58. Philadelphia: University of Pennsylvania Press.

Copjec, Joan. 1994. *Read My Desire: Lacan Against the Historicists*. Cambridge, MA: MIT Press.

Coraggio, José Luis. 1992. *Economia y Educación en América Latina: Notas para una Agenda para los 1990*. Quito: Instituto Fronesis.

Cortina, Regina. 1992. "Gender and Power in the Teachers' Union of Mexico." In *Women and Education in Latin America*, ed. Nelly Stromquist. Boulder, CO: Lynne Rienner.

Coser, Rose L. 1960. "Laughter Among Colleagues: A Study of the Social Functions of Humor Among the Staff of a Mental Hospital." *Psychiatry* 23: 112–38.

Darling-Hammond, Linda. 1990. "Instructional Policy into Practice: The Power of the Bottom Over the Top." *Educational Evaluation and Policy Analysis* 12(3):339–48.

———. 1993. Introduction to *Review of Research in Education* 19:xi–xviii.

———. 1997. *The Right to Learn: A Blueprint for Creating Schools That Work*. San Francisco: Jossey-Bass Publishers.

Davini, María C. 1995. *La Formación Docente En Cuestión: Política y Pedagogia*. Buenos Aires: Paidós.

Davini, María C., and Andrea Alliaud, eds. 1995. *Los Maestros Del Siglo XXI: Un Estudio Sobre El Perfil De Los Estudiantes De Magisterio*. Buenos Aires: Miño y Dávila Editores.

Delamont, Sara. 1990. *Sex Roles and the School*. 2d ed. New York: Routledge.

Dicker, Gabriela, and Flavia Terigi. 1994. *Panorámica De La Formación Docente En Argentina*. Buenos Aires: Ministerio de Cultura y Educación/ Organización de los Estados Americanos.

Donald, James. 1992. *Sentimental Education: Schooling, Popular Culture, and the Regulation of Liberty*. London: Verso.

Dove, L. 1986. *Teachers and Teacher Education in Developing Countries*. London: Croom Helm.

Duncan, Judith. 1996. "Gendered Discourses of New Zealand Kindergarten Teachers." *Gender and Education* 8(2):159–70.

Duranti, Alessandro. 1993. "Language in Context and Language As Context: The Samoan Respect Vocabulary." In *Rethinking Context: Language as an Interactive Phenomenon*, ed. Alessandro Duranti and Charles Goodwin, 77–100. Cambridge: Cambridge University Press.

Duranti, Alessandro, and Charles Goodwin, eds. 1992. *Rethinking Context: Language as an Interactive Phenomenon*. Cambridge, MA: Cambridge University Press.

Dussel, Inés. 1997. *Curriculum, Humanismo y Democracia En La Enseñanza Media*. Buenos Aires: FLACSO-CBC.

———. 1999. "Foucault's Conception of History: Reflections on the Use(s) of Genealogy." Paper presented at the annual conference of the American Educational Research Association (Montreal).

————. forthcoming. "What Can Multiculturalism Tell Us About Difference?: The Reception of Multicultural Discourses in France and Argentina." In *The Ideals and Realities of Mutlicultural Education in Global Contexts*, ed. Carl Grant and Joy Lei, 1–25. New Jersey: Lawrence Erlbaum Associates.

Dussel, Inés, Guillermina Tiramonti, and Alejandra Birgin. 2000. "Decentralization and Recentralization in Argentine Educational Reform: Reshaping Educational Policies in the 1990s." In *Educational Knowledge: Changing Relationships Between the State, the Civil Society, and the Educational Community*, ed. Thomas S. Popkewitz, 155–72. Albany: SUNY University Press.

Eagleton, Terry. 1991. *Ideology: An Introduction*. London: Verso.

ECLAC (Economic Commission for Latin America and the Caribbean). 1992. *Education and Knowledge: Basic Pillars of Changing Production Patterns with Social Equity*. Santiago, Chile: ECLAC.

The Economist. 1996. "Latin America's Backlash." *The Economist* 341(7994):19–23.

Edwards, Beth. 1994. "Women, Work and Democracy in Latin America." *Convergence* 27(2–3):51–57.

Eisner, Elliot. 1997. "The Promise and Perils of Alternative Forms of Data Representation." *Educational Researcher* 26(6):4–11.

————. 1998. *The Enlightened Eye: Qualitative Inquiry and the Enhancement of Educational Practice*. New Jersey: Merrill-Prentice Hall.

Elbaz, Frank. 1991. "Research on Teacher's Knowledge: The Evolution of a Discourse." *Journal of Curriculum Studies* 23(1):1–19.

Ellsworth, Elizabeth. 1997. *Teaching Positions: Difference, Pedagogy and the Power of Address*. New York: Teachers College Press.

Elon, Amos. 1986. *Letters from Argentina*. Buenos Aires: Asamblea Permanente por los Derechos Humanos.

Elshtain, Jean. 1994. "The Mothers of the Disappeared: Passion and Protest in Maternal Action." In *Representations of Motherhood*, ed. Donna Bassin, Margaret Honey, and Meryle Marher Kaplan, 75–91. New Haven: Yale University Press.

Etchart de Bianchi, Maria. 1976. *Costos De La Educación En La Argentina: Metodología y Principales Resultados*. Buenos Aires: FIEL/ECIEL.

Etchart de Bianchi, María. 1993. *Descentralización De La Escuela Primaria y Media: Una Propuesta De Reforma*. Buenos Aires: FIEL-CEA.

Ezpeleta, Justa. 1991. *Escuelas y Maestros: Condiciones Del Trabajo Docente En La Argentina*. Buenos Aires: CEAL-UNESCO-REC.

Fajnzylber, Fernando. 1992. "Transformación Productiva Con Equidad." *Revista de la CEPAL* (47): 39–60.

Ferguson, Kathy. 1984. *The Feminist Case Against Bureaucracy*. Philadelphia: Temple University Press.

Ferguson, Mary W. 1991. "Juggling the Categories of Race, Class and Gender: Aphra Behn's Oroonoko." *Women's Studies* 19(1):159–81.

Fischman, Gustavo E. 1997. "Love It or Leave It: The Gendered Dimensions of Teachers' Education in Argentina." Paper presented at the annual conference of the International Education Society (Mexico City).

———. 1998. "Re-Pensando o Ensino: Brincando Co o Bom, o Feo e o Imaginario." In *A Escola Cidada No Contexto De Globaliçaçao*, ed. Luiz Heron da Silva, 130–57. Petrópolis, Brazil: Vozes Editora.

Fischman, Gustavo E., and Peter McLaren. 2000. "Schooling for Democracy: Towards a Critical Utopianism." *Contemporary Sociology* 29(1): 168–80.

Folette, Marcel C. 1990. *Making Science Our Own: Public Images of Science 1910–1950*. Chicago: Chicago University Press.

Foster, Hal. 1988. *Vision and Visuality*. Seattle: Bay Press.

Foucault, Michel. 1977. *Discipline and Punish: The Birth of the Prison*. Trans. Alan Sheridan. New York: Pantheon Books.

———. 1978. "The History of Sexuality." vol. 1 Trans. Robert Hurley. New York: Pantheon Books.

———. 1980. In *Power and Knowledge: Selected Interviews and Other Writings, 1972–1977*, ed. Colin Gordon. New York: Pantheon Books.

———. 1981. "The Order of Discourse." In *Untying the Text: A Poststructuralist Reader*, ed. Robert Young, 48–78. Boston:Routledge.

———. 1982. "The Subject and Power." In *Michel Foucault: Beyond Structuralism and Hermeneutics*, ed. H. Dreyfreus and P. Rabinow, 76–100. Chicago: University of Chicago Press.

———. 1984. "Nietzsche, Genealogy, History." Trans. D. Bouchard and S. Simon. In *The Foucault Reader*, ed. Paul Rabinow, 76–100. New York: Pantheon Books.

———. 1986. "Of Other Spaces." *Diacritics* 16:22–27.

———. 1988. "Technologies of the Self." In *Technologies of the Self: A Seminar with Michel Foucault*, ed. L. Martin, H. Gutman, and P. Hutton, 16–49. Amherst: University of Massachusetts Press.

———. 1990a. *The History of Sexuality: The Use of Pleasure*. New York: Vintage Books.

———. 1990b. The Use of Pleasure. Vol. 2 of the History of Sexuality. Trans. R. Hurley. New York: Vintage Books.

———. 1991. "Governmentality." Trans. Rosi Braidotti and C. Gordon. In *The Foucault Effect: Studies in Governmentality*, ed. G. Burchell, C. Gordon, and P. Miller, 87–104. Chicago: University of Chicago Press.

———. 1993. "Space, Power and Knowledge." In *The Cultural Studies Reader*, ed. Simon During. London: Routledge.

Francoeur, Robert T., Martha Cornog, Timothy Perper, and Norman A. Scherzer, eds. 1995. *The Complete Dictionary of Sexology*. New York: Continuum.

Fraser, Nancy. 1989. *Unruly Practices: Power Discourse and Gender in Contemporary Social Theory*. Minneapolis: University of Minnesota Press.

Freire, Paulo. 1985. *The Politics of Education: Culture, Power, and Liberation*. South Hadley, MA: Bergin and Garvey.

———. 1989. *Education for the Critical Consciousness*. New York: Continuum.

———. 1993. *Professora Sim, Tia Nao: Cartas a Quem Ousa Ensinar*. Sao Paulo: Olho d'Agua.

Freire, Paulo, Moacir Gadotti, Sergio Guimaraez, and Isabel Hernández. 1988. *Pedagogia, Dialogo y Conflicto*. Buenos Aires: Ediciones Cinco.

Fullan, Michael. 1993. *Change Forces: Probing the Depth of Educational Reform*. New York: Falmer Press.

Gadotti, Moacir. 1994. *Reading Paulo Freire*. Albany: SUNY Press.

Galeano, Eduardo. 1991. *The Book of Embraces*. Trans. Cedric Belfrage. New York: W.W. Norton and Company.

Gallart, Maria A., Martin J. Moreno, and Marcela Cerrutti. 1993. *Educación y Empleo En El Gran Buenos Aires (1980–1991)*. Buenos Aires: CENEP.

García Canclini, Nestor. 1995. *Hybrid Cultures: Strategies for Entering and Leaving Modernity*. Trans. Christopher Chiappary and Silvia L. Lopez. Minneapolis: University of Minnesota Press.

Geertz, Clifford. 1983. *Local Knowledge: Further Essays in Interpretive Anthropology*. New York: Basic Books.

Genro, Tarso. 1999. "Cidadãnia, Emancipação e Cidade." In *Escola Cidadã: Teoria e Práctica,* ed. Luiz Heron da Silva, 6–12. Petrópolis, Brazil: Vozes Editora.

Gentili, Pablo. 1994a. *Poder Económico, Ideología y Educación*. Buenos Aires: Miño y Dávila.

———. 1994b. *Proyecto Neoconservador y Crisis Educativa*. Buenos Aires: Centro Editor de América Latina.

Gibaja, Regina. 1986. *Fuentes y Límites Del Discurso Acerca De La Mujer*. Buenos Aires: Centro de Investigaciones en Ciencias de la Educación.

Giddens, Anthony. 1993. *Sociology*. 2d ed. Cambridge, U.K.: Polity Press.

Gilbert, Rob. 1992. "Citizenship, Education and Democracy." *British Journal of Sociology of Education* 13(1):51–68.

Gilligan, Carol. 1992. *In a Different Voice*. Cambridge: Harvard University Press.

Giroux, Henry. 1988. *Teachers as Intellectuals*. New York: Bergin and Garvey.

———, ed. 1990. *Postmodernism, Feminism and Cultural Politics*. Albany: SUNY Press.

Giroux, Henry, and Peter McLaren, eds. 1989. *Critical Pedagogy, The State and Cultural Struggle*. Albany: SUNY Press.

Giroux, Henry, and Roger I. Simon, eds. 1989. *Popular Culture: Schooling and Everyday Life*. South Hadley, MA: Bergin and Garvey.

Gitlin, A., and F. Margonis. 1995. "The Political Aspect of Reform: Teacher Resistance As Good Sense." *American Journal of Education* 103:377–405.

Goffman, Erving. 1981. *Forms of Talk*. Philadelphia: University of Pennsylvania Press.

Goldwerth, Marvin. 1985. "The Meaning of Macho: The Flight from Femininity." *The Psychoanalytic Review* 72(1):161–69.

Goodlad, John, Robert Soder, and K. Sirotnik, eds. 1997. *Places Where Teachers Are Taught*. San Francisco: Jossey-Bass.

Gore, Jeniffer. 1993. *The Struggle for Pedagogies*. New York: Routledge.

Grabb, Edward. 1990. *Theories of Social Inequality: Classical and Contemporary Perspectives*. 2d ed. Canada: Holt, Rinehart and Winston.

Gramsci, Antonio. 1971. *Selections from the Prison Notebooks*. New York: International Publishers.

Graziano, Frank. 1992. *Divine Violence: Spectacle, Psychosexuality and Radical Christianity in the Argentine "Dirty War."* Boulder, CO: Westview Press.

Griffin, Gary A., ed. 1999. *The Education of Teachers: Ninety-Eighth Yearbook of the National Society for the Study of Education*. Part 1. Chicago: University of Chicago Press.

Grossberg, Lawrence. 1999. "Speculations and Articulations of Globalization." *Polygraph* 11:11–48.

Grumet, Madeleine R. 1988. *Bitter Milk: Women and Teaching*. Amherst: University of Massachusetts Press.

Guinsburg, Mark. 1992. "Educators/Politics." *Comparative Education Review* 36(4):417–45.

Guinsburg, Mark, and B. Lindsay, eds. 1995. *The Political Dimension in Teacher Education*. London: Falmer Press.

Gutierrez, Kris, and Joanne Larson. 1994. "Language Borders: Recitation As Hegemonic Discourse." *International Journal of Education Reform* 3(1):22–36.

Gutierrez, Kris, Joanne Larson, and Betsy Kreuter. 1995. "Cultural Tensions in the Scripted Classroom." *Urban Education* 29(4):410–42.

Gutmann, Mathew C. 1996. *The Meaning of Macho: Being a Man in Mexico*. Berkeley: University of California Press.

Hall, Stuart, and James Donald, eds. 1986. *Politics and Ideology: A Reader*. Philadelphia: Open University Press.

Hall, Stuart, and Martin Jacques, eds. 1989. *New Times: The Changing Face of Politics in the 1990s*. London: Lawrence and Wishart and Marxism Today.

Hamilton, David. 1989. *Towards a Theory of Schooling*. East Sussex: Falmer Press.

Harding, Sandra. 1987. "Introduction: Is There a Feminist Method?" In *Feminism and Methodology*, ed. Sandra Harding, 7–14. Bloomington: Indiana University Press.

———. 1991. *Whose Science? Whose Knowledge? Thinking From Women's Lives*. Ithaca: Cornell University Press.

————. 1994. "Is Science Multicultural?" *Configurations* 2:301–30.

Hargreaves, Andy. 1994. *Changing Teachers, Changing Times: Teachers' Work and Culture in the Postmodern Age*. New York: Teachers College Press.

Hartley, John. 1992. *The Politics of Pictures: The Creation of the Public in the Age of Popular Media*. London: Routledge.

Hebdige, Dick. 1988. *Hiding in the Light*. London: Routledge .

Held, David. 1995. *Democracy and the Global Order*. Palo Alto: Stanford University Press.

Henke, Robin R., Susan P. Choy, Chen Xianglei, Sonya Geis, and Martha N. Alt. 1997. *America's Teachers: Profile of a Profession, 1993–94*. Washington, D.C.: U.S. Department of Education, National Center for Education Statistics.

Henke, Robin R., Sonya Geis, Jennifer Giambattista, and Paula Knepper. 1996. *Out of the Lecture Hall and into the Classroom: 1992–93 College Graduates and Elementary/Secondary School Teaching, with an Essay on Undergraduate Academic Experiences*. Washington, D.C.: U.S. Department of Education. National Center for Education Statistics.

Hernández, Adriana. 1997. *Pedagogy, Democracy and Feminism: Rethinking the Public Sphere*. Albany: SUNY Press.

Heywood, Ian, and Barry Sandywell, eds. 1999. *Interpreting Visual Culture: Explorations in the Hermeneutics of the Visual*. London: Routledge.

Hill Collins, Patricia. 1990. *Black Feminist Thought: Knowledge, Consciousness, and the Politics of Empowerment*. Boston: Unwin Hyman.

Hollan, Douglas. 1994. "Suffering and the Work of Culture: The Case of Magical Poisoning in Toraja." *American Ethnologist* 21(1):74–87.

Hollan, Douglas, and Jane C. Wellenkamp. 1994. *Contentment and Suffering: Culture and Experience in Toraja*. New York: Columbia University Press.

————. 1996. *The Thread of Life: Toraja Reflections on The Life Cycle*. Honolulu: University of Hawaii Press.

Holquist, Michael. 1990. *Dialogism: Bakhtin and His World*. London: Routledge.

hooks, bell. 1994. *Outlaw Culture*. New York: Routledge.

Hoskin, Keith. 1990. "Foucault Under Examination: The Crypto-Educationalist Unmasked." In *Foucault and Education*, ed. Stephen Ball. London: Routledge.

Houston Luiggi, Alice. 1959. *Sesenta y cinco valientes: Sarmiento y las Maestras Norteamericanas*. Buenos Aires: Agora.

Hunter, Ian. 1994. *Rethinking the School: Subjectivity, Bureaucracy and Criticism*. New York: St. Martin's Press.

INDEC (Instituto Nacional de Estadística y Censos). 1998. *Boletin Oficial*. Buenos Aires: INDEC.

IDB (Inter-American Development Bank). 1991. *Economic and Social Progress in Latin America*. Washington, D.C.: Inter-American Development Bank.

Isuani, Ernesto, Ruben Lo Vuolo, and Emilio Tenti Fanfani. 1991. *El Estado Benefactor: Un Paradigma En Crisis.* Buenos Aires: CIEPP-Miño y Davila.

Jameson, Frederick. 1984. "Postmodernism, or the Cultural Logic of Late Capitalism." *New Left Review* 146:53–92.

Jay, Martin. 1994. *Downcast Eyes: The Denigration of Vision in Twentieth-Century French Thought.* Berkeley: University of California Press.

Jelin, Elizabeth, ed. 1987. *Ciudadania e Identidad: Las Mujeres En Los Movimientos Sociales En Latino-Americanos.* Ginebra, Switzerland: Instituto de Investigaciones de las Naciones Unidas para el Desarrollo Social.

John, Smyth. 1992. "Teachers' Works and Politics of Reflection." *American Educational Research Journal* 29(2):267–302.

Jones, Alan. 1998. Introduction to *Teacher Education Quarterly* 25(2):1–12.

Jones, Jacqueline. 1995. *Labor of Love, Labor of Sorrow: Black Women, Work, and the Family from Slavery to the Present.* New York: Vintage Books.

Jones, Robert. 1990. "Educational Practices and Scientific Knowledge." In *Foucault and Education,* ed. Stephen Ball. London: Routledge.

Jung, Carl G. 1964. *Man and His Symbols.* New York: Dell.

Kabeer, Naila. 1994. *Reversed Realities: Gender Hierarchies in Development Thought.* London: Verso.

Kanpol, Barry, and Peter McLaren, eds. 1995. *Critical Multiculturalism: Uncommon Voices in a Common Struggle.* Westport: Bergin and Garvey.

Katz, M. B. 1995. *Improving Poor People: The Welfare State, the "Underclass," and Urban Schools as History.* Princeton: Princeton University Press.

Kellner, Douglas, and Steven Best. 1991. *Postmodern Theory: Critical Interrogations.* New York: Guilford Press.

Kenway, Jane, and Lindsay Fitzclarence. 1997. "Masculinity, Violence and Schooling: Challenging 'Poisonous Pedagogies.'" *Gender and Education* 9(1):117–35.

Khun, Thomas S. 1970. *The Structure of Scientific Revolutions.* Chicago: University of Chicago Press.

Kincheloe, Joe L. 1991. *Teachers As Researchers: Qualitative Inquiry as a Path to Empowerment.* London: Falmer Press.

Kohli, Wendy, ed. 1995. *Critical Conversations in Philosophy of Education.* New York: Routledge.

Kohn, Alfie. 1999. *The Schools Our Children Deserve.* Boston: Houghton Mifflin Company.

Krawczyc, Nora. 1993. "A Utopia Da Participação: A Posição Dos Movimientos Docentes Na Formulação Da Politica Educativa Na Argentina." Ph.D. dissertation, Universidad Estadual da Campinas, Campinas, Brazil.

Kugler, Bernardo. 1991. *Argentina: Reallocating Resources for the Improvement of Education.* Washington, D.C.: The World Bank.

Kundera, Milan. 1996. *Slowness*. Trans. Linda Asher. New York: HarperCollins.

Laclau, Ernesto. 1989. "Politics and the Limits of Modernity." In *Universal Abandon: The Politics of Postmodernism*, ed. A. Ross. Edinburgh: Edinburgh University Press.

Laclau, Ernesto, and Chantal Mouffe. 1985. *Hegemony and Socialist Strategy*. London: Verso.

Lankshear, Colin, and Peter L. McLaren, eds. 1993. *Critical Literacy: Politics, Praxis and the Postmodern*. Albany: SUNY Press.

Larrosa, Jorge. 1998. *Pedagogia Profana: Danças, Piruetas e Mascaradas*. Porto Alegre, Brazil: Contra*Bando.

Lather, Patricia A. 1991. *Getting Smart: Feminist Research and Pedagogy with/in the Postmodern*. New York: Routledge.

Le Tendre, Gerard K. 1999. "The Problem of Japan: Qualitative Studies and International Educational Comparisons." *Educational Researcher* 28(2):38–45.

Leonard, Pauline. 1998. "Gendering Change? Management, Masculinity and the Dynamics of Incorporation." *Gender and Education* 10(1):71–85.

Lightfoot, Sara L. 1983. *The Good High School*. New York: Basic Books.

Lightfoot, Sara L., and Jessica Hoffman-Davis. 1997. *The Art and Science of Portraiture*. San Francisco: Jossey Bass Publishers.

Lincoln, Yvonna, and Egon Guba. 1985. *Naturalistic Inquiry*. Beverly Hills: Sage.

Lindstrom, Lamont. 1992. "Language in Context and Language As Context." In *Rethinking Context: Language As an Interactive Phenomenon*, ed. Alessandro Duranti and Charles Goodwin, 77–100. Cambridge, MA: Cambridge University Press.

Lipman, Martin. 1997. "Restructuring in Context: A Case Study of Teacher Participation and the Dynamics of Ideology, Race, and Power." *American Educational Research Journal* 34:3–37.

Lord, M. G. 1994. *Forever Barbie: The Unauthorized Biography of a Real Doll*. New York: Morrow and Co.

Lortie, Dan C. 1977. *Schoolteacher: A Sociological Study*. Chicago: University of Chicago Press.

Luke, Carmen, ed. 1996a. *Feminisms and Pedagogies of Everyday Life*. Albany: SUNY Press.

————. 1996b. "Feminist Pedagogy Theory: Reflections on Power and Authority." *Educational Theory* 46(3):283–302.

Lyotard, Jean F. 1984. *The Postmodern Condition*. Minneapolis: University of Minnesota Press.

Mac an Ghaill, Máirtín. 1994. *The Making of Men: Masculinities, Sexualities and Schooling*. Buckingham: Open University Press.

Maeroff, Gene, ed. 1998. *Imaging Education: The Media and Schools in America*. New York: Teachers College Press.

Margolis, Eric. 1994. "Images in Struggle: Photographs of Colorado Coals Camps." *Visual Sociology* 9(1):4–26.

————. 1998. "Picturing Labor: Photographs of the Coal Mine Labor Process." *Visual Sociology* 13(2):5–35.

————. 2000. "Class Pictures: Representations of Race, Gender and Ability in a Century of School Photography." *Visual Sociology* 14:10–39.

Marshall, James D. 1995. "Needs, Interests, Growth, and Personal Autonomy: Foucault on Power." In *Critical Conversations in Philosophy of Education*, ed. Wendy Kohli, 364–78. New York: Routledge.

Martin, Emily. 1997. "The End of the Body?" In *The Gender Sexuality Reader*, ed. Roger N. Lancaster and Micaela di Leonardo, 543–58. New York: Routledge.

Martin, Luther H., Huck Gutman, and Patrick H. Hutton. 1988. *Technologies of the Self: A Seminar with Michael Foucault*. Amherst: University of Massachusetts Press.

Matthews, Brian. 1996. "Drawing Scientists." *Gender and Education* 8(2):231–46.

McCarthy, Cameron. 1988. "Rethinking Liberal and Radical Perspectives on Racial Inequality in Schooling: Making the Case for Nonsynchrony." *Harvard Educational Review* 58(3):265–79.

McLaren, Peter. 1993. *Schooling as a Ritual Performance: Towards a Political Economy of Educational Symbols and Gestures*. London: Routledge.

————. 1995. "Moral Panic, Schooling and Gay Identity: Critical Pedagogy and the Politics of Resistance." In *The Gay Teen*, ed. Gerald Unks, 105–25. New York: Routledge.

McLaren, Peter, and Gustavo E. Fischman. 1998. "Reclaiming Hope: Teacher Education and Social Justice in the Age of Globalization." *Teacher Education Quarterly* 25(4):125–33.

McLaren, Peter, and James M. Giarelli, eds. 1995. *Critical Theory and Educational Research*. Albany: SUNY Press.

McLaren, Peter, and Colin Lankshear, eds. 1994. "Politics of Liberation: Paths From Freire." London: Routledge.

McLaren, Peter, and Peter Leonard, eds. 1993. *Paulo Freire. A Critical Encounter*. New York: Routledge.

McQuillan, Jeff. 1998. *The Literacy Crisis: False Claims, Real Solutions*. Portsmouth, NH: Heinemann.

Medina, Cecilia. 1994. "Toward a More Effective Guarantee of the Enjoyment of Human Rights by Women in the Inter-American System." In *Human Rights of Women*, ed. Rebecca Cook, 257–85. Philadelphia: University of Pennsylvania Press.

Mekler, Víctor M., ed. 1993. *Juventud, Educación y Trabajo*. Vols. 1 and 2. Buenos Aires: Centro Editor de América Latina.

Melhuus, Marit, and Kristi A. Stølen, eds. 1996. *Machos, Mistresses, Madonnas: Contesting the Power of Latin American Gender Imagery*. London: Verso.

Mellibovsky, Matilde. 1997. *Circle of Love over Deaath: Testimonies of the Mothers of the Plaza de Mayo*. Willimantic, CT: Curbstone Press.

Messner, Michael A. 1992. *Power at Play: Sports and the Problems of Masculinity*. Boston: Beacon Press.

———. 1997. *Politics of Masculinities*. Thousand Oaks: SAGE.

Middleton, Sue. 1998. *Disciplining Sexuality: Foucault, Life Stories, and Education*. New York: Teachers College Press.

Miles, Matthew B., and Michael Huberman. 1984. *Qualitative Data Analysis: A Sourcebook of New Methods*. Beverly Hills: Sage Publications.

Minujin, Alberto, ed. 1992. *Cuesta Abajo. Los Nuevos Pobres: Efectos De La Crisis En La Sociedad Argentina*. Buenos Aires: UNICEF/LOSADA.

Mirandé, Alfredo. 1997. *Hombres y Machos: Masculinity and Latino Culture*. Boulder, CO: Westview Press.

Mitchell, Claudia, and Sandra Weber. 1998. "Picture This! Class Line-Ups, Vernacular Portraits and Lasting Impressions of School." In *Image-Based Research*, ed. Jon Prosser, 197–214. London: Falmer Press.

Mitchell, William J. 1992. *The Reconfigured Eye: Visual Truth in the Post-Photographic Era*. Cambridge, MA: MIT Press.

Molyneux, Maxine. 1992. "Jo Fisher: Mothers of the Disappeared." *History Workshop Journal* 34:186–88.

Montecino, Sonia. 1988. *Identidad Femenina y Mundo Mariano En Chile*. Santiago, Chile: Centro de Estudios de la Mujer.

Morgade, Graciela. 1992a. *El Determinante De Género En El Trabajo Docente De La Escuela Primaria*. Buenos Aires: Miño y Dávila Editores-Instituto de Investigaciones en Ciencias de la Educación.

———. 1992b. "La Docencia Para Las Mujers: Una Alternativa Contradictoria En El Camino De Los Saberes 'Legítimos.'" *Propuesta Educativa* 4(7):53–62.

———. 1993. "¿Quienes Fueron Las Primeras Maestras?" *Revista Del Instituto De Ciencias De La Educación* 2(2):52–61.

———. 1995. "Mujeres y Educación Formal." *Revista Del Instituto De Investigaciones En Ciencias De La Educación* 4(6):26–35.

———, ed. 1997. *Mujeres En La Educación: Género y Docencia En La Argentina 1870–1930*. Buenos Aires: Miño y Dávila Editores.

Morrow, Raymond, and Carlos A. Torres. 1995. *Social Theory and Education*. New York: SUNY Press.

Mosse, George L. 1984. *Formations of Nations and People*. London: Routledge.

———. 1985. *Nationalism and Sexuality: Middle-Class Morality and Sexual Norms in Modern Europe*. Madison: University of Wisconsin Press.

Mouffe, Chantal. 1992. "Feminism, Citizenship, and Radical Democratic Politics." In *Feminist Theorize Politics*, ed. Judith Butler and Joan W. Scott, 369–85. New York: Routledge.

Narodowski, Mariano. 1996. *La Escuela Argentina De Fin De Siglo*. Buenos Aires: Novedades Educativas.

Narodowski, Mariano, and Patricio Narodowski. 1988. *La Crisis Laboral Docente*. Buenos Aires: Centro Editor de America Latina.

NCTAF (National Commission on Teaching and America's Future). 1996. *What Matters Most: Teaching and America's Future*. New York: NCTAF.

Nikola-Lisa, W., and Gail Burnaford. 1994. "Mosaic: Contemporary Schoolchildren's Images of Teachers." In *Images of Schoolteachers in Twentieth-Century America*, ed. P. Bolotin Joseph and Gail Burnaford, 116–42. New York: St. Martin's Press.

Noddings, Nel. 1984. *Caring: A Feminine Approach to Ethics & Moral Education*. Berkeley: University of California Press.

———. 1991. "Caring From a Feminist Perspective." In *Ethics for Professionals in Education*, ed. Kenneth Strike and Lance P. Ternasky. New York: Teachers College Press.

———. 1992. *The Challenge to Care in Schools: An Alternative Approach to Education*. New York: Teachers College Press.

———. 1995. *Philosophy of Education*. Boulder: Westview.

———. 1999. "Caring and Competence." In *The Education of Teachers*, ed. Gary A. Griffin, 205–20. Chicago: University of Chicago Press.

O'Donnell, Guillermo, and Philippe C. Schmitter. 1986. *Transitions From Authoritarian Rule: Tentative Conclusions About Uncertain Democracies*. Baltimore: Johns Hopkins University Press.

O'Hanlon, Rosalin. 1988. "Recovering the Subject: Subaltern Studies and Histories of Resistance in Colonial South Asia." *Modern Asian Studies* 22(1):222–33.

O'Shea, David. 1993. "Review: Sentimental Education: Schooling, Popular Culture and the Regulation of Liberty." *Media Culture and Society* 15:501–10.

Oakes, Jeannie, and Martin Lipman. 1999. *Teaching to Change the World*. Boston: McGraw-Hill College.

Oakes, Jeannie, Amy Wells, M. Jones, and A. Datnow. 1997. "Detracking: The Social Construction of Ability, Cultural Politics, and Resistance to Reform." *Teachers College Record* 98(3):482–510.

Parker, Andrew, Mary Russo, Doris Sommer, and Patricia Yaeger, eds. 1992. *Nationalism and Sexualities*. New York: Routledge.

Parker, Pat. 1997–99. Argentina's Grandmother of Kindergartens. <www.departments.bucknell.edu/pr/BucknellWorld/1997–9/glance>.

Parsons, Talcott. 1956. *Economy and Society: A Study in the Integration of Economic and Social Theory*. Glencoe: Free Press.

Pateman, Carole. 1984. *The Disorder of Women: Democracy, Feminism and Political Theory*. Cambridge, U.K.: Polity.

Paulston, Rolland, ed. 1996. *Social Cartography: Mapping Ways of Seeing Educational Change*. New York: Garland.

Paviglianitti, Norma. 1991. *Neo-Conservadurismo y Educación*. Buenos Aires: Libros del Quirquincho.

Peterson, Spike, ed. 1992. *Gendered States: Feminist (Re)Visions of International Relations Theory*. Boulder: Lynne Rienner.

Pineau, Pablo. 1997. *La Escolarización De La Provincia De Buenos Aires: Una Versión Posible*. Buenos Aires: FLACSO-CBC.

Popkewitz, Thomas S. 1991. *A Political Sociology of Educational Reform*. New York: Teachers College Press.

———, ed. 1993. *Changing Patterns of Power: Social Regulation and Teacher Education Reform*. Albany: SUNY Press.

———. 1996. "Rethinking Decentralization and the State/Civil Society Distinctions: The State As a Problematic of Governing." *Journal of Educational Policy* 11:27–51.

———. 1998a. "Dewey, Vygotsky, and the Social Administration of the Individual: Constructivist Pedagogy as Systems of Ideas in Historical Spaces." *American Educational Research Journal* 35(4):535–70.

———. 1998b. *Struggling for the Soul: The Politics of Schooling and the Construction of the Teacher*. New York: Teachers College Press.

———. 1999. "A Social Epistemoplogy of Educational Research." In *Critical Theories in Education: Changing Terrains of Knowledge and Politics*, ed. Thomas S. Popkewitz and Lynn Fendler, 17–45. New York: Routledge.

———. 2000a. "The Denial of Change in Educational Change: Systems of Ideas in the Construction of National Policy and Evaluation." *Educational Researcher* 29(1):17–30.

———, ed. 2000b. *Educational Knowledge: Changing Relationships Between the State, the Civil Society, and the Educational Community*. New York: SUNY Press.

Popkewitz, Thomas S., and Marie Brennan. 1998. *Foucault's Challenge: Discourse, Knowledge, and Power in Education*. New York. Teachers College Press.

Poulantzas, Nicolas. 1978. *State, Power, Socialism*. London: New Left Books.

Prawda, Juan. 1990. *Decentralization and Educational Bureaucracies*. Washington, D.C.: The World Bank.

Prosser, Jon. 1998. "The Status of Image-Based Research." In *Image-Based Research*, ed. Jon Prosser, 97–113. London: Falmer Press.

Pruyn, Marc. 1996. *Gotham City Wars*. Boulder: Westview.

Przeworski, Adam. 1991. *Democracy and the Market: Political and Economic Reforms in Eastern Europe and Latin America*. Cambridge, MA: Cambridge University Press.

Puiggrós, Adriana. 1986. *Democracia y Autoritarismo En La Pedagogia Argentina y Latinoamericana*. Buenos Aires: Editorial Galerna.

———. 1987. *Discusiones Sobre Educación y Política*. Buenos Aires: Editorial Galerna.

————. 1990. *Sujetos, Disciplina y Curriculum En Los Origenes Del Sistema Educativo Argentino*. Buenos Aires, Editorial Galerna.

————, ed. 1991. *Sociedad Civil y Estado En Los Origenes Del Sistema Educativo Argentino*. Buenos Aires: Galerna Editorial.

Puiggrós, Adriana, and Jose Balduzzi, eds. 1989. *Hacia Una Pedagogia De La Imaginación En América Latina*. Buenos Aires: Contrapunto.

Radcliffe, Sarah, and Sallie Westwood. 1996. *Remaking the Nation: Place Identity and Politics in Latin America*. London: Routledge.

Reimers, Fernando. 1990. *Deuda Externa y Financiamiento De La Educacion. Su Impacto En Latinoamérica*. Santiago: UNESCO-OREALC.

————. 1991. "The Impact of Economic Stabilization and Adjustment on Education in Latin America." *Comparative Education Review* 35(2):319–53.

Reimers, Fernando, and Luis Tiburcio. 1993. *Education, Adjustment, Reconstruction: Options for Change*. Paris: UNESCO.

Rhoten, Diana. 1999. *Global-Local Conditions of Possibility: The Case of Education Descentralization in Argentina*. Palo Alto: Stanford University.

Rose, Mike. 1995. *Possible Lives*. Boston: Houghton Mifflin.

Rose, Nikolas S. 1990. *Governing the Soul: The Shaping of the Private Self*. New York: Routledge.

Rosenthal, Robert, and Lenore Jacobson. 1968. *Pygmalion in the Classroom; Teacher Expectation and Pupils' Intellectual Development*. New York: Rinehart and Winston.

Ross, Andrew, ed. 1988. *Universal Abandon? The Politics of Postmodernism*. Edinburgh: Edinburgh University Press.

Roth, James. 1992. "Of What Help Is Foucault?" *American Educational Research Journal* 29(4).

Rubin, Gayle. 1975. "The Traffic in Women: Notes on the 'Political Economy' of Sex." In *Towards an Anthropology of Women*, ed. R. Reiter, 157–210. New York: Monthly Review Press.

Ruby, Jay. 1996. "Visual Anthropology." In *Encyclopedia of Cultural Anthropology*, ed. D. Levinson and M. Ember, 1341–51. New York: Henry Holt and Co.

Rust, Val. 1991. "Postmodernism and Its Comparative Education Implications." *Comparative Education Review* 35(4):611–26.

————. 1996. "From Modern to Postmodern Ways of Seeing Social and Educational Change." In *Social Cartography. Mapping Ways of Seeing Social and Educational Change*, ed. Rolland Paulston, 29–53. New York: Garland Publishing.

Said, Edward W. 1978. *Orientalism*. New York: Pantheon.

Salessi, Jorge. 1995. *Medicos, Maleantes y Maricas*. Buenos Aires: Beatriz Viterbo Editora.

Samoff, Joel, ed. 1994. *Coping With Crisis: Austerity, Adjustment and Human Resources*. London: Cassell.

————. 1999. "Institutionalizing International Influence." In *Comparative Education: The Dialectic of the Global and the Local*, ed. Robert F. Arnove and Carlos A. Torres, 51–90. Lanham, MA: Rowman & Littlefield.

Sara-Lafosse, Violeta. 1998. "Machismo in Latin America and the Caribbean." In *Women in the Third World: An Encyclopedia of Contemporary Issues*, ed. Nelly Stromquist, 107–14. New York: Garland.

Saramago, José. 1998. *Blindness*. New York: Harcourt & Brace Company.

Sarlo, Beatriz. 1998. *La Maquina Cultural: Maestras, Traductores y Vanguardistas*. Buenos Aires: Editorial Ariel.

Savigliano, Marta E. 1995. *Tango and the Political Economy of Passion*. Boulder: Westview Press.

Sawicki, Jana. 1991. *Disciplining Foucault: Feminism, Power and the Body*. New York: Routledge.

Schieffelin, Bambi B. 1990. *The Give and Take of Everyday Life: Language Socialization of Kaluli Children*. Cambridge, MA: Cambridge University Press.

Schmukler, Beatriz. 1992. "Women and the Microsocial Democratization of Everyday Life." In *Women and Education in Latin America*, ed. Nelly Stromquist. Boulder: Lynne Rienner.

Schrift, Alan D. 1995a. *Nietzsche's French Legacy: A Genealogy of Poststructuralism*. New York: Routledge.

————. 1995b. "Reconfiguring the Subject As a Process of Self." *New Formations* 25:28–40.

Schugurensky, Daniel. 1994. *Global Economic Restructuring and University Change: The Case of University of Buenos Aires*. Ph.D. dissertation, Edmonton: University of Alberta.

Schutz, Aaron. 1998. "Caring in Schools Is Not Enough: Community, Narrative, and the Limits of Alterity." *Educational Theory* 48(3):373–93.

Scott, Joan W. 1992. "Experience." In *Feminist Theorize the Political*, ed. Judith Butler and Joan W. Scott, 22–40. New York: Routledge.

Shakeshaft, Carolyn. 1989. *Women in Educational Administration*. Newbury Park, CA: Sage.

Shapiro, Svi. 1995. "Postmodern Dilemmas." In *Critical Conversations in Philosophy of Education*, ed. Wendy Kohl, 298–309. New York: Routledge.

Shulman, Lee S., and Gary Sykes, eds. 1983. *Handbook of Teaching and Policy*. New York: Longman.

da Silva, Tomaz Tadeus. 1998. "Radical Historicism or Principled Conformism? Review of Ian Hunter: Rethinking the School: Subjectivity, Bureaucracy, Criticism." *Journal of Curriculum Studies* 3(3): 317–24.

Smith, Frank. 1995. *Between Hope and Havoc: Essays into Human Learning and Education*. Portsmouth, NH: Heinemann.

Smyth, John. 1992. "Teachers' Works and Politics of Reflection." *American Educational Research Journal* 29(2):267–302.

Sontag, Susan. 1977. *On Photography*. New York: Farrar-Strauss-Giroux.

Steiner-Khamsi, Gita. 1999. "Teacher Education Reform." *Comparative Education Review* 43(3):353–61.

Stromquist, Nelly, ed. 1992. *Women and Education in Latin America: Knowledge, Power, and Change*. Boulder: Lynne Rienner.

———. 1993. "The Political Experience of Women: Linking Micro and Macro Democracies." *La Educación* 37(116):541–59.

———, ed. 1996a. *Gender Dimensions in Education in Latin America*. Washington, D.C.: Organization of the American States.

———. 1996b. "Gender Delusions and Exclusions in the Democratization of Schooling in Latin America." *Comparative Education Review* 40(4):404–25.

———. 1997. *Literacy for Citizenship: Gender Grassroots Dynamics in Brazil*. Albany: SUNY Press.

Stuart Wells, Amy, and Todd W. Serman. 1998. "Education against All Odds: What Films Teach Us about Schools." In *Imaging Education*, ed. Gene I. Maeroff, 181–95. New York: Teachers College Press.

Suarez, Daniel. 1993. "Formación Docente y Prácticas Escolares." *Revista Del Instituto De Investigaciones De Ciencias De La Educación* 2(2):28–42.

———. 1994. "Formación Docente, Curriculum e Identidad." *Revista Argentina De Educación* 12(22):29–56.

———. 1995. "Formación Docente y Curriculum En Acción." Informe de Avance. Buenos Aires: Universidad de Buenos Aires.

Sugg, Redding S. 1978. *Motherteacher: The Feminization of American Education*. Charlottesville: University Press of Virginia.

Tagg, John. 1993. *The Burden of Representation: Essays on Photographies and Histories*. Minneapolis: University of Minnesota Press.

Tatto, Maria T. 1999. "Education Reform and State Power in Mexico: The Paradoxes of Decentralization." *Comparative Education Review* 43(3):251–82.

Taylor, Julie M. 1979. *Eva Peron, the Myths of a Woman*. Chicago: University of Chicago Press.

———. 1998. *Paper Tangos*. Durham: Duke University Press.

Tedesco, Juan C. 1980. *Conceptos De Sociología De La Educación*. Buenos Aires: Centro Editor de América Latina.

———. 1982. *Educación y Sociedad En La Argentina (1880–1900)*. Buenos Aires: Centro Editor de América Latina.

———. 1986. *Educación y Sociedad En La Argentina: (1880–1945)*. Buenos Aires: Ediciones Solar.

———. 1991. *Algunos Aspectos De La Privatización En América Latina*. Quito: Instituto Fronesis.

Tedesco, Juan C., Cecilia Braslavsky, and Ricardo Carciofi. 1983. *El Proyecto Educativo Autoritario: Argentina, 1976–1982*. Buenos Aires: Facultad Latinoamericana de Ciencias Sociales-GEL.

Teitel, Simon, ed. 1992. *Towards a New Development Strategy for Latin America*. Washington, D.C.: Inter-American Development Bank.

Tenti Fanfani, Emilio. 1993. *La Escuela Vacía. Deberes Del Estado y Responsabilidades De La Sociedad*. Buenos Aires: UNICEF-Losada.

Terigi, Flavia, and Gabriela Dicker. 1997. *La Formación de Maestros y Profesores: Hoja de Ruta*. Buenos Aires: Paidós.

Thurer, Shari. 1994. *The Myths of Motherhood: How Culture Reinvents the Good Mother*. Boston: Houghton Mifflin.

Timperley, Helen, and Viviane M. J. Robinson. 1998. "The Micropolitics of Accountability: The Case of Staff Appraisal." *Educational Policy* 12(1–2):162–76.

Tiramonti, Guillermina. 1996. "La Crisis Docente." *Clarín* (March 25): 5.

Tiramonti, Guillermina, and María C. Nosiglia. 1991. *La Normativa Educativa De La Transición Democrática*. Buenos Aires: Universidad de Buenos Aires, Facultad de Filosofía y Letras.

Tironi, Eugenio, and Ricardo A. Lagos. 1991. "The Social Actors and Structural Adjustment." *CEPAl Review* (44):12–37.

Todd, John M. 1982. *Luther, a Life*. New York: Crossroad.

Torres, Carlos A. 1990. *The Politics of Nonformal Education in Latin America*. New York: Praeger.

———. 1992. *The Church, Society and Hegemony*. Westport: Praeger.

———. 1994. "Paulo Freire As Secretary of Education in the Municipality of Sao Paulo." *Comparative Education Review* 38:181–214.

Torres, Carlos A., and Gustavo E. Fischman. 1994. "Popular Education: Building From Experiences." In *Learning Through Action Technologies*, ed. Annie Brooks and Karen Watkins. San Francisco: Jossey-Bass.

Torres, Carlos A., and Adriana Puiggrós. 1995. "The State and Public Education in Latin America." *Comparative Education Review* 39(1):1–27.

Tuckey, Catherine. 1992. "Who Is a Scientist? Children's Drawings Reveal All." *Education* 13(3):30–32.

Turner, Victor W., and Edward M. Bruner. 1986. *The Anthropology of Experience*. Urbana: University of Illinois Press.

U.S. Department of Education. 1997. *The Condition of Education*. Washington, D.C.: U.S. Department of Education. National Center for Education Statistics.

UNICEF. 1993. *All for Education, Education for All*. New York: UNICEF.

Vare, Jonathan. 1995. "Gendered Ideology: Voices of Parents and Practice in Teacher Education." *Anthropology and Education* 26(3):251–70.

Wallerstein, Immanuel. 1991. *Unthinking Social Science: The Limits of Nineteenth-Century Paradigms*. Cambridge, U.K.: Polity Press.

Weber, Sandra, and Claudia Mitchell. 1995. *That's Funny, You Don't Look Like a Teacher*. Bristol: Falmer Press.

Weedon, Chris. 1987. *Feminist Practice and Poststructuralist Theory*. Oxford: Blackwell.

Weiler, Hans. 1990. "Comparative Perspectives of Educational Descentralization: An Exercise in Contradiction?" *Educational Evaluation and Policy Analysis* 12(4):433–48.

Weiler, Kathleen. 1988. *Women Teaching for Change: Gender, Class and Power*. New York: Bergin and Garvey Publishers.

———. 1991. "Freire and a Feminist Pedagogy of Difference." *Harvard Educational Review* 16(4):230–61.

———. 1996. "Myths of Paulo Freire." *Educational Theory* 46(3):353–72.

———. 1997. *Gender, Race and Class Photographs*. New York: American Educational Research Association.

Weimberg, Gregorio. 1983. *Modelos Educativos En América Latina*. Buenos Aires: Kapeluz.

Welch, Anthony. 1999. "The Triumph of Technocracy or the Collapse of Certainty? Modernity, Postmodernity, and Postcolonialism in Comparative Education." In *Comparative Education: The Dialectic of the Global and the Local*, ed. Robert Arnove and Carlos A. Torres, 25–50. Lanham, MD: Rowman and Littlefield.

Wells, Amy, Martin Hirschberg Lipton, and Jeannie Oakes. 1995. "Bounding the Case Within Its Context: A Constructivist Approach to Studying Detracking Reform." *Educational Researcher* 24(5):18–25.

Whitty, Geoff. 1997. "Creating Quasi-Markets in Education: A Review of Recent Research on Parental Choice and School Autonomy in Three Countries." *Review of Research in Education* 22:3–47.

Wilensky, Harold L. 1975. *The Welfare State and Equality: Structural and Ideological Roots of Public Expenditures*. Berkeley: University of California Press.

———. 1976. *The New Corporatism: Centralization and the Welfare State*. Beverly Hills: Sage.

Williams, Raymond. 1976. *Keywords: A Vocabulary of Culture and Society*. Oxford: Oxford University Press.

Willis, Paul. 1977. *Learning to Labour: How Working Class Kids Get Working Class Jobs*. Aldershot: Gower.

Wong, Kenneth K., and Dorothea Anagnostopoulos. 1998. "Can Integrated Governance Reconstruct Teaching? Lessons Learned From Two Low-Performing Chicago Schools." *Educational Policy* 12(1–2):19–30.

Woodward, Kathryn, ed. 1997. *Identity and Difference*. London: Sage-Open University Press.

World Bank, The. 1991. *The Dividends of Learning*. Washington, D.C.: The World Bank.

———. 1997. *World Development Report*. New York: Oxford University Press.

———. 2000. *World Development Report 1999/2000*. Washington, D.C.: World Bank.

Yannoulas, Silvia. 1996. *Educar:¿Una Profesión De Mujeres?* Buenos Aires: Kapeluz.

Zeichner, Ken. 1999. "The New Scholarship in Teacher Education." *Educational Researcher* 28(9):4–15.

Zizek, Slavoj. 1991. *Looking Awry: An Introduction to Jacques Lacan through Popular Culture*. Cambridge, MA: MIT.

INDEX

ABOUT THE AUTHOR

Gustavo E. Fischman (Ph.D., UCLA) is assistant professor in the College of Education at Arizona State University. He works in the areas of teacher education, comparative and international education, cultural studies, and qualitative research methodologies. This book is a revised version of his doctoral dissertation which was awarded the 1998 Gail P. Kelly outstanding dissertation for the Comparative and International Education Society.